SHAKESPEARE, LANGUAGE AND THE STAGE

THE ARDEN SHAKESPEARE

SHAKESPEARE AND LANGUAGE

GENERAL EDITORS
Lynette Hunter, Lynne Magnusson and Ann Thompson

Available
Shakespeare and the Language of Translation
Ton Hoenselaars (editor)

Forthcoming
Reading Shakespeare's Bodies   *Keir Elam*

Further titles are in preparation

SHAKESPEARE, LANGUAGE AND THE STAGE

The Fifth Wall:
Approaches to Shakespeare
from Criticism, Performance
and Theatre Studies

Edited by
Lynette Hunter and Peter Lichtenfels

The Arden website is at
http://www.ardenshakespeare.com

This edition of *Shakespeare, Language and the Stage*
first published 2005 by the Arden Shakespeare

Editorial matter and selection
© 2005 Lynette Hunter and Peter Lichtenfels

Arden Shakespeare is an imprint of Thomson Learning

Thomson Learning
High Holborn House
50–51 Bedford Row
London WC1R 4LR

Typeset by Gray Publishing, Tunbridge Wells, Kent
Printed in Hong Kong by C+C Offset

British Library Cataloguing in Publication Data
A catalogue record for this book is available from the British Library

Library of Congress Cataloguing in Publication Data
A catalogue record has been requested

ISBN–10: 1-90427-149-9
ISBN–13: 978-1-90427-149-9

NPN 9 8 7 6 5 4 3 2 1

CONTENTS

ACKNOWLEDGEMENTS

The editors would like to thank Gresham College for its generous support of this experimental programme, the British Academy for support toward the visit of a United States scholar, Shakespeare's Globe London especially the indefatiguable Education Department for inspiration, and Manchester Metropolitan University for a grant to aid publication.

Our sincere thanks go to Sarah Poulton for copy-editing an exceptionally difficult text, and to the Arden Shakespeare publishing team for patience and encouragement.

Lynette Hunter and Peter Lichtenfels

SHAKESPEARE AND LANGUAGE
SERIES STATEMENT

Building on the Arden Shakespeare editions and, more specifically, *Reading Shakespeare's Dramatic Language* (2001), this series aims to provide focused studies of Shakespeare's language in relation to particular contexts and methodologies in which it has yet to be fully explored. Individual volumes address topics such as the language of translation, theatre language, the language of film, language and society, language and history, and the language of Shakespeare's contemporaries.

A renewed investigation of Shakespeare's achievements in relation to such topics is timely because the various materialist and historicist approaches of recent criticism have broadened our understanding of the range of cultural contexts pertinent to Shakespeare's works but have largely neglected the details and artistry of the language. Without wishing to deny the important achievements of materialist and historicist criticism, this series aims to bridge the gap between Shakespeare's language and its cultural contexts. It includes both single-authored and collaborative volumes, and authors are drawn from the international scholarly and theatre communities; some volumes involve an interdisciplinary approach, using, for example, methods from linguistics and film studies. The readership envisaged is similar to that for the Arden Shakespeare editions, ranging from those studying Shakespeare in their final years at secondary school through teachers, undergraduates and postgraduates, scholars, theatre practitioners and general readers with an interest in Shakespeare and/or language.

The aim of each volume is to illuminate how a specific context or approach opens up fresh perspectives on Shakespeare's language in a way which is accessible and gives the reader a clearer understanding or a new way of thinking about the verbal achievement or impact of Shakespeare's texts. The series aims to publish one volume per year – and the General Editors would be pleased to hear from people with appropriate proposals.

Lynette Hunter, Lynne Magnusson and Ann Thompson
General Editors

CONTRIBUTORS

Annabel Arden read English at Cambridge, trained with Philippe Gaulier and Monika Pagneux, and co-founded Théâtre de Complicité in 1983. Her work as an actor and director for Complicité includes *A Minute Too Late*, *Anything For A Quiet Life* and *The Winter's Tale*; and as artistic collaborator, *The Three Lives of Lucie Cabrol* and *Mnemonic*. Other theatre directing includes *Women of Troy* (National Theatre) and *India Song*, both with Annie Casteldine. She has directed opera extensively in Europe and for ENO, won Olivier awards in both opera and theatre, and taught actors and singers all over the world.

Calixto Bieito is Artistic Director of the Teatre Romea in Barcelona. His early work ranged from Marivaux and Rodoreda to Shakespeare (*Two Gentlemen of Verona*, *A Midsummer Night's Dream*). Subsequent productions have included work by Synge, Plath, Brecht, Sondheim, Molière, Schoenberg, Lorca, Shakespeare's *The Tempest* and Valle-Inclan's *Barbaric Comedies* (Edinburgh Festival, Abbey Theatre), which was awarded The Irish Times–ESB Theatre Award in 2000. Recent projects include *Così fan tutte* for the WNO; *Don Giovanni* for the Hannover Staatsoper, ENO and the Liceu, Barcelona, and *Macbeth* for the Salzburg Festival, Münchner Kammerspiele, Teatre Romea and the Barbican.

Anne Bogart is Artistic Director of the SITI Company, which she founded with Japanese director Tadashi Suzuki in 1992. She is a recipient of two Obie Awards, a Bessie Award and a Guggenheim Fellowship and is an Associate Professor at Columbia University where she runs the Graduate Directing Programme. Recent works with SITI include: *A Midsummer Night's Dream*; *La Dispute*; *Short Stories*;

bobrauschenbergamerica; *Cabin Pressure*; *Alice's Adventures*; *Bob*; *Miss Julie*; and Charles Mee's *Orestes*. Other recent productions include *Lilith* and *Seven Deadly Sins* (New York City Opera) and *Gertrude and Alice* (Foundry Theatre).

David Bradby is Professor of Drama and Theatre Studies at Royal Holloway, University of London, a post he has held since 1988. His books include *Modern French Drama 1940–1990* and *Beckett: Waiting for Godot* (Cambridge, 1991 and 2001 respectively), *The Theater of Michel Vinaver* (University of Michigan Press, 1993) and (with Annie Sparks) *Mise en Scène: French Theatre Now* (Methuen, 1997). He has translated Lecoq's *The Moving Body* (Methuen, 2000) and has translated and edited plays by Michel Vinaver and Bernard-Marie Koltès. With Maria M. Delgado, he edits the *Contemporary Theatre Review* and published *The Paris Jigsaw: Internationalism and the City's Stages* (Manchester University Press, 2002).

Tim Carroll is Associate Theatre Director at Shakespeare's Globe. He has been Master of Play for *Richard II* (2003), *Twelfth Night* and *The Golden Ass* (2002), *Macbeth* (2001), *The Two Noble Kinsmen* (2000) and *Augustine's Oak* (1999). He has also worked with the English Shakespeare Company, as director of productions such as *Cymbeline*, *Julius Caesar* and *The Tempest*, and as Associate Director of the Northcott Theatre in Exeter. As an opera director, his productions include Benjamin Britten's *The Prodigal Son* and Monteverdi's *Orfeo* (Kent Opera); Sir Peter Maxwell Davies' *Eight Songs for a Mad King* and Hans Werner Henze's *El Cimarron* (Psappha). Recent work includes *Acis & Galatea* for New Kent Opera, for whom he is Director of Productions.

Maria M. Delgado is Professor in Drama and Theatre Arts and Head of Drama at Queen Mary, University of London. She is also co-editor of *Contemporary Theatre Review*. Her recent publications include '*Other' Spanish Theatres: Erasure and Inscription on the Twentieth-Century Spanish Stage* (Manchester University Press, 2003). Co-edited volumes include *In Contact with the Gods?: Directors Talk Theatre*, *The Paris Jigsaw: Internationalism and the City's Stages* and *Theatre in Crisis: Performance Manifestos for a New Century* (all Manchester University Press, 1996 and 2002) and *Conducting a Life: Reflections on the Theatre of Maria Irene Fornes* (Smith and Kraus, 1999).

Greg Doran has been an Associate Director of the RSC since 1996. His productions there include a double bill of *The Taming of the Shrew* and Fletcher's sequel *The Tamer Tamed*; *Macbeth* with Antony Sher and Harriet Walter (which was filmed by Channel 4/Illuminations); *The Winter's Tale*; *Much Ado About Nothing*; *Timon of Athens*; *King John*; *All is True (Henry VIII)*; *As You Like It* and *The Merchant of Venice*. In 2002 he was Artistic Director of a series of rare Jacobean plays in the Swan Theatre, for which he received the Olivier Award for Outstanding Achievement of the Year. He is co-author with his partner, Sir Antony Sher, of *Woza Shakespeare!* (St Martin's Press, 2000), which tells the story of their experience of mounting a production of *Titus Andronicus* at the Market Theatre in Johannesburg.

Bridget Escolme is Lecturer in Theatre Studies at the University of Leeds, where she teaches Renaissance drama, contemporary performance and theatre in education. She is currently working on a monograph, *Talking to the Audience: Shakespeare, Performance, Self*, and has recently performed in Chris Thorpes' *Static* and *Safety* for Leeds-based Unlimited Theatre. Escolme has also taught drama in secondary and further education.

Margo Hendricks is Associate Professor of Literature at the University of California, Santa Cruz. She is co-editor of *Women, 'Race', and Writing in the Early Modern Period* (Routledge, 1994). She has published on Shakespeare, Renaissance concepts of race, and Aphra Behn. Her recent work includes essays on 'Response: Monstrosity and the Mercurial Female Imagination' and 'Visions of Colours: Spectacle, Spectators and the Performance of Race'.

Lynette Hunter is Professor of the History of Rhetoric at the University of Leeds and a professor in the Department of Theatre and Dance at the University of California, Davis. Her research interests include Renaissance rhetoric, particularly in the areas of science, women's history and politics. She has worked in many areas of theatre practice including acting, directing, stage management and make-up, and for the past ten years has developed an international reputation for a series of performance pieces relating to critical theory and literary texts.

Nicholas Hytner is Director of the Royal National Theatre where he recently directed *Henry V* and *The Winter's Tale*. Other recent productions include Mark Ravenhill's *Mother Clap's Molly House*, Nicholas Wright's *Cressida*, and Alan Bennett's *The Lady in the Van*. His films include *The Madness of King George* and *The Crucible*.

Russell Jackson is Director of the Shakespeare Institute in Stratford-upon-Avon and Professor of Shakespeare Studies at the University of Birmingham. His publications include *The Oxford Illustrated History of Shakespeare on Stage* (with Jonathan Bate) and *Romeo and Juliet* in the series Shakespeare at Stratford (New Arden, 2002). With Robert Smallwood, he has co-edited two volumes in the Players of Shakespeare series for Cambridge University Press. He has written an annual review of Shakespearean performances at Stratford for *Shakespeare Quarterly* since 1993. As a text adviser, he has worked on many stage, film and radio productions, including Kenneth Branagh's *Henry V, Much Ado About Nothing, Hamlet* and *Love's Labour's Lost*.

Janelle Jenstad, at the University of Windsor at the time of The Fifth Wall workshop, is now an Assistant Professor of English at the University of Victoria, where she teaches Shakespeare and Renaissance literature. Research interests include Renaissance finance, civic pageantry, theatre history and Shakespeare in performance. She has taught and lectured at Canada's Stratford Festival, reviews plays for *Shakespeare Bulletin*, and consults on theatrical productions. Her publications have appeared in *Early Modern Literary Studies* and *Elizabethan Theatre*. She is currently writing a book on usury and the theatre.

Peter Lichtenfels has directed over 60 professional productions in Europe and North America. He is a former Artistic Director of the Traverse Theatre in Edinburgh, and Executive Director of the Leicester Haymarket, as well as former Associate Director of the Liverpool Playhouse. Lichtenfels also has an international scholarly reputation, having contributed to numerous publications, including *Reading Shakespeare's Dramatic Language: A Guide* (Arden Shakespeare, 2001) and *In Arden: Editing Shakespeare* (Thomson Publishers, 2002), and a critical theatre commentary on *The Merchant of Venice* (Applause, 2000) for directors and actors. He is currently a Professor of Theater at the University of California, Davis.

Lynne Magnusson is a Professor of English at the University of Toronto and has published on Shakespeare's language, early modern women's writing, the genre of the letter, and discourse analysis. She is the author of *Shakespeare and Social Dialogue: Dramatic Language and Elizabethan Letters* (Cambridge, 1999), a co-author and co-editor of *Reading Shakespeare's Dramatic Language: A Guide* (Arden Shakespeare, 2001), and co-editor of *The Elizabethan Theatre*, volumes 11 to 15. Currently she is working on a book on the language of early modern women's letters.

Patricia Parker is the Margery Bailey Chair Professor of English and Dramatic Literature, and Professor of Comparative Literature, at Stanford University. She is the author of *Inescapable Romance* (Princeton, 1979), *Literary Fat Ladies: Rhetoric, Gender, Property* (Routledge, 1987), and *Shakespeare from the Margins* (University of Chicago Press, 1996), and co-editor (with Geoffrey Hartman) of *Shakespeare and the Question of Theory* (Routledge, 1985) and (with Margo Hendricks) *Women, 'Race', and Writing in the Early Modern Period* (Routledge, 1994). She is currently at work on a new Arden edition of *A Midsummer Night's Dream*.

Janelle Reinelt is Associate Dean and Professor of Drama in the Claire Trevor School of the Arts at the University of California, Irvine. She is also President of the International Federation for Theatre Research, and Vice President for Research and Publications of the Association for Theatre in Higher Education. She is the former editor of *Theatre Journal*. Her books include *After Brecht: British Epic Theatre* (University of Michigan Press, 1994), *Crucibles of Crisis: Performance and Social Change* (University of Michigan Press, 1996), *The Performance of Power* with Sue-Ellen Case (University of Iowa Press, 1991), and *The Cambridge Companion to Modern British Women Playwrights* with Elaine Aston (Cambridge, 2000). Her current project is *Public Performances: Race and Nation in the Theatre of Our Time*.

Emma Smith teaches Renaissance literature at Hertford College, Oxford, and has published on Shakespeare in performance on stage and screen. Her current research is on the role of the author in the reception of early modern drama on stage and in print.

Patrick Spottiswoode is the Director of Globe Education, a position he has held since 1989. In 1999 he created The Globe MA, Shakespeare Studies: Text and Playhouse, with King's College, London, and last year (2003) he oversaw the launch of Globe Education's first one-year Bachelor of Fine Art (BFA) acting course for undergraduates. As well as running numerous other educational programmes and his commissioning activities, Patrick is currently working on a special part-time MA for primary and secondary school teachers, Creative Arts and the Classroom, which he hopes will be launched in the autumn of 2004.

Ann Thompson is a professor of English Language and Literature and Head of the School of Humanities at King's College, London. She is a general editor of the Arden Shakespeare (3rd series) and is co-editing *Hamlet* with Neil Taylor. She has published widely in Shakespeare studies, mainly on editing, feminist criticism and metaphor.

Martin White is Professor of Theatre and Provost of the Institute for Advanced Studies at the University of Bristol. He also coordinates the research programme at London's Globe. He has written extensively on the drama and theatre practice of the early modern period, and directed a number of less well-known plays from the period, most recently Massinger's *Believe As You List* and *The Bondman*. He is currently writing a book on *A Midsummer Night's Dream* and editing a volume of essays on early modern theatre and the modern stage and screen.

W.B. Worthen is Professor and Chair of the Department of Theater, Dance and Performance Studies at the University of California, Berkeley. He is the author of *Shakespeare and the Force of Modern Performance* (Cambridge, 2003), *Shakespeare and the Authority of Performance* (Cambridge, 1997), *Modern Drama and the Rhetoric of Theater* (California, 1992), and *The Idea of the Actor* (Princeton, 1984); he is also the editor of *The Heinle Anthology of Drama*, past editor of *Theatre Journal*, and current co-editor of *Modern Drama*.

INVITED PARTICIPANTS TO THE CONFERENCE

Patricia Baillie trained in voice studies at the Central School of Speech and Drama in London and then, in Oxford with Elisabeth Walker, to be a teacher of the Alexander Technique. She has taught voice and speech in drama schools in London, Oxford and Rome and since completing her Alexander Technique (AT) training, has been the Head of Voice at Manchester Metropolitan University School of Theatre.

Alan Cox is an actor and director who trained at the London Academy of Music and Dramatic Art. His many acting credits include seasons at the Royal Shakespeare Company (RSC), the National Theatre and the Chichester Festival Theatre. As a director he has coordinated perfomances for the 'Read Not Dead' series at The Globe and worked extensively on the London Fringe.

Michael Gould is an actor and has appeared at The Globe on numerous occasions – as Edmund in *King Lear*, Polixenes in *The Winter's Tale* and Diphilus in *The Maid's Tragedy*. At the RSC he played Rosencrantz in Kenneth Branagh's *Hamlet*, Benvolio in *Romeo and Juliet* and Creon in *The Phoenician Women*. He has appeared at theatres around the UK including The Royal Exchange in Manchester, Birmingham Rep and Salisbury Playhouse. On television he has appeared in *Eastenders*, *State of Play*, *Wire in The Blood* and on film, in *Mary Shelley's Frankenstein*.

Joy Richardson trained at the Webber Douglas Academy of Dramatic Art in London. Her many acting credits include Paulina in *The Winter's Tale* and Lucrece in *The Ghost of Lucrece* (both at The Globe), Della in *The Royal Family* (Theatre Royal, Haymarket) and Hermia in *A Midsummer Night's Dream* (Young Vic). She has also acted extensively at the National Theatre playing, among others, Thaisa in Phyllida Lloyd's production of *Pericles* and Stella in *Racing Demon*, directed by Richard Eyre. Richardson has also worked in TV, radio and film.

Leon Rubin is Professor of Drama and Theatre Arts at Middlesex University, England. He is also Programme Leader for an internationally known MA and MFA programme in professional theatre directing. He has written a number of books and articles, and has a specialist interest in South East Asian theatre. Rubin is also a well-known theatre director with professional credits all over the world, including recent work at the Stratford Festival in Canada such as *Pericles*, *Henry VI* parts 1, 2 and 3 and Giradoux's *Electra*.

PREFACE

In his letter to the reader of *The Malcontent*, John Marston apologised for publishing a play that he had 'invented merely to be spoken'. All he could hope was that readers would remember 'the pleasure it once afforded you when it was presented with the soul of lively action'. For self-effacing Marston, the printed text was, at best, a keepsake that would help a reader recall the original energy of the live event. The 'soul of lively action' was ephemeral not eternal. Less successful plays of the period were literally ephemeral and lasted only a day before disappearing without text.

With the 1623 Folio the actors Hemings and Condell set out to eternise texts of Shakespeare's plays for readers. 'Reade him, therefore; and againe, and againe: And if then you doe not like him, surely you are in some manifest danger, not to vnderstand him.' They acknowledged their interest in promoting a readership: 'to read and censure' and added wryly 'but buy it first'. The Shakespeare industry was born and with it the beginnings of a divide between readers and stage playmakers.

Playmakers are not entirely overlooked. The last page of the prolegomena before the printing of *The Tempest* is not a paean to Shakespeare but a list of the plays' 26 principal actors, an acknowledgement of the people who had been responsible for providing the 'soul of lively action'.

Professional readers and playmakers approach texts from different points of view, of course, and prepare work for different publics. Playmaking is a collaborative and ephemeral act and responds to 'now'. Scholarship is a lonely pursuit in comparison and aspires to print and shelf-life.

The scholar Lynette Hunter and the director Peter Lichtenfels like to promote and provoke collaboration between scholars and playmakers. They had participated in The Globe's Winter Playing workshops to address staging issues that arise in *Romeo and Juliet*, and their positive experience prompted them to approach Globe Education to host The Fifth Wall symposium.

One of this book's contributors almost ruefully admits: 'in the end, Fifth Wall proved somewhat less antagonistic than I hoped'. The good-natured atmosphere may in part have resulted from Lynette and Peter's choice of contributors, but it also stemmed from the mutual respect that participants had for one another's very different disciplines. No animosity surfaced between 'gown' and 'clown', although people did not always see eye to eye. As another contributor writes, 'for a trained critical reader "what is there on the page" may be quite different from what is there for a trained actor. The skills involved in each training are different but commensurate and each can inform the other.'

Each can indeed inform the other. Like The Globe itself, this book is proof positive that collaboration between researcher and playmaker can help nurture the 'soul of lively action'.

Patrick Spottiswoode
Director, Globe Education

INTRODUCTION

The impetus for this collection of essays is quite simple: the theatre director Peter Lichtenfels and critic Lynette Hunter got together in 1994 to carry out some research on *Romeo and Juliet*. Lichtenfels had some academic background and Hunter some theatre experience, and both thought that collaboration would be a fruitful interchange of ideas. Ten years later this has in fact turned out to be the case, but only after a series of seemingly impossible contradictions in vocabulary and profound disciplinary lacunae were recognised and troubled over.

In the course of learning how to speak sensibly to each other, and giving joint presentations to academic conferences and to groups of theatre practitioners, it became clear that while there is an area of performance studies beginning to address the borderland between the different approaches to understanding dramatic texts, for many others there is a 'fifth wall'. If the 'fourth wall', the barrier between the actor and the audience introduced by theatre conventions, is an invisible artefact between the stage and the audience, the fifth wall may be thought of as the invisible wall between critics or readers and theatre practitioners. Most scholars of Shakespeare's writing, and of other writers for the theatre, although highly sophisticated as audience participators, have not trained for the theatre in any sustained manner. Neither have many theatre practitioners much sense of what is involved in theatre scholarship, apart from a dim memory of secondary school or undergraduate essays. Yet precisely because of that interaction across the fourth wall, each thinks they understand what the other is doing.

There are few occasions when detailed and expansive discussions can take place between critics of Shakespeare's texts and theatre practitioners, partly because there has been an unspoken consensus that there is no need to do so. But the collaborative work that has gone into this collection of essays has been inspired by a sense among many of the participants that there can be real benefits from exploring new inter-actions between people working in these different areas. The essays mark a desire for a more substantial dialogue than programme theatre notes or directors doing pre-performance talks for audiences, and a feel-ing that the dramaturge's role of bringing intellectual and critical material to the theatre could be more public and open out wider debate. Many of the contributors are also involved in new and innovative programmes being developed within universities that attempt to bring together the different practices. More widely, these changes are further indications of a growing understanding that greater collaboration and exchange of practice can not only enrich both worlds but also the appre-ciation and engagement of the general public.

At the start of the process, when the theatre practitioners and the critics began their conversations through the mediation of the performance theorists, most of the contributors found that there was little common vocabulary for the discussion. Yet several of the theatre practitioners felt that if they were able to speak to critics about the detail of their practice, then they would begin to get a handle on ways of talk-ing about this to others as well. In a parallel move, some of the critics, although not all, voiced their hope that if they could speak to directors and actors about the complexity of their art, then they might also be able to open up what is often a rather solitary engagement with the texts of Shakespeare to a much wider audience. Readers of this collection have the opportunity to engage with these interactions, to compare and possibly extend their own interdisciplinary practices, or to explore an entirely new way of thinking about the language of Shakespeare's plays that self-consciously breaks down that invisible fifth wall.

A few examples may delineate the construction of the fifth wall in more concrete terms. One of the first contradictions in vocabulary experienced by Hunter and Lichtenfels was that around the word 'char-acter'. As a well-trained post-deconstruction and subject-constitution critic, Lynette Hunter found it difficult to accept the description of actors drawing on *authentic personal experience* as a basis for identi-fying the essence of character, not 'a character', but character that involves others on stage. Even the word 'essence' proved problematic for her in a critical world where 'essentialising' signified the blind acceptance of social representations as 'true'. On the other hand, it turned out that this was not in effect what was being signified when Peter Lichtenfels used the words 'character', 'experience' and 'essence'. An actor may work on a set of lines and find anger or grief being released in them because of their personal body memories, but this is not a copying of a type (or stereotype) they have 'experienced before'. Rather it is a mimetic repetition of context that in the re-hearsal or the per-formance (hyphenated to emphasise the way that acting forms character through interweaving of the text with the body) materialises a particular action in the moment. What this means in practice takes a thorough understanding of acting training to comprehend. An actor may subsequently explain why 'they cried' in terms of private memory or of psychology, but in this they simply reproduce a culturally dominant vocabulary for the construction of character which would be unlikely to engage an audience.

A more pragmatic example emerged from the editorial approach to stage directions such as '[*Aside*]'. Lichtenfels argued that to include this stage direction in all cases where it is conventionally found could be misleading. A particular production might well play the line straight into the dialogue for a different effect, and to fix the line as an '[*Aside*]' would pre-judge a rehearsal practice. Hunter's response was that readers needed stage directions like this because they are not watching a specific production, and may not recognise the implications of a decision to include or exclude the line from ongoing dialogue. Hence '[*Aside*]' would alert the reader to possibilities, not necessarily fix a specific action.

Versions of this debate concerning 'what the theatre practitioner wants' or 'what the reader/critic wants' have a wide impact in other areas of stage direction: for example, do you include a stage direction on the page if it is already clear in the text that such action takes place? The debate also affects punctuation: do you include punctuation, thus imposing syntax to enable a particular reading, or leave it sparse to encourage a variety of readings, even though this may be confusing? Although editing is only part of the critical response and the readers' concern, these questions recognise that producing an edition is analogous to directing a production, with the significant difference that an edition has a much longer shelf-life. On the other hand, even a three-week run of a stage production has an audience far more alert to its production elements than a printed edition that will usually be read by people with few skills for understanding and interacting with the textual performance it offers.

Even more challenging is the way that those people who take up the different approaches work on the verbal text. Here it is vital to understand the detailed practice of the actor and director on the one hand and the scholarly critic on the other. For example, when Lichtenfels described part of the actor's verse training as an attempt to break down all conventional connection between sound and meaning leaving only the physical sound in the body, Hunter objected that as social creatures who are what they are because they learn how to be so, human beings cannot *not* make these connections. This kind of debate is so prevalent in the essays of this collection that another title for this book could have been Lynne Magnusson's query during the workshop: 'Is it *true* that consonants relate to action and vowels register emotional temperature?' However, having had training in the basic actor's voice exercise that works on vowels and consonants independently, it becomes apparent that conventional and stereotypical associations *can* lose their tether to culturally expected meanings, with the result that their range of reference becomes unstable.

Curiously, the process involved in the breaking down of the sounds of words is similar to the work a critic may do on etymological derivation, a staple of editorial commentary that many readers let alone theatre practitioners frequently skip, and which is often central to extending critical knowledge. Working back through the history of a word, as do a number of contributors to the following essays, we may see the forks in meaning become apparent, the residual significances emerge from centuries of verbal sedimentation into different cultures and eventually different languages. The process can radically destabilise the contemporary meaning of a word, even before one gets to the stage of 'false' etymology, the historically 'illegal' but often highly evocative association of a verbal fragment with a completely different set of meanings.

These issues are familiar, or becoming so, both to critics and to theatre practitioners, yet there are few opportunities to discuss them collaboratively and in depth. The Fifth Wall research workshop was intended to bring theatre practitioners and critics together for exactly this purpose and within the context of Shakespeare's writing. All of the issues mentioned above, and many more, are part of the discussion that follows, and while this discussion is focused on a number of different

Shakespearian plays, the issues to a greater or lesser extent run through the concern with any dramatic language. The format for the workshop was to have one theatre practitioner, one critic and one respondent, in a grouping that would discuss a particular area of Shakespeare's writing, language and the stage. The workshop, which ran over two days, also invited three actors, Alan Cox, Michael Gould and Joy Richardson, the director Leon Rubin and voice trainer Patricia Baillie, and Patrick Spottiswoode, the director of Globe Education, to participate.

The first day focused largely on elements that accompany language on the stage: on gesture (Annabel Arden, Margo Hendricks, Lynette Hunter), on visual and verbal interaction particularly in film (David Bradby, Greg Doran, Russell Jackson), and on the effects of time and space on production (Anne Bogart, William Worthen, Bridget Escolme). The second day shifted the emphasis on to the verbal texture of dramatic language, looking at verse (Janelle Jenstad, Peter Lichtenfels, Lynne Magnusson), text (Calixto Bieito, Maria Delgado, Patricia Parker), script (Tim Carroll, Emma Smith, Martin White), and heightened language (Nicholas Hytner, Janelle Reinelt, Ann Thompson). The order of sessions has been slightly rearranged in the collection to reflect the development of ideas and issues that emerged over the two days.

Each grouping prepared for the workshop in quite different ways, some with extensive prior interaction and some with very little. The workshop was open only to participants and most attended the full two days. After the workshop, transcripts were made of all sessions and circulated to all participants. The respondents, drawing upon their own work, on the transcripts, the preparatory material and post-workshop interactions in conversation or by email, and their knowledge of the wider work of those in their group, wrote the essays. The essays are collaborative productions, with the respondent as the writer, or if you like, the director, each attempting to climb over, or possibly to dismantle or dissolve, the fifth wall.

The collection begins with an essay based on the collaboration of Lynne Magnusson with Peter Lichtenfels, for which Janelle Jensted acted as correspondent and essay writer. Magnusson's recent critical work has been focused on analysing the social interactions that language and dialogue convey. Her interests parallel those of the theatre director Peter Lichtenfels, who also trains actors in voice, body movement and interaction on stage. Demonstrating some techniques with the actor Joy Richardson, and discussing *A Midsummer Night's Dream*, they negotiate each other's practices, having difficulty with the differences in vocabulary, but moving toward an understanding of each other's techniques. Theatre scholar and performance critic Janelle Jensted uses a considerable amount of her collaborators' work to frame the exchange into one about the different kinds of 'text' with which each works, and offers an array of commentary from the workshop that was sparked off by the debate.

Martin White's essay is written with director Tim Carroll, who has worked extensively at Shakespeare's Globe Theatre which has a specific commitment to historical research, and with Emma Smith an academic at Oxford University who researches textual and historical contexts for early modern drama. White is himself an 'academic practitioner-critic' and the work he collaborates on continues to probe the differences between the world of the critic and of the stage, as he posits 'script' as a conceptual tool for talking about the text in performance. In a remarkably frank exchange of doubts about whether either side can ever resolve their 'frictive relationship', the three examine editorial and theatrical issues raised by several scenes in *Twelfth Night*, in particular the 'scenic turns' in 2.1 that was acted for the workshop by Alan Cox and Michael Gould, and pays some attention to the work of Philip Massinger.

Scenic turns are gestures that the text makes to which actors, and arguably readers, need to pay attention. Annabel Arden, opera director and director at Théâtre Complicité, Margo Hendricks, dramaturge and critic devoted to understanding race, ethnicity and gender, and respondent Lynette Hunter, editor, critic and performer, pursued the idea of textual gesture and bodily gesture in studies of both *Titus Andronicus* and *The Winter's Tale*. Drawing extensively on workshop contributions as well as communications among the participants, this third essay takes a detailed look at how actors train, and what kinds of gesture they learn about. Hunter contributes an element missing from the analysis when she argues for the need explicitly to recognise the training of the reader as well, because reading is also an embodied practice. The discussion also considers textual gesture, the critic's skills in understanding it, and the way that the audience's and reader's responses are central to gestural signification, looking both at language and the body (Hendricks) and movement and the text (Arden).

The fourth essay brings together the Royal Shakespeare Company director Greg Doran, Shakespeare Institute Director Russell Jackson, and David Bradby, an eminent theatre and film scholar and critic. In the workshop itself, this session followed that of Arden, Hendricks and Hunter, and developed the discussion of bodily and textual gesture specifically into visual gesture on the stage and in film. Doran's contribution compares a stage production of *Macbeth* to his film of the same play, analysing the difficulties that film poses to the expansiveness of Shakespearean language and positing a number of technical devices that he used to get his audience to 'listen' to the film. Picking up on this study with an analysis of a film version of *Richard III*, Jackson developed a complex study of the way cultural expectations add to and interfere with filmic gesture. Missing from these contributions was any sense that theatre could use visual, even spectacular, display to engage an audience in listening to the text. However, Bradby, an expert on the physical theatre of Jacques Lecoq in which Arden trained, as well as French theatre more broadly, contextualised this issue through the work of Arian Mnouchkine. He explored her direction of *Richard II*, suggesting that her special approach to actor training develops a range and repertoire of gestural movement that can match the playwright's vocabulary in flexibility and variety.

The concentration of visual image was extended by the extensive discussion of design and dramaturgy in the work of Calixto Bieito, director of the Teatre Romea in Barcelona, particularly in his *Macbeth*. The theatre critic and Spanish theatre scholar Maria Delagdo worked with Bieito and Patricia Parker, editor of *A Midsummer Night's Dream* and an exceptionally subtle and sophisticated commentator on Shakespeare's language. Delgado brought extensive interviews with Bieito together with Parker's contributions to highlight the way translation, either within a language or from one to another, can engender resistant political readings that open up convention. Bieito's *Macbeth* recasts not only the language but the structure and physical dimensions of the play so that it addresses the contemporary issues he wants to foreground, often using gestures from film and popular culture. His claim that translation into a foreign language can produce a play that is fully current in the way that a production of a play in Shakespearean English cannot, is implicitly contested by Parker. Although concurring that many fruitful readings emerge from remembering that English is a 'foreign' language, she demonstrates that the modern reader of a Shakespeare text has just as much translating to do.

The issue of resistance is central to the contributions from Anne Bogart, theatre director of the SITI company in New York, and William Worthen, performance studies theorist and Shakespeare critic. As respondent Bridget Escolme, a critic of theatre and performance, notes that each contributor takes 'making things difficult' as a common purpose, and provides a constant counterpoint to their discussion in a reading of a production of *Richard II*. They do so in superficially different ways, as Bogart's contemplation of her working practices and a future production of *A Midsummer Night's Dream*, and Worthen's analysis of a performance of the play in Finland, demonstrate. Worthen's theorisation of the understanding of cultural materialism that underlies what productions mean, seems a world away from the shortlist of things 'needed' in a production by Bogart. However, the contributors to this session were remarkably able to negotiate common ground, agreeing that 'sourcework' was not aimed at authenticity but social grounding, that references to the 'body' mediating the text did not imply an irrational or arbitrary expression, and that an attempt to find the energy 'of the original production' was in effect an attempt to put the play into a constellation of social and cultural immediacy today.

The happy concurrence of the theatre practitioners and critics in some sessions was insistently corrected by others. The final session of the workshop, and the final essay in this collection, brought together Nicholas Hytner, director of the Royal National Theatre in London, Shakespeare scholar and a general editor of the Arden Shakespeare Ann Thompson, and internationally recognised performance studies critic Janelle Reinelt. Unlike most other participants, Hytner had not contributed in advance to the discussion, so his comments on heightened language were coming directly from a public perception of Shakespeare's language. As a result, the essay is able to engage with a debate that has not had the mediating influence of conversation and negotiation. Not surprisingly, the essay recounts a series of impasses between the editorial scholar and the public director. But at the same time also finds a number of *rapprochements* about physicality and speech, the need for context, and the usefulness of an understanding of syntax, grammar and semantics.

Reinelt's concluding thoughts on the collection as a whole begin by citing Robert Weimann's suggestion that the writer's pen and the actor's voice may delineate a fundamental disjunction, and move to the distinction made by Arden and Hendricks, the first saying that the body animates the text and the second that the text animates the body. Following a number of examples from specific sessions, she suggests that institutions encourage practitioners and critics to think quite differently, but that they need each other. Reinelt goes on to argue for a 'doctrine of separate but overlapping spheres' that could generate far more dialogue. We need to do rather more that peer through this chink in the wall, but no one says it's going to be easy.

Lynette Hunter, University of Leeds
Peter Lichtenfels, Manchester Metropolitan University

Both editors are currently working at the
University of California, Davis
October 2004

NOTE ON CITATIONS

Because this collection draws from oral presentation as well as written, many citations are to the transcripts subsequently prepared for circulation among the participants of the workshop, and several are to emails and letters that were exchanged both before and after the event. Each session has an individual transcript with unique pagination. All citations, in brackets following a quotation, to a session transcript are to the page numbers from that transcript; some essays cite transcripts from other sessions, and when this is the case the citation contains the title of that session, followed by the page number from that transcript. Where it is not clear in the text of the essay that a particular participant is speaking, the page number will be preceded by the name of that speaker; this is often the case when a member of the session audience made a contribution, or when a citation is being made to a transcript from another session. Because of the prior preparation and considered practice and research that participants made for the workshop, the oral contributions made by participants are cited in a way analogous to citations to printed published texts for research. Exchanges of emails and letters that took place before and after the workshop, are cited as (Writer, email) or (Writer, letter). Citations from printed published works are cited in the style adopted by the Arden Shakespeare.

1

TEXT AND VOICE

Janelle Jenstad (University of Victoria): respondent
Peter Lichtenfels (University of California, Davis)
Lynne Magnusson (University of Toronto)

Theatre practitioners often train and rehearse so there is a vocal preci-
sion and consciousness of sound that arises when actors are saying what
they think and thinking what they say. Critics on the other hand engage
with a wide variety of strategies for engaging with the 'voice' of the text
and understanding the social interactions displayed. While discussing voice
training techniques such as vowel/consonant exercises, rhythm and silence,
as well as more literary techniques such as punctuation and rhetorical
strategy, the exchange turns into a substantial debate between people try-
ing to negotiate each other's practices, that demonstrates the considerable
difficulty arising from disciplinary vocabularies and expectations.

The eye of man hath not heard, the ear of man hath not seen …
Nick Bottom in *A Midsummer Night's Dream*[1]

DIVERGENCE AND CONVERGENCE

Theatre practitioners and literary critics come to this discussion with
different ideas about 'voice' and 'text' and what we do with them. In
our pre-workshop exchanges, we found ourselves having to articulate,
question and clarify basic assumptions and terminology.

Shakespeare's texts, our texts

Both Peter Lichtenfels and Lynne Magnusson work extensively with the
first *printed texts* of Shakespeare's plays. It is important to recognise
that we have no unmediated access to what Shakespeare actually wrote.
Shakespeare's *manuscripts* have not survived for us to consult, and the

scribes who copied those manuscripts and the compositors who type-set the copies may have changed punctuation, spelling and lineation. Nineteen plays have survived in quarto format (small, single-play texts); 36 plays were collected in the large folio volume of *Mr. William Shakespeares Comedies, Histories & Tragedies* of 1623. Of those plays that appeared in both quarto (Q) and folio (F) texts, the two or more versions often differ significantly, from punctuation right up to scenes that are present in one text but absent from the other(s). The 'bad quartos' – memorial reconstructions of the play in question[2] – may record early performance cuts and rearrangements, and can be useful to theatrical practitioners today. Peter Lichtenfels refers later to a performance direction in the bad quarto (Q1) of *Romeo and Juliet.*

The multiplicity of early texts means that editors who create *editions* must either choose between the texts or produce a *conflated* text. The long tradition of editing Shakespeare began in the eighteenth century, with Nicholas Rowe's edition of 1709. Editors have usually corrected certain aspects of the early texts, such as peculiarities of typography (*u* and *v* were not distinguished, nor were *i* and *j*, as you will notice in some of the early texts we quote later) and punctuation (which Lynne Magnusson discusses at length).[3] Recently, editing has taken a turn towards *unediting*, or removing the accretions of generations of editor-ial intervention.[4] Both Peter Lichtenfels and Lynne Magnusson are editors, bringing to the early texts their different perspectives as theatre director and literary critic.

Theatre practitioners benefit from the work of textual scholars, but often choose to ignore much of it. Full *editorial stage directions* are usually meant to guide the reader's imagination rather than the actor's gestures. However, as Peter Lichtenfels goes on to explain, actors need to discover the *implied stage directions* of the text for themselves. It has often been said that editors put everything into their editions and directors take everything out when preparing their scripts. In creating a *performance script*, the director may have many objectives: shorten-ing the performance time, clarifying obscurities, emphasising a parti-cular aspect of the play, or even shaping its message.[5] To do so, directors may cut scenes, conflate or eliminate characters, change words, trim speeches and rearrange the sequence of events. During rehearsal, this text may undergo further cuts and changes.

When most of us use the word *text* in ordinary conversation, we are thinking either of a written utterance made up of words, or a book or script made of paper and ink. But to literary theorists, a text is any 'structure composed of elements of signification,'[6] which means that a *theatrical production* is also a text. Costume, music, lighting, scenery, properties, blocking and, most importantly, the actors' *voices* and *bodies* all make meanings that are 'read' by the playgoer. Performance critics, who share with theatre practitioners the idea that the 'written text of a play' is 'a script to be realized in performance,'[7] will thus take as their object of inquiry the text created in part by the actors' voices.

Shakespeare's voices, our voices

The theatre practitioner and literary critic often work from radically different assumptions about what 'voice' is. For the theatre practitioner, voice can be something one brings *to* the text, while for literary critics, voice is something one identifies *from* or *in* the text. To Peter Lichtenfels, the voice is a tool – an instrument to realise the text. Like the rest of the muscles in the body, the voice has to be exercised and trained.

To critics of dramatic literature, voice means the personality, power, education, wit, social class, authority, intelligence and volubility of the character as they are expressed through syntax, diction and style. Is the language prose or verse? rhymed or blank verse? How much does the character speak and to whom? Shakespeare critics are trained to distinguish a variety of distinct voices being created within the text, none of which can or should be identified with Shakespeare himself. It used to be that critics would think of these as the voices of many different 'individuals'. It is becoming more common to think of them as a concert of social voices, and to consider the relationship of each voice to other voices. For example, the Nurse has a different voice in private with Juliet than she does with the Friar or with Romeo and his friends. Her voice power depends on how her age, class, gender, learning, and knowledge compare to those of the other voices in the scene.

In the next section, Peter Lichtenfels describes his methods for training the voice. His techniques, though very much his own, share commonalities with the work of Cicely Berry, Head of Voice at the Royal Shakespeare Company (RSC) for many years, and author of a number of influential books, beginning with *Voice and the Actor* in 1973. Berry, her colleague Patsy Rodenburg and their American counterpart Kristin Linklater have each produced a pair of books dealing with voice

and text respectively.[8] However, 'nobody ever learned to act from reading a book', nor did anyone ever learn to teach acting from a book.[9]
Both actor and coach learn from practice and experience.

WORKING ON VOICE: THE THEATRE PRACTITIONER

Peter Lichtenfels

Part of my work as a theatre professor and director entails teaching
young actors to be 'on *voice*', a state in which the *text* is integrated into
the body, so that when actors come to perform they are able to respond
in the moment to other characters as if they are hearing the others' lines
for the first time and speaking their own thoughts as they think them.
It is much easier to describe the consequences of not being on voice
than to define the state of being on voice. Actors who are not on voice
speak Shakespeare's text as if it were an opinion they do not share; if
asked to explore what the line says, they will instead explain what the
line means; their inflections tend to rise at the ends of words and lines;
they accent non-substantives (pronouns and possessives like 'I', 'me',
and 'my') in unstressed positions; and they take unearned pauses, using
conjunctions like 'and' or 'but' as holidays while they think about the
next phrase. These 'holidays' kill energy for the actor and the audience
precisely when the line and the thought should be driving forward.

 Age, confidence, peer pressure, class and geography impact the degree
to which we habitually vocalise. Would-be actors have to give themselves permission to use their vocal instruments. In developing from
infancy to adulthood, we all learn to censor ourselves into relative silence.
We are socialised to listen politely, to suppress our voices, not to sing
or mutter when we are around other people, not to interrupt other
people and not to talk at the theatre or a concert. Young actors need to
recognise the internalised messages of social regulation in everyday life
so that they can respond otherwise to the need to speak when on stage.

 This self-censorship is particularly acute when we live our daily lives
in close proximity to other people. Having taught until recently mainly
in the UK, I find that some of my students (rural Irish, Welsh, northern
English and Scots) have grown up with the vestiges of an oral culture,
but most (from cities or the south) have grown up travelling in cars
from building to building, where they spend much of their time in
silent, non-interactive activities in front of the television or computer.
Not only are these students unaccustomed to making sound, they have

also lost their ability to hear certain sounds because noise pollution cuts out higher frequencies. Students cannot vocalise what they cannot hear, and have to expand their auditory sensitivity before they can develop the full range of their voices.

While we do have voice lessons, we teach the student that voice is part of the body. Voice involves the lips, tongue, mouth, resonating cavities in the head, throat and neck muscles, vocal cords, lungs, diaphragm, hips and feet. The first step to being on voice is correcting posture. Raising the heels off the floor predisposes the actor to let the spoken word run ahead of the body breathlessly. Collapsing the body into the hips produces a ponderous and leaden voicing of the text. The 'grounded' actor keeps the heels on the floor, connected to the earth, with the body up and forward from the hips; this posture helps the voice to move forward from word to word. I work with stances, from traditional Chinese physical culture,[10] that put the weight over a specific area of the body and promote the floor–body connection. The next step is softening the habitual tensions of the adult body – around the solar plexus, for example – through extensive vocalisation. Then the tongue – a muscle group – has to be trained and strengthened like any other muscle.

When I work with students on a text, I get them to build it up sound by sound first, then word by word, then line by line, then sentence by sentence. One of the first exercises is to take all the words in a speech down to their consonant and vowel sounds.[11] The actor will speak the sound of the consonants aloud (as they sound within the context of that word, omitting any that are silent) for the entire speech, keeping the shape of the word alive. For example, Hermia's reply to Helena in 3.2 of *A Midsummer Night's Dream*:

> 'Puppet'! Why, so? Ay, that way goes the game!
> Now I perceive that she hath made compare
> Between our statures; she hath urg'd her height;
> And with her personage, her tall personage,
> Her height, forsooth, she hath prevail'd with him.
> And are you grown so high in his esteem
> Because I am so dwarfish and so low?
> How low am I, thou painted maypole? Speak:
> How low am I? I am not yet so low
> But that my nails can reach unto thine eyes.

(3.2.289–98)

would sound as follows:

P·P·T W S Th·T W G·Z Th G·M
N P·R·S·V Th·T Sh H·Th M·D K·M·P·R
B·T·W·N R S·T·T·R·Z Sh H·TH R·J·D H·R H·T
N·D W·Th H·R P·R·S·N·J H·R T·L P·R·S·N·J
H·R H·T F·R·S·Th Sh H·Th P·R·V·L·D W·Th H·M
N·D R Y G·R·N S H N H·Z S·T·M
B·K·Z M S D·W·R·F·Sh N·D S L
H L M Th P·N·T·D M·P·L S·P·K
H L M M N·T Y·T S L
B·T Th·T M N·L·Z K·N R·Ch N·T Th·N Z

The actor then repeats the exercise for the vowels, preserving the shape and meaning of each word as much as possible while making only the vowel sounds (as they sound in the context of the word, so silent letters are not sounded here):[12]

u e ai O ai a A O ə A
ow ai ə E a E a A o A:
ə E ow a u: E a u: ə: ai
a i ə: ə: o a ə: a ə: o a
ə: ai o: oo E a E A i i
a a: oo O O I i i e E
E u I a O a: i a O O
ow O a ai ow A ə A O E
ow O a ai ai a o e O O
u a ai A a E u oo ai ai

If you try to speak the consonants only, and then the vowels only, you will discover that it takes a surprising amount of energy and effort to articulate all these sounds separately. In a one-minute speech, then, the actor's jaw and tongue need to do about five minutes' worth of work. The point of the exercise is not to get the actor to say the vowels and consonants in a particular way, but to isolate each of the sounds the actor will make in his or her unique way. Actors need to be specific about each word and to value its particularity, in order to avoid running words together or using the same energy to homogenise or generalise a number of distinct words as one sound. Theatre can be exciting only if the particularities of each word, and the clash of each of its sounds, can be heard.

This work with sounds allows one to hear when a particular vowel, consonant or consonantal cluster predominates.[13] Alliterative effects provide auditory clues to aspects of characterisation. One way of thinking about the exercise is to imagine that the consonants are allied to the actions, and the vowels to the emotions of the character. For example, breaking down the opening exchange between Theseus and Hippolyta in *A Midsummer Night's Dream* into its component sounds reveals that it contains a high proportion of 'ow', 'oh' and 'oo' sounds: 'Now' (1.1.1), 'our' (11), 'hour' (1), 'Four' (2, 7, 8), 'moon' (3, 4, 9), 'O' (3), 'how slow' (3), 'dowager' (5), 'out' (6), 'bow' (9), 'Now-bent' (10, in Q and F texts; 'New-bent' is a Rowe emendation) and 'behold' (10). These sounds might suggest to the English-speaking actor that the relationship is vulnerable on some level because of the way the sounds call on deep resonances below the solar plexus. We do not know precisely how Elizabethans pronounced their words, but, from an actor's or director's point of view, there is enough of a pattern to support the sense that the relationship is full of potential hurt.

In *Romeo and Juliet*, after hearing the Nurse's garbled account of the duel and not knowing if Romeo is dead or alive, Juliet's response is:

> What devil art thou that dost torment me thus?
> This torture should be roar'd in dismal hell.
> Hath Romeo slain himself? Say thou but 'Ay'
> And that bare vowel 'I' shall poison more
> Than the death-darting eye of cockatrice.
> I am not I if there be such an 'I'
> Or those eyes shut that makes thee answer 'Ay'.
> If he be slain say 'Ay', or if not, 'No'.
> Brief sounds determine of my weal or woe.
>
> (3.2.43–51)

Juliet's repetition of the sound 'Ay'/'I'/'eye' – foregrounded by her own use of the phrase 'bare vowel' – has something to do with the destabilisation of her identity in this moment of grief, her version of what Romeo has said earlier ('Tut, I have lost myself, I am not here. / This is not Romeo, he's some other where' [1.1.195–6]). But as one says these sounds aloud, what one hears is the sound of keening: believing that Romeo is dead, Juliet grieves. These examples suggest that what one sees on the page is not necessarily what one hears on the stage and that Shakespeare's text can be accessed on different levels. One needs to see *and* hear it to get a full feeling for the dialogue. Perhaps Bottom is right when he says that 'The eye of man hath not heard, the ear of man hath not seen … what my dream was' (*MND* 4.1.209–10, 212).

Going from word to word teaches young actors where stress should be laid. Many of them seem to put more energy into mispronouncing a word than into being simple and getting it right. This tendency is partly rooted in an assumption that they have to try harder with Shakespeare's text – which leads to oddly exaggerated words – but much of it lies in our daily habits. These habits include hanging on to sounds instead of giving the word closure. 'I' becomes 'Iiiiiiiii', for example, or 'my' becomes 'myyyyyyyy'. Another habit is hitting only the first sylla-ble in a word and not seeing the energy of the word through (to the 'ing' or 'ly' suffix, for instance). The actor has to go from word to word, leaving the energy of the last word behind and choosing the next word, embracing its energy, then leaving that one behind. Modern speech patterns, if applied to Shakespeare, encourage actors to wrench the metre by emphasising the first word of a verse line (often a conjunction, or 'I' or 'My') and the second-last word, which runs against the iambic pentameter heartbeat of the verse line. Teaching Shakespeare properly requires making students aware of their own voice habits and patterning new habits if necessary.

But these new habits do not mean that the actor cannot shape the rhythm and stress to colour the thought, or cannot pause in order to create an effect. The goal is a precision and consciousness of sound that arises when people are saying what they think, and thinking what they say, instead of simply reciting someone else's words. We want actors to *choose* actively these particular words. Shakespeare's characters are on stage precisely because they want to change somebody, or influence the outcome of an event, either by speaking or by remaining silent. Either way it is an active choice, as if the actor *is* the character thinking in the moment: a character elects to remain silent but could speak at any moment, or a character elects to speak but could have remained silent. By choosing the word and meaning what it says, the actor takes responsibility for the words, which then begin to be powerful again.

Having built from sounds to the word, I then get the actor going from word to phrase to line to complete thought. This process destabilises the written text in that it takes words from the printed text and puts them into the musculature, which is where they have their life henceforth in the process. Once we are at the point of working with thoughts and dialogue, an actor has to read for what the text asks one to *do* rather than for what the text *means*. Hermia's speech near the end of 3.2 in *A Midsummer Night's Dream* asks the actor to enact a number of different things:

> Never so weary, never so in woe,
> Bedabbled with the dew, and torn with briars,
> I can no further crawl, no further go;
> My legs can keep no pace with my desires.
> Here will I rest me till the break of day.
> Heavens shield Lysander, if they mean a fray!
>
> (3.2.442–7)

Hermia must crawl onstage during her speech (444), show her weariness (442), cease crawling (444), designate what is meant by 'Here' (446), and pray (447). This kind of reading looks for the directions that many people claim Shakespeare gives to the actor within the text.[14] Although the actor/director/production may ultimately decide not to observe these implicit stage directions, it must be a conscious decision either to follow or reject them.

Even if there is no implied physical stage direction, the actor has to identify a practical task that the written text asks him or her to do at any one time. This task can usually be understood in a few words, such as 'I want Romeo out of the house' (Tybalt in *RJ* 1.5) or 'I want Romeo to remain in my house' (Capulet in *RJ* 1.5). These are *objectives*. The reasons Tybalt and Capulet give to sustain their objectives are *tactics*. Juliet's prothalamium (*RJ* 3.2.1–31) is a good test case because, unlike Hermia's speech, it does not require any physical action. Juliet's objective is to hasten the coming of her wedding night. In the first two lines, 'Gallop apace, you fiery-footed steeds, / Towards Phoebus' lodging' (1–2), her tactic is to order night to come. Night does not come, so Juliet needs to go on. In lines 2 to 4, her tactic is to make comparison, and shame night into coming: 'Such a waggoner / As Phaeton would whip you to the west / And bring in cloudy night immediately'. Of course, there is a dramatic irony here in that Juliet's invocation of Phaeton forebodes an end that the playgoer anticipates but Juliet does not. Here, because the *meaning* of the line differs from what Juliet *means*, we can see how important it is that the actor be able to identify and articulate what the line says rather than (or before) what the line means.

Throughout the speech, Juliet's objective remains constant, but her tactics are constantly changing.

Being on voice then, requires a number of levels of work: posture, bodywork and confidence-building; strengthening the tongue and sensitising the ear; replacing habits inimical to verse with new ones; working with the basic sounds of the language; building from sounds to words; getting actors to speak through the words and not take unearned pauses; getting them to choose the words actively; building from words to sentences; and understanding all of the things a speech asks the actor to do.

KNOWING THE STOP: THE LITERARY CRITIC

Lynne Magnusson

One of the critical questions for this topic of text and voice must be (bending a formulation in Robert Weimann's *Author's Pen and Actor's Voice*) 'is there any necessary relation between performance and text?' To what extent and how is the 'actor's voice' guided by the 'author's text'?[15] Shakespeare himself knew about the 'unearned pause' that Peter Lichtenfels has talked about: in the Rude Mechanicals' play in *A Midsummer Night's Dream*, he gives us an incompetent actor who pauses in the wrong places. Peter Quince's garbled prologue makes Theseus comment that 'This fellow doth not stand upon points'; Lysander concurs, offering the criticism that 'He hath rid his prologue like a rough colt; he knows not the stop', and Hippolyta observes that 'he hath played on this prologue like a child on a recorder; a sound, but not in government' (5.1.118–23). Does Shakespeare's text tell the actors how 'to stand upon points' and 'know the stop'? If we turn to it for signals to help the actor's voice, in which features of his language will we find them: (1) the punctuation, (2) the metre and versification, (3) the syntax and sentence structure, or (4) some combination of all three? Will those aspects of their individual speeches tell actors everything they need to know, or do they need to look at the give and take of dialogue as well?

Punctuation and breath

My starting point is the punctuation; my example the apparently simple prose exchange between Moth and Don Armado in 1.2 of *Love's*

Labour's Lost; and my problem the placement of the punctuation in this dialogue. Even if we decide that it is the modern editor's responsibility to punctuate in such a way as to aid understanding, we still need to ask if editors should punctuate for silent reading (sense) or performance (voice). Let us compare the passage as it appears in the Q1 text (1598) and in the H.R. Woudhuysen Arden 3 edition (1998):

Enter Armado and Moth his page.
Armado. Boy, What signe is it when a man of great spirite growes
   melancholy?
Boy. A great signe sir that he will looke sadd.
Ar. Why? sadnes is one & the selfe same thing deare imp.
Boy. No no, O Lord sir no.

[Sig. B1v][16]

Enter ARMADO *and* MOTH, *his Page.*
ARMADO Boy, what sign is it when a man of great spirit
   grows melancholy?
MOTH A great sign, sir, that he will look sad.
ARMADO Why, sadness is one and the selfsame thing,
   dear imp.
MOTH No, no, O Lord, sir, no.

(1–6)

In the third spoken line of the Q1 passage, there is a question mark after Armado's 'why'. This word and punctuation combination, 'why?', appears a number of times in the scene. When Woudhuysen removes the question mark in his edition, he changes the sense of 'why' from an interrogative expressing curiosity to an interjection expressing surprise, but perhaps his punctuation is the better guide for the actor's *voice*. In the subsequent line, contrary principles seem to apply. Q1's 'No no, O Lord sir no' does not meet current standards of correctness, and Woudhuysen could scarcely reproduce it; he gives us instead, 'No, no, O Lord, sir, no'. But isn't the Q1 punctuation a much more effective guide for the actor's voice?

Early modern writers about punctuation make an explicit link between punctuation and control of breath, which may take us some way towards linking textual signs to the actor's voice as an instrument of the body. According to Richard Mulcaster's *Elementarie* (1582), an important pedagogical manual, the comma 'warneth us to rest there, and to help our breath a little', while a period requires a longer pause 'to help our breath at full'; the colon marks a pause of intermediate length. Other marks indicate the tone and pace of the voice: parenthesis, he says, signals a 'lower & quicker voice', and the mark of interrogation presumably a rising intonation. Altogether, these five main punctuation marks (the semicolon was only just coming into use):

> are helps to our breathing, & the distinct utterance of our speech … they are creatures to the pen, & distinctions to pronounce by, & therefore, as they are to be set down with judgement in writing, so they are to be used with diligence in the right framing of the tender child's mouth.[17]

Mulcaster offers what Bruce Smith (following Walter Ong) calls a 'physiological' system of punctuation, as opposed to a 'syntactical' system that 'marks the separation of sentence elements according to the logic of … grammar'.[18]

This recognition of historical differences in the use of punctuation can help us to see why Theseus, Lysander and Hippolyta might elevate to such high importance the standing upon 'points'. The issue in this language of 'stops' is not to demarcate moments empty of speech, but to demarcate, through control of the breath, oratorical units of utterance. To know the stop is, in their words, 'to speak true' (5.1.121), to 'govern' the articulation of sound, to produce orderly speech with the harmonious disposition of music.

However promising this recognition, we must be clear about why the punctuation of the early modern text will always be an insufficient guide for the actor seeking to 'speak true'. One intractable problem is that we know virtually nothing about the punctuation of Shakespeare's dramatic manuscripts. We have no evidence to tell us if Shakespeare's own punctuation habits were in any way calculated to *help* the actor 'know the stop'. Those who see Shakespeare in Hand D in *The Booke of Sir Thomas More* have described it as 'remarkably *under*punctuated',[19] and certainly not serving to demarcate oratorical units according to Mulcaster's prescriptions.

In addition, as Jonathan Crewe has argued, early modern punctuation shows the signs of both a rhetorical and a syntactical system of pointing: 'the history of print does not move along a simple trajectory from orality to literacy, or from rhetoric to logic, and no study of Shakespearean punctuation can be organized simply on that basis'.[20] For example, George Puttenham's *The Arte of English Poesie* (1589) offers, like Mulcaster's *Elementarie*, definitions of comma, colon and periodus as 'resting places', but describes a function of the comma that is very like the modern syntactical one: 'In a verse of six syllables and under is needefull no *Cesure* [cæsura] at all, because the breath asketh no relief: yet if ye give any *Comma*, it is to make distinction of sense more then for any thing else'.[21] We have no idea how the theories outlined by Mulcaster and Puttenham impinged on the practices of printing houses,[22] never mind how or if they were the guiding principles of Shakespeare's own punctuation. For many reasons, then, we cannot simply turn to the earliest texts for implied breathing directions the way we can for implied stage directions.

Assuming that Shakespeare had nothing to do with the punctuation of the quarto and folio texts, modern editors silently repunctuate without explaining when or how they have done so. The New Cambridge Shakespeare's guide for editors instructs that editorial emendations to punctuation should be recorded 'only where they affect meaning'. In fact, modern editorial practice performs a radical 'cultural translation' every time it replaces punctuation that does constitute a guide for the voice with a syntactical guide instead. Perhaps it is not feasible for the editor to provide directions that would enable actors to govern the sound of their bodily instruments. As Crewe puts it, there can probably never be more than a 'messy compromise'[23] between modernised punctuation (aimed at the mind and eye) and the practices of early texts (insofar as they were aimed at the voice and ear). But no service is done to the theatre practitioner when scholarly editors exercise their power over the stops without any effort at transparency.

Voice in dialogic interaction

Knowing the stops can never have been solely or even primarily a matter of simply paying attention to the punctuation. In this passage from 1.2 of *Love's Labour's Lost*, the actors must pay attention to *voice* as it is born out of *dialogue* and as it takes its signals from *rhetorical figures of sound*. The boy page, Moth, cannot really be said to have a voice apart from the way in which he plays off Armado's utterances. The basic pattern of interaction in this interchange is the most fundamental in language use: alternating questions and answers. The passage, quoted below from the Q1 text, continues from the text quoted previously and starts out with the asymmetrical pattern of question and answer that seems to set up a simple hierarchical arrangement of questioning master, answering page. But then the voice flavour of the dialogue begins to alter, as the page's deprecating tone marked by obedient answer-words slips into imitative repetition of his master's utterances:

Arm. How canst thou part sadnes and melancholy, my tender Iuuenall?
Boy. By a familier demonstration of the working, my tough signeor.
Arma. Why tough signeor? Why tough signeor?
Boy. Why tender iuuenall? Why tender iuuenall?
Arm. I spoke it tender iuuenal, as a congruent apethaton apperteining
　　to thy young dayes, which we may nominate tender.
Boy. And I tough signeor, as an appertinent title to your
　　olde time, which we may name tough.
Arma. Prettie and apt.

[Sig. B2r]

We do not need to provide the rhetorical labels to spell out what is happening here; but if we did, we would note the parallel constructions (parison) of approximately matching length (isocolon). Soon, in this dialogue of two voices, it is the boy who has taken over the rising intonation of the questioner, with the master being increasingly put to his answer: 'How meane you sir, I prettie, and my saying apt? or I apt, and my saying prettie?' asks Moth; 'Speak you this in my praise Maister?' and then, a few lines later, 'How many is one thrice told?' [Sig. B2r]. Here, voice grows out of simple patterns of dialogue and rhetoric, as the clever and cheeky page establishes his intellectual ascendancy over his ponderous and self-important master.

Metre and syntax

Just as notoriously difficult to talk about as the elusive effects of punctuation in providing signals for the actor's voice may be the interaction of metre and syntax. How do they productively interfere in ways that can guide the actor's voice? One of the problems inherent in our attempt to talk across the literary and theatrical disciplines may be that it is unfashionable in literary criticism at the moment to look at things in formalist ways.[24] Few critics other than George T. Wright and, to a lesser extent, Russ McDonald have taken up the issue of Shakespeare's prosody in recent years,[25] and yet surely it is so obtrusive and central a fact of Shakespeare's language that it has to be addressed in identifying textual signals for the actor's voice. For example, in *A Midsummer Night's Dream*, after Oberon's plot has entangled Bottom in Titania's arms and she has relinquished to Oberon the contested Indian boy, the Fairy King directs Puck as follows:

> And gentle Puck, take this transformed scalp
> From off the head of this Athenian swain,
> That he awaking when the other do,
> May all to Athens back again repair,
> And think no more of this night's accidents
> But as the fierce vexation of a dream.
>
> (4.1.63–8)

Far from confirming the old truism about the harmonious match between iambic pentameter and the rhythms of English syntax, the metrical requirements of the blank verse here seem to complicate the simple instructions that Oberon must give. That is, the needs of the metre distort what needs to be said, in the first line by stretching out 'transformed' into three syllables and reducing 'Athenian' in the second line to three syllables; throwing the preceding word 'this' into un-accustomed relief in a stressed position; and causing strangely contracted forms in the elliptical 'he awaking when the other do'; and redundancy and unmotivated syntactic inversion in the fourth line's 'May all to Athens back again repair' (would not 'May all repair to Athens' suffice?). What can the actor's voice do with the strange proportions signalled by the metrical disposition of these lines?

In one possible interpretation, the metrical dynamics throw an un-accustomed emphasis on 'this' in two consecutive lines – '*this* trans-formed scalp' and '*this* Athenian swain'. Such an emphasis would suggest that the actor/character is to make some link between his voice and the stage spectacle before us. But if Shakespeare's words do guide the voice to this emphasis (and, of course, they need not), I am not convinced that the metrical stress is required to make Oberon's imperative clear. This instance of deictic pointing is not like Polonius' 'Take this [my head] from this [my body] if this [information] be otherwise' (*Ham* 2.2.156), which Keir Elam analyses so skilfully in *Reading Shakespeare's Dramatic Language*.[26] Clearly, the metrical stress there points to some required stage action that clarifies each otherwise ambiguous 'this'. In the passage from *A Midsummer Night's Dream*, however, the first and second 'this' are both followed by the nouns they modify. The verbal pointers seem redundant, unless the text means to make a sharp distinction between Bottom's ass head and his human body.

Maybe all that can be said here about how metre drives syntax is that the resulting strangeness reinforces the sense of ceremony and fairy-like other-worldliness. But perhaps we cannot always afford to put Shakespeare's language under this kind of microscope, nor to expect it to provide all the signals an actor needs. Maybe the actor has to find the character's objectives and tactics in creative collaboration with – or even in spite of – the writer's text. As Weimann suggests in exploring the 'bifold authority' of the early modern 'author's pen' and 'actor's voice',[27] we need to recognise the *disjunction* between the writer's 'literary "endeavors of art" derived from a university or grammar school education in rhetoric and composition' and the actor's 'largely oral, physical, spectacular, body-centered practices of performance and display'. 'In their (dis)continuity', he remarks, 'writing and playing, pen and voice, allowed for both reciprocity and difference at the heart of their relations in theatrical production.'[28]

To 'find the stop' in Shakespeare's language, we need to look not just to punctuation, vowels, consonants and words, but also to the interactions and interferences of metre and syntax as well as other levels of dialogue and pragmatics. Knowing the stops, then, for an actor, must not only mean matching English syntax to voice emphasis and stress as Peter Lichtenfels has described. It also means attending to the patterning of uptake and speaker change, and identifying the social dynamic behind it, even in a dialogue as artificial as the one in 1.2 of *Love's Labour's Lost.*

WORKING TOGETHER: TEXTS AND VOICES

PL: I'm glad you've brought up the issue of dialogue, which is an important later stage of the process I was describing. I may have inadvertently implied that I work with actors in isolation. Occasionally I do, if one actor has extended monologues or soliloquies, but for dialogue all the actors involved always remain in the room. I work with each speech in the order it appears in the text, so that each speaker hears and responds to the other voices in the dialogue. It is important that all the actors be present for two reasons: (1) at the beginning of this process, the actor might not recognise the difference between his or her normal voice and a rooted voice, but the other actors can attest to it, and (2) actors need to learn to listen as well as speak. One cannot respond in the moment unless one has truly heard what the other character is saying. Everyone has to be on voice; everyone has to speak as if thinking the thought for the first time; and everyone has to respond as if hearing the others' thoughts for the first time.

LM: Thinking about this account of voice as an expression of the body, and about these exercises that contribute to being 'on voice', I have two incompatible responses. On the one hand, I now recognise the importance of understanding this process before asking questions about how the author's or the editor's text comes together with the actor's voice. On the other hand, I suspect that the business of acting – like running, doing a job interview, giving an important speech, leading a government, hosting a dinner party, or even using everyday language effectively – is a *practice* in which competence or practical mastery does not require an analytical understanding of how it works.[29] Is it *true* that consonants relate to action and vowels register emotional temperature? But 'Is it true?' may simply be the wrong question to ask when one tries to articulate the logic of a complex practice like coming into voice. Perhaps it would be better to ask 'Does it work?' This particular narrative, a story one can tell young actors to orient their voice practice, must be effective. Is it *the* story or simply one of many workable stories that might be told?

PL: Is it *true* that vowels represent emotion and consonants action? No, not in any absolute way, although it is perhaps a shorthand. What is 'true', I think, is that vowel and consonant sounds affect the body and breath differently. If you voice only the consonants in a Shakespearean speech, you will begin to feel light-headed, but the shape of the word will be there. Vowels will be easier on your breathing, but keeping the shape of the word alive will be harder. On the whole, vowel sounds seem to blend more into each other, and clusters of consonantal sounds retain their constituent sounds more clearly. The value of the exercise lies somewhere between 'it's true' and 'it works'.

LM: While I can believe that the physical dimension of sounds matters to the actor, I find it almost impossible to say anything critical about them. I hear sound clusters or internal rhymes and find them satisfying, as in the following examples:

EMILIA … had *mi*ne ea*r* / Stol'*n* so*m*e *n*ew ai*r*

(consonance and end rhyme;
TNK 1.3.74–5; Magnusson's emphasis)

2 QUEEN … Sp*ea*k't in a woman's *key*; like such a woman / As any of us *three*; w*ee*p ere you fail. / Lend us a *knee*

(assonance and internal rhyme;
TNK 1.1.94–6; Magnusson's emphasis)

But I usually have little to say about their significance or the work they do.

JJ: Alliterative effects may serve to create the *body memory* that Peter has alluded to. Many actors say that they find it easy to memorise verse (rhyming couplets especially) because of its melodic and mnemonic qualities. Lynne, you suggested that speaking true produced the harmonious disposition of music; what if musicality helped the actor speak true? Try *saying* the words of a song, and you might find that you can't recite them even though you can sing them. Brain researchers think that we store and reproduce song using a different part of the brain to that for spoken words. Maybe these aural effects serve to push verse into the part of the brain that remembers song, to access alternate and possibly better memory pathways. Working as an actor and writing for actors, Shakespeare must have intuited what kind of language helped them remember the many different roles the repertory system required. Or perhaps assonance, consonance and rhyme were the aural equivalent of spectacle, intended mainly for pleasure and entertainment.

LM: Certainly I tend to be suspicious of using onomatopoeia as a key to characterisation. While it does make sense to me to imagine some level of hurt in the relationship of Theseus and Hippolyta, I find it hard to hear the hurt specifically in the 'ow' sounds, partly because, as a historicist scholar, my first recourse is to the *Oxford English Dictionary*, where I don't find 'ow' as an 'exclamation expressing sudden pain' until George Bernard Shaw's use of the word in 1919. This etymology does not invalidate your remark: performance happens in the present, and 'ow' is certainly available to be heard now as hurt. And perhaps it was indeed a sound associated in Shakespeare's day with grief and keening that has simply gone unrecorded.

But I can offer a critical commentary on the assonance in these lines (*MND* 1.1.3–4). After two lines of fairly regular iambic pentameter, the 'oh' and 'oo' sounds retard the rhythm of the thought: 'but *O*, methinks, h*ow* sl*ow* / This *o*ld m*oo*n wanes!' (Magnusson's emphasis) is impossible to say quickly, given the necessary rounding and pushing forward of the lips. What I hear in this line is a reinforcement of Theseus' frustration that Time obstructs the will of a powerful man. What Hippolyta has to say in response (1.1.7–11) seems wonderfully upbeat in comparison, the quickness and lilt of its pace reinforcing the radiantly beautiful simile of the silver bow that replaces his negative (and woman-limiting) image of the dowager. Theseus' 'O' of impatience and sexual frustration is then transformed in his second speech, moving from the 'O' of passive reaction to the 'Go' of active command followed by a series of imperatives: 'Go … Stir up … Awake … Turn melancholy forth …' (11–14).

His next address to Hippolyta, even if it keeps him in control ('*I* woo'd', '[*I*] won', '*I* will' [16–18; Magnusson's emphasis]), does seem to me to express a kind of integrity in that he acknowledges the terms under which he has brought her to Athens. The switch in key of their relations is echoed by a mimetic switch in rhythm, from the monosyllables of 'I woo'd thee with my sword' to the changed measure of the lengthening phrases, 'With pomp, with triumph, and with revelling' (1.1.16, 19).

PL: As conqueror of the Amazons, he could be reminding Hippolyta that she, as his slave, owes love to him, and then offering to change that relationship from one of power to one of friendship: 'But I will wed thee in another key' (1.1.18). It is difficult not to read 'sword' as 'penis'.

JJ: Hippolyta does not reply to this speech, for at this point Egeus enters with Hermia, Lysander and Demetrius. The text does not tell us how she feels about Theseus' rescripting of their relationship, nor about the reference to the sword/phallus that has conquered her. However, it has become conventional in performance to make her lack of voice throughout the rest of the scene meaningful, and to have her indicate through her silence that she disapproves of Theseus' support of Egeus. When Theseus, just before their exit, says 'Come, my Hippolyta' (another imperative), many productions will have her reject the hand he extends to her. This staging makes good sense of Theseus' 'what cheer, my love?' (1.1.122). Hippolyta may sweep past Theseus and exit before him. He then turns to Demetrius and Egeus to cover his embarrassment and reassert his authority.

PL: Hippolyta's silence in *A Midsummer Night's Dream* is fascinating and problematic. It may indeed register her objection to the violence of the patriarchal state represented by the Duke and Egeus. She says nothing yet has to witness the violence of a father against his daughter: 'As she [Hermia] is mine, I [Egeus] may dispose of her; / Which shall be either to this gentleman, / Or to her death, according to our law / Immediately provided in that case' (1.1.42–5).

LM: Theseus doesn't overrule Egeus, but does present a third option. Many of the lines we have been discussing are end-stopped, a feature typical of the early plays, but Theseus' answer to Hermia's request to 'know / The worst that may befall' her (1.1.62–3) contains a long sentence made of enjambed lines. It is also periodic (in the nineteenth-century sense of a sentence that holds off its logical completion to the end), the syntax and metre demanding the actor's sustained breath and force over many lines:

THESEUS [to Hermia] Take time to pause; and by the next new moon,
    The sealing-day betwixt my love and me
    For everlasting bond of fellowship,
    Upon that day either prepare to die
    For disobedience to your father's will,
    Or else to wed Demetrius, as he would,
    Or on Diana's altar to protest,
    For aye, austerity and single life.

                    (1.1.83–90)

As Ben Jonson said,

> Some men are tall, and bigge, so some Language is high and great. Then the words are chosen, their sound ample, the composition full, and absolution plenteous, and powr'd [poured, but probably with a pun on power] out, all grave, sinnewye and strong.[30]

Theseus' language here is full, plenteous, and poured out, as the completed logic of his sentence awaits the fulfilment of its sound. And yet there is an odd feature of the syntax, as it presses majestically forward, that demands interpretation in the actor's voice: the triplet of alternatives beginning with the word 'or'. Theseus has previously proposed Hermia a choice of X *or* Y punishment if she does not wed Demetrius: 'Either to die the death, or to abjure / For ever the society of men' (65–6). Here, however, the choices seem to multiply on the page. What is an actor to do? Propose three alternatives (which seems anticlimactic), or subordinate with voice and intonation the second, and make the third alternative to the first? I think the latter, since it sustains 'the composition full, and absolution plenteous'[31] of Theseus' utterance, which seems appropriate, even when his voice is quietly challenged by the power that makes Hermia 'bold' (59). But the utterance is, of course, open to other possibilities, especially since Theseus later mentions how his 'mind', 'being over-full of self-affairs', lost track of the relevant detail that Demetrius has been chasing Helena (1.1.113, 114). Can an actor speak this 'being over-full', as if Theseus is only haphazardly organising his thoughts as he speaks?

JJ: He could, but a performance solution that gives Hippolyta a role here might have Theseus achieve the completed logic at the end of the second option, with sinewy, strong words all poured out – and then hastily reiterate the less harsh alternative when he recognises her disapproval. '[T]he sealing-day betwixt my love and me' (84) may provide a cue for him to direct part of his speech implicitly to her, talking to Hermia but looking at Hippolyta for approval. Clearly, we need to consider the ramifications of silent characters. How do they affect the voices of, and dialogic interaction between, speaking characters?

LM: Peter's account of people – perhaps most of us and probably women in particular – who censor themselves into relative silence is fascinating. In my research, I am interested in Shakespeare's *representation* of voice power, status, self-confidence and timidity in the texts. Is there room to turn around and restore timidity and lack of voice as an aspect of what is represented in performance?

PL: Of course. The actor/character can use either words or silence to achieve the objective; silence itself is a powerful tactic. But either way, it is an active choice: a character chooses to speak or to remain silent.

LM: The idea of silence as something an actor/character chooses works well for Hippolyta; she cannot be entirely happy with her lot, but she is courteous in her speech and any hurt she feels is registered only in silence. In some instances, however, I would argue that actors may need to be aware that their characters have silence forced upon them, either by direct coercion or internalised self-censorship.

PL: Characters in Shakespeare's plays silence themselves or are silenced for many reasons. One example that comes to mind immediately is from 3.7 of *Richard III*, where the Citizens refuse to endorse Richard's coronation.[32] After *Romeo and Juliet*, there are characters reduced to silence instead of dying. Think of the apparent deaths of Hero in *Much Ado About Nothing*, Hermione in *The Winter's Tale*, or Guiderius/Polydore and Arviragus/Cadwal in *Cymbeline*. Kate in *The Taming of the Shrew* would be a fascinating study, not in silence *per se*, but in pressing a voice to change so that it is more socially acceptable and compliant.

There are other kinds of silencings in *Romeo and Juliet*. For example, the Nurse is reduced to repeating phrases in her vexation after the ill treatment by Mercutio and Benvolio in 2.4: 'Scurvy knave' (151, 161 and 'knave' at 154) and 'as they say' (165–6). Capulet is uncharacteristically silent while on stage in the latter part of 3.1 when the Prince comes to deal with Mercutio's and Tybalt's deaths. In 4.2, Juliet comes from the Friar 'Where I have learnt me to repent the sin / Of disobedient opposition / To you and your behests, and am enjoin'd / By holy Laurence to fall prostrate here, / To beg your pardon' (17–21). She silences herself still further in 4.3 by drinking the Friar's potion.

JJ: Many of these silencings pertain to women. In a scene that has much to say about the appropriate voices for various kinds of characters, the voice Quince prescribes for Francis Flute's Thisbe is 'small' (*MND* 1.2.46). Early modern culture allowed women relatively little voice power and characterised them as monstrous or anomalous when they did speak. Our discussion thus far has focused on the early comedies, but in the tragedies and tragicomedies women who speak freely are punished. In *Othello*, the more Desdemona exercises her voice on Cassio's behalf the more she seems to corroborate Iago's lies. Emilia is killed because she does not 'hold [her] peace' (5.2.219): 'So speaking as I think, alas, I die' (5.2.252). In *The Winter's Tale*, Hermione's troubles begin when her persuasive voice turns out to be more 'potent' than Leontes' (1.2.51); the play ultimately validates women's voices, for Leontes encourages Paulina to 'Go on, go on: / Thou canst not speak too much' (3.2.214–15), but this seems to be an exception to the rule that death is the ultimate stop for the speaking woman.

PL: I too am fascinated by punctuation and its effects on the voice power of a character. Along with Lynette Hunter, I have observed in *Romeo and Juliet* that modern editorial practice has tended to give Juliet less voice power than the early texts did.[32] The last line of Juliet's speech in 3.2 (quoted in full earlier in the chapter) is usually punctuated as 'Brief sounds determine of my weal or woe'; editors usually assume that 'Brief sounds' refers to the previous line's 'Ay' and 'No', which makes good sense. But Q2 punctuates this last line rather differently: 'Briefe, sounds, determine my weale or wo'. With this punctuation, 'brief' can be an imperative ('Be brief'), referring to the Nurse's repeated failure to clarify if Romeo is alive or dead. 'Sounds!' often doubles for 'Zounds!' (God's wounds!), which is the way the Nurse seems to hear the last line because she next says 'I saw the wound [picking up the vowel and consonant cluster of 'zounds'], I saw it with mine eyes'. If we adopt the Q2 punctuation, which has Juliet so frustrated that she utters an oath, we give Juliet a different register of power. I find that it changes one's perception of her.

While researching *Romeo and Juliet*, I did productions of the Q1 (the 'bad quarto' of 1597), Q2 (1599) and Q4 (c.1616–27) texts, paying particular attention to punctuation to see what it could release for the actors. On the whole, these early texts were more lightly punctuated than most modern editions. Although we do not know whose punctuation is represented in Q1, Q2 and Q4, the punctuation worked better for the actor's breath than that in modern editions. The grammatical commas in modern editions, if taken as breath cues, produce many unearned pauses for the actor. With fewer punctuation marks, the quarto texts allow actors to keep going forward until the whole thought has been completed. This process of acting the early quarto texts confirmed for me that Shakespearean characters think as they speak and speak as they think. The more lightly punctuated quartos have another advantage in that they keep alive several possible meanings; they ask the actor/reader to take responsibility for the phrasing and meaning of the text. Often modern texts are so punctuated they insist on a particular phrasing and meaning. In my research I worked hard to strip away the accretions that had been accumulating since the seventeenth century.

A CONCERT OF WORKSHOP VOICES

Michael Gould: My experience with early texts has been similar to Peter's. Take Sebastian's 'This is the air, that is the glorious sun' (*TN* 4.3.1) speech, in which he wonders if Olivia's favour is real or if he's going mad. I find that modern punctuation makes me more rational, while the folio punctuation, which contains fewer full stops, helps me enter the madness. I lean towards folio punctuation in that case, but not in every case. Actors are opportunists when it comes to techniques: whether the folio punctuation is right is irrelevant to them; what matters is what the punctuation can do for them in a given speech on a given day.

Bridget Escolme: I'm deeply conflicted about the ideologies of voice training, and find the idea of stripping back modern mannerisms to reveal a voice that's free of cultural contingency very troubling.

PL: The goal is not to achieve a neutral accent. Indeed, an actor with a strong Northern Irish accent who adopted 'received pronunciation'[34] would probably not be 'on voice'. Voice work is a starting place to make young actors aware of their individual qualities. You have to unpack and take apart the habits before you put them together again, but the point is not to unpack Northumberland and put it back together as RP; you want to keep Northumberland.

LM: Shakespeare brings together a wide diversity of voices from different social and occupational groups. How can the linguistic variety of the Shakespearean text and the linguistic variety in the voices of the actors come together productively?

PL: Marrying the individual actor to the character is important to me. One encourages actors to join their own rhythms, dialects and personal temperaments with the needs of their characters.

Bridget Escolme: Regional accents are a political issue in Britain, as is the notion that there may be something inherently better about certain sounds. Some regional accents don't offer closure on some words, and I *want* to hear 'Iiiiiii' sometimes. I like the clashes, awkwardness and strangeness that arise from different voices.

JJ: Regional accents are represented in the plays themselves (particularly the history plays) and a production might well capitalise on the native voices of its actors, but I think what you are suggesting, Bridget, is that someone with a Northumberland accent shouldn't simply play Hotspur or the Earl of Northumberland (to a King Henry who speaks RP), but should play Hal or King Henry IV in a production that is 'accent-deaf' in the way that productions can be colour-blind.

Bill Worthen: The work of voice coaches does have an ideological component: the way the text and the body are coupled in training actually *produces* for us our sense of what we think works, which is radically different from what David Garrick, say, would have thought in the eighteenth century. He was interested in how one should stand too, but he had a different idea of what was 'natural'. The relationship between training, performance, human behaviour and texts is one of the hardest things to talk about, because everything one says seems to sound either prescriptive or analytical in a way that somehow belies the 'practice' that Lynne spoke about.

Michael Gould: Most actors I know get their clues from the metaphoric litter bins that surround the theatre. If someone suggests that vowels represent emotion and consonants action, you'll try it and see what it does for you.

Joy Richardson: Working with a variety of directors, actors are asked to approach the text in new ways every time. That process makes us aware of choices, suggests the arbitrary nature of the exercises and forces us to question assumptions about what is 'natural'.

Ann Thompson: Does it matter to people who do this kind of work that many of the vowel sounds have changed since Shakespeare's time? One can see this change in end-rhymes that no longer rhyme. The 'ow' sound is doubly historically contingent in that it neither meant what it does now nor sounded as it does now.

Lynette Hunter: My understanding (as a critic) is that these exercises are a way of providing the actor with an internal gesture – a melody – to work on. It doesn't necessarily matter how the words sound in any given accent or may have sounded at various points in history.

PL: Sometimes Shakespeare seems to create music in a formal way, as in 4.5 of *Romeo and Juliet* when Juliet has taken the potion and is apparently dead in her bed. The Q1 stage direction asks that Capulet, Paris, Lady Capulet and the Nurse 'All at once cry out' [sig. I2r]; in the Q2 and subsequent texts, each usually has six lines to speak before the Friar silences them. Capulet begins with 'Despis'd, distressed, hated, martyr'd, kill'd', Paris with 'Beguil'd, divorced, wronged, spited, slain', and Lady Capulet with 'Accurs'd, unhappy, wretched, hateful day'. Together, these lines create a cacophony of hard consonantal sounds (d, t, k in particular). The Nurse's 'O woe! O woeful, woeful, woeful day' cuts through the harder sounds with a wailing 'oh' sound (4.5.49). It's very much a verbal piece of music.

Patricia Parker: But one good thing about Shakespeare is that it's not all music on the same level; the melodic is punctuated with the rough.

NOTES

1 *A Midsummer Night's Dream*, ed. Harold F. Brooks (London: Methuen, 1979), p. 99, 4.1.209–10.

2 See Peter W.M. Blayney, 'The Publication of Playbooks', in *A New History of Early English Drama*, ed. John D. Cox and David Scott Kastan (New York: Columbia University Press, 1997), 393–4. Note that 'bad quarto' was a term applied pejoratively

by bibliographers early in the twentieth century to distinguish these play texts from the 'good quartos' that seemed closer to what Shakespeare actually wrote. We now recognise that these texts have intrinsic interest.

3   Editors also systematise speech prefixes (and sometimes reassign speeches if it appears that a mistake has been made); correct verse set as prose or prose set as verse; and re-line the verse if it has been divided or distributed oddly (if the compositors had too much or too little room on their page, they would divide or join verse lines).

4   Leah S. Marcus, in *Unediting the Renaissance: Shakespeare, Marlowe, Milton* (London and New York: Routledge, 1996), proposes a 'temporary abandonment of modern editions in favor of Renaissance editions that have not gathered centuries of editorial accretion', 5.

5   For example, in his book *Henry V* (Shakespeare in Performance Series; Manchester: Manchester University Press, 1997), James N. Loehlin states that the play is notorious for being capable, with the right cuts, of becoming either a nationalistic pageant or an exploration of 'ruthless expediency', 2.

6   Bernhard Radloff, 'Text', in *Encyclopedia of Contemporary Literary Theory: Approaches, Scholars, Terms*, ed. and comp. Irena R. Makaryk (Toronto: University of Toronto Press, 1993), 639.

7   C.E. McGee, 'Performance Criticism', in Makaryk, 133.

8   These books are: Cicely Berry, *Voice and the Actor* (London: Harrap, 1973) and *The Actor and His Text* (London: Harrap, 1987; later retitled *The Actor and the Text*); Patsy Rodenburg, *The Right to Speak: Working with the Voice* (London: Methuen, 1992); and *Voice and the Text* (London: Methuen, 1993); and Kristin Linklater, *Freeing the Natural Voice* (New York: Drama Book Specialists, 1976) and *Freeing Shakespeare's Voice: The Actor's Guide to Talking the Text* (New York: Theatre Communications Group, 1992). Follow-up books include Berry, *Text in Action* (London: Virgin, 2001) and Rodenburg, *Speaking Shakespeare* (New York: Palgrave Macmillan, 2002). Another valuable source is John Barton's *Playing Shakespeare: An Actor's Guide* (1984; rpt. New York: Anchor Books, 2001), based on the television series in which Barton, a director, used actors to demonstrate the voice directions implicit in Shakespeare's text. Barton received his academic training in literature from F.R. Leavis (a New Critic) at Cambridge and has brought his close-reading skills to bear on the dramatic text throughout his directorial career.

9   W.B. Worthen, *Shakespeare and the Authority of Performance* (Cambridge: Cambridge University Press, 1997), 96–7.

10   Peter Lichtenfels trains with the College of Chinese Physical Culture, the recognised system employed by the International Daoist Society headed by Desmond Murray.

11   See Cicely Berry, *The Actor and the Text*, 151–2, for another version of this exercise; and Kristin Linklater, *Freeing Shakespeare's Voice*, 11–29, for other exercises one can do with vowels and consonants.

12   In this transcription, long vowels are represented by upper-case characters, short vowels by lower-case characters, the vowel of 'moon' as oo, and diphthongs by two

letters. The schwa (ə) indicates the sound in 'the'. The colon indicates that a subsequent R colours the vowel. The exact quality of the vowels will depend on the regional accent of the speaker.

13. These forms of alliteration are what literary critics call *assonance* (repetition of a vowel sound) and *consonance* (repetition of a consonantal sound).

14 Language contains many implied stage directions, from the relatively explicit directions that one has to do something (draw a sword, turn away, hesitate) to the less explicit directions that guide the speed of dialogue. John Barton is helpful on the latter in his television series and subsequent book, *Playing Shakespeare*. See also Ann Pasternak Slater, *Shakespeare the Director* (Sussex: Harvester, 1982).

15 Robert Weimann, *Author's Pen and Actor's Voice: Playing and Writing in Shakespeare's Theatre* (Cambridge: Cambridge University Press, 2000). The phrases 'author's pen' and 'actor's voice' in Weimann's title come from line 24 of the Prologue to *Troilus and Cressida.*

16 The long 's' has been normalised, and spaces have been silently inserted after punctuation marks. All other peculiarities of typography, orthography and lineation are preserved in this and other quotations from the early texts of Shakespeare's plays.

17 Richard Mulcaster, *The First Part of the Elementarie* (1582; rpt. Menston: Scolar Press, 1970), 148–9; typography and orthography modernised. Mulcaster goes on to describe a system of accents – not much used in the early printed texts of Shakespeare's plays – that indicate 'sharp and high' or 'flat and quick' pronunciation of vowels, 151.

18 Bruce R. Smith, *The Acoustic World of Early Modern England: Attending to the O-Factor* (Chicago and London: University of Chicago Press, 1999), 239.

19 *Ibid.*, 240; writer's emphasis.

20 Jonathan Crewe, 'Punctuating Shakespeare', *Shakespeare Studies* 28 (2000), 32–3.

21 George Puttenham, *The Arte of English Poesie* (1589), introduction by Baxter Hathaway (1906; rpt. Kent, Ohio: Kent State University Press, 1970), 88-9.

22 Crewe, *op. cit.*, 36–7.

23 *Ibid.*, 29, 37.

24 According to M.H. Abrams in *A Glossary of Literary Terms* (Boston: Heinle & Heinle, 1999, 7th edn), formalism focuses on 'the formal patterns and technical devices of literature'. In its main incarnations, Russian Formalism (1910s–1920s) and American New Criticism (1920s–1960s), it did so 'to the exclusion of … subject matter and social values', 102.

25 In his essay 'Troubles of a Professional Meter Reader', in *Shakespeare Reread: The Texts in New Contexts*, ed. Russ McDonald (Ithaca and London: Cornell University Press, 1994), George T. Wright gives the following advice to actors: 'In preparing a speech, study the sentence and study the metrical line, and work out a way of speaking the words that is consistent with the stress requirements of both, that seems to spring from both, and that fits with your whole reading of the character and the dramatic

situation. Then take advantage of your own voice and its special powers of timbre, volume, pitch, and pace to register nuance and expression', 67. See also the other essays in this volume and Wright's *Shakespeare's Metrical Art* (Berkeley: University of California Press, 1988). A recent volume on *Hamlet* in a popular American teaching series (*Approaches to Teaching Shakespeare's* Hamlet, ed. Bernice W. Kliman [New York: Modern Language Association, 2002]) includes two essays under the rubric 'Introducing Verse and Meter'; that both essays address the need to hear or feel metre in the body suggests that the *rapprochement* between formalism, performance and contextual criticism may already be happening in the classroom.

26 Keir Elam, 'Language and the Body, in *Reading Shakespeare's Dramatic Language. – A Guide*, ed. Sylvia Adamson *et al.* (London: The Arden Shakespeare, 2001), 181.

27 'Bifold authority' is also from *Troilus and Cressida* (5.2.151).

28 Weimann, *op. cit.*, 55.

29 Here, Lynne Magnusson uses the term 'practice' in the way it has been defined by French sociologist Pierre Bourdieu, as 'a mode of practical knowledge not comprising knowledge of its own principles'. See *Outline of a Theory of Practice*, trans. Richard Nice (Cambridge: Cambridge University Press, 1977), 19.

30 Quoted in Bruce R. Smith, *op. cit.*, 96. The comment is Lynne Magnusson's.

31 Ben Jonson, *Complete Works*, ed. C.H. Herford, Percy Simpson and Evelyn Simpson, 11 vols (Oxford: Clarendon Press, 1925–63), vol. 8, pp. 625–7.

32 See Peter Lichtenfels' reading of this scene in 'Shakespeare's Language in the Theatre', in *Reading Shakespeare's Dramatic Language*, 162–3.

33 Leah S. Marcus makes a similar point about editors whose editorial practices (including punctuation) have tamed Kate in 'The Editor as Tamer: *A Shrew* and *The Shrew*', in *Unediting the Renaissance*, 101–31.

34 Received pronunciation, or RP, is 'the regionally neutral, prestige accent of British English'. See David Crystal, *The Cambridge Encyclopedia of the English Language* (Cambridge: Cambridge University Press, 1995), 457.

2

PURPOSEFUL PLAYING?
PURPOSEFUL CRITICISM?

Tim Carroll (Shakespeare's Globe)
Emma Smith (Hertford College, Oxford)
Martin White (University of Bristol): respondent

Taking the question 'What exactly is the relationship between the practitioner and the literary critic?', the collaborators on this discussion turn to the kinds of analysis brought to bear on a text by an editor and how helpful this may or may not be to the theatre. Cautiously negotiating scenic 'turning points', approaches to character and the use of social and historical background, a particular focus develops whether the literary critic should even attempt to be of relevance to the theatre. Given that the disciplines are so different, consideration is given to strategies that each can bring to benefit from knowledge in the other's field.

STARTING POINT

In the emails we exchanged prior to the conference, in which we each argued from our own standpoint of professional practitioner (Carroll), text/performance history critic (Smith) and academic practitioner-critic (White) – standpoints between which we (initially, at least) tried to draw and hold firm lines – we identified a number of key issues: does performance have priority? does the critic have any responsibility towards the performer and vice versa? and, if so, how are we to tell him or her? Is there, in fact, really any *need* for academics and practitioners (assuming for the moment this separation) to talk to each other? If so, how (email)?[1]

> The word written to be spoken is an entirely different thing from the word written to be read
>
> Edward Gordon Craig[2]

During his workshop session, Peter Lichtenfels worked through a passage from 3.2 of *Romeo and Juliet* with the actor Joy Richardson:

> Say thou but 'ay',
> And that bare vowel 'I' shall poison more
> Than the death-darting eye of cockatrice.
> I am not I, if there be such an 'ay',
> Or those eyes shut, that makes thee answer 'ay'.
> If he be slain, say 'ay', or if not, 'no'.
> (45–50 G. B. Evans, New Cambridge Shakespeare, 1984)

As they worked on the speech, seeking the physicality of the words and their expression, my eye[3] caught the note provided by the (unidentified) editor on our photocopied hand-out: 'Here … Shakespeare plays *tiresomely* on "ay" (= yes, spelled "I" in Elizabethan orthography) and "I", as well as on the homonym "eye"' (emphasis added). It was a revealing comment, showing that the editor had simply, it appeared, failed to notice that dramatic language is intended first to be spoken and listened to, and only subsequently read. It is worth, therefore, recalling how Shakespeare's actors received the lines they would be required to fill out vocally and physically. Unlike modern actors they did not receive the whole play, but only their own parts, comprising just their own lines, with each speech preceded by two or three words to provide the cue. Much is made in critical-historical writing on the early modern theatre of the idea that an audience went to hear, rather than see, a play. But it is undoubtedly also as true of the contemporary actor's experience: he received the play, other than his own part in it (rather as his audience would) as predominantly a 'heard' rather than 'read' text, learning it through the process of listening and rehearsing. The director Matthew Warchus experimented with cue scripts while rehearsing his 1994 production of *Henry V* for the Royal Shakespeare Company (RSC). He commented:

> It's very exciting, with all the actors waiting to hear their cue in the scene and simply not knowing when it's going to come. Or for the actor who is speaking, not knowing exactly who is going to intervene, or when. It raises the whole level and energy of listening, which in turn makes the spoken language more active, more persuasive.[4]

To the performance-based critic (White), practices such as the use of 'parts' suggest that we should, when working on such a text, seek to explore it primarily as a spoken, physical event, examining how language activates physical and emotional action, between actor and actor, actor and spectator, within a specific space. Study that does not involve some practical engagement with the spoken word and implied gestural performance is, White argued, in significant ways incomplete, since some knowledge about plays is accessible *only* through practice, and whereas practice invariably involves engagement with other modes of textual investigation, the opposite is not the case: if the editor of that piece from *Romeo and Juliet* had read it aloud, or listened to it in a theatre, he or she might have had more of an inkling of how the sounds of the words operate in performance (White, 13). It's something actors are fully alert to.

At the time of The Fifth Wall workshop, Antony Sher – a very experienced player of Shakespeare – was performing two roles in the RSC's ground-breaking season of less well-known and even less often performed Elizabethan and Jacobean plays.[5] The first role was the Emperor Domitian in Philip Massinger's *The Roman Actor*, the other, Malevole, in the *Malcontent* by John Marston. In an essay in the *Guardian*, Sher tried to establish how these and other contemporary dramatists were different from Shakespeare from an actor's perspective of speaking their words. He looked back at a variety of his own experiences, identifying Tourneur's 'jagged verse … like twists of barbed wire on the tongue'; Marlowe's 'mighty lines' that 'flow easily – too easily, in fact. Magnificent but repetitive and seemingly endless, they threaten to trap you in one long droning boom'; the 'effortless variety' of the verse in *The Winter's Tale*; Macbeth's 'more ordered' speeches; Massinger's 'deceptively straight-forward' verse, the 'speeches laid out almost like legal arguments'; and Marston, 'a bit like Tourneur', with language that 'twists and turns in the mouth, yet is surprisingly delicious'.[6] Ben Jonson once wrote that 'Language most shows a man; speak that I may see thee',[7] and without trying to engage with the taste, texture and sound of the language we are failing to engage wholly with the dramatic, theatrical text, and do so more directly from a *performer's* perspective.

Challenging this claim for the primacy of performance, or White's definition of practice-based study, Emma Smith put forward reading as, in effect, a 'practice', that can respond to texts in ways unavailable to those who look solely to the validation of interpretation through performance:

Dividing the play into cue scripts, experiencing it as a diachronic aural event, thinking about it from the point of view of an actor in a single role – all these approaches disintegrate the play even as they alert us to its verbal texture. Criticism enables us – indeed requires us – to read asequentially, to read anachronistically, and to read for an academic, rather than theatrical, context, in which questions of history, language, reception and interpretation are interleaved with questions of the literary discipline, and its academic hierarchies. Academic and theatrical display and iteration are not identical, although each commands its own territory in similar ways. What works in the essay, or classroom, or monograph is not the same as what works in the theatre, and nor, perhaps, should it be.

(Smith, email)

On this point, Carroll agreed with Smith, observing that:

a lot of things that I love about Shakespeare, or that have filled me with delight or excitement about Shakespeare, have been things I have read which I know I could not use in a production, that I don't believe an audience would get. And you can always fall back on the lazy thing of 'Oh, they get it subconsciously', but what's the point of saying that – it's meaningless. When I read an essay pointing out various structures in a play – 'have you noticed that this happens in this act, or this happens in that act, and they balance each other', for example – I can be excited, and I don't need it to go into what I do in a rehearsal room for it to have value.

(Carroll, 15)

Nevertheless, White wanted to draw a distinction at this stage 'between reading the play text itself, and reading the things that surround and seek to explicate that text' (White, 15), seeing them as different practices, but still arguing the need always to be alert to a play-text as something that is conceived of in specific space, and under specific material conditions and pressures. Citing the reaction to the RSC's recent season and The Globe's 'Read Not Dead' seasons, he argued that it is the *presentation* of neglected plays, for example, that is likely to demonstrate their quality, rather than their inclusion in critical studies (White, email).[8]

SCHOLARSHIP AND PRACTICE

In recent years, many books that collect together the ideas of theatre practitioners have been published, and much academic scholarship in the performing arts is currently carried out as practice. But examples are still reasonably sparse of direct dialogue between practitioners and scholars (from White's and Smith's different camps), of the kind The Fifth Wall workshop or The Globe's own 'Winter Playing' project have sought to promote.[9] And in these rare dialogues it has been essential that the different perspectives – the varying kinds of critical and performance-focused approaches – are seen as mutually central to the interpretative process. In a highly relevant essay in *Shakespeare Quarterly*, Janette Dillon noted that:

> The alliance between theater and the academy is not really so new … but its currency may result from the desire of each to have its practices validated by the other. Theater perhaps looks to scholars to provide a theoretical authentication for its practices, while scholars look to theater to provide an authenticating material dimension in a slippery intertextual world.[10]

Dillon's is a valuable essay. Nevertheless it tends to position the practitioner and critic, and the responses each produces to the dramatic text, as potentially separate, describing the stage as the '"authenticity factor" behind the play text',[11] whereas one might argue that the aim should be to harmonise *and* integrate these approaches, seeking the benefits of each to performer and critic. White offered an example from his own experience while working on an edition of Massinger's *The Roman Actor*, during which time he had been given access to rehearsals of the play, which was being staged by the RSC in the 2002 to 2003 season at the Swan Theatre in Stratford-upon-Avon.[12] At the opening of the second play-within-a-play, Paris (played by Joe Dixon) enters (3.2.148). He is described by the Empress Domitia: 'How do you like / That shape?' she asks of her fellow audience (presumably both the fictitious and actual spectators seated onstage at the Blackfriars), 'Methinks it is most suitable / To the aspect of a despairing lover' (149–50). The noose he carries ('this fatal halter', 279)[13] will probably (and would have certainly to its original audience) be read as an ominous sign, but clearly the actor playing Paris is required to adopt an appropriate posture, a 'shape'. But what should this be?

Dixon offered the director (Sean Holmes) a range of 'shape[s]', all of which were variations on the 'back of the hand to the forehead, head and eyes inclined upwards' gesture that one generally associates with nineteenth-century acting or with early film 'melodrama'.[14] That the Jacobean actor would have had a suitable 'pose' in his repertoire is clear: it explains why characters in these plays can identify each other's moods without specific reference in the text.[15] White offered a possible gestural pose, based on visual and dramatic examples drawn from the play's own period: that melancholy was invariably represented by folding the arms across the chest, accompanied by crossing the feet. If a hat were worn, it might be held in front, crown downwards or pulled down over the eyes, as shown on the frontispiece of Richard Burton's *Anatomy of Melancholy*. Nathan Field, a sometime collaborator of Massinger's, described a (rather over-the-top) lover who 'Lay mine arms o'er my heart … / Walk with mine eyes in a hat, sigh and make faces'.[16] Dixon adopted the pose (but not the overdoing of it). It was unlikely to 'read' to a modern audience, but the fact that the actor knew it was 'authentic' gave him confidence: it rooted his action in a reality. It was not a 'theoretical' but practical interchange between the actor and scholar. (Questions of 'authenticity' – itself a particularly slippery concept – have a slightly different weighting in the work done at The Globe, and figured in the final part of our session.)

Tim Carroll offered an example from the other direction. Responding in an email to White's writings on early modern acting, and the vocal demands The Globe would have made on the performers, Carroll had stated:

> You question whether the actors would have had to speak loudly to be heard in The Globe. At Globe 3, as you call it, we have the same problem: how to be loud and clear and true. I think some of this problem has been exaggerated, and that we are now discovering that it is possible to communicate without bellowing; but one of the ways we have done this is perhaps in contradiction to another piece of evidence you cite.[17] You quote one contemporary's criticism of those actors who turned out to the audience instead of the person they were addressing. I happen to think that such a device is not only a useful way of being heard in The Globe, but a way of responding to the most distinctive feature of The Globe: the fact that it puts us all in the same light. I'm not talking about playing every line

out front; but I do think that our policy of never pretending the audience were not there ensured that the actors were always aware of how far they had to project their thoughts and in how many directions.

(email)

While such examples demonstrate the benefits of bringing more scholarship into direct contact with practice and more practice into scholarship, what, if any, are the specific issues that must be addressed if that process is to succeed? In another email Tim Carroll made the point from the outset that editors/critics did not always address the questions that seemed to preoccupy those reading a scene as something to be performed, or those rehearsing it. White offered an example of the problems actors performing early modern drama face constantly with the language of the plays, drawing on *The Bondman* by Massinger.[18] There is no single edition of this neglected play (by a too-neglected dramatist) and the notes and glossary in the five-volume Oxford edition (apart from being in separate sections in a different volume from the play, making cross-referencing more awkward) are not especially helpful to a *performer*. Archidamus, a middle-aged senator, unexpectedly taking up arms, warns his son, Timagoras, and his son's friend, Leosthenes, of the dangers of too much sexual indulgence before war. The young men admit they have been 'wild' (in the sense of debauched) and ask what he concludes from that. 'What you'll groan for, I fear' he replies:

> … when you come to the test. Old stories tell us
> There is a month called October, which brings in
> Cold weather; there are trenches, too, 'tis rumoured,
> In which to stand all night to the knees in water,
> In gallants breeds the toothache; there's a sport, too,
> Named *lying perdue*, do you mark me? 'Tis a game
> Which you must learn to play at: now in these seasons,
> And choice variety of exercises,
> (Nay, I come to you) and fasts – not for devotion –
> Your rambling hunt-smock feels strange alterations;
> And, in a frosty morning, looks as if
> He could with ease creep into a pottle-pot,
> Instead of his mistress's placket. Then he curses
> The time he spent in midnight visitations,

And finds what he superfluously parted with
To be reported good at length and well-breathed,
If but retrieved into his back again
Would keep him warmer than a scarlet waistcoat,
Or an armour lined with fur.

$$(2.1.25–44)^{19}$$

The actor will face problems. The opening is reasonably straightforward, as Archidamus lists some trials of the battlefield: the cold, the trenches filled with water icy enough to make your teeth ache, and (though the phrase itself is obscure) the fear when you're '*lying perdue*' (the furthest guard from the camp). But the language carries other connotations, too, in the pun on 'trenches/trenchers' and in the use of the words 'stand', 'breeds', 'tooth', 'lying', 'game', 'sport', 'exercises', 'devotion', all of which in other contexts could refer directly to satisfying their (especially sexual) appetites. Each term, therefore, that refers to deprivation has a close partner that refers to depravity: they are what Peter Brook calls 'vibrating' words, that cannot be restricted to a single meaning.

The second part of the speech (line 35 on) introduces different problems – understanding words, foreign to us now, that Massinger uses ('hunt-smock', 'pottle-pot', 'placket'); being aware that words still in our vocabulary did not necessarily mean the same to the Jacobeans ('strange', 'visitations'); and sorting out the meaning of phrases ('what he superfluously parted with', 'good at length and well-breathed', 'retrieved into his back again'), etc. The first section of the speech (if we've been alert to the undercurrent of sexual reference) will probably signal the way the speech as a whole is going. But whereas the reader, armed with more or less precise glosses on individual words can, to some extent, content himself or herself with a general sense of the passage, an actor cannot: the actor, who has to try to convey the levels of meaning, must, in Ian McKellen's phrase, 'explore every little corner' of the text – it is not possible to act a generalised emotion or argument. And, in this respect, White argued:

> in my own experience (as with directing *The Bondman*), it is actors who force me to engage with the text in this level of detail and it is why, in my view, a practical engagement with the text is crucial. Of course, the actor's task is often too great. As with the passage I've quoted, the actor had to admit a degree of frustration: you can't act a footnote. This raises, of course, the issue of how knowledge that

is embedded in a written form can be translated into practice for the performer. But as with the issue of the 'aspect of a despairing lover', the actor found confidence, and felt more rooted, as a result of his own knowledge of the underlying meaning in the words he had to speak, and that inevitably influenced his vocal tones and gestural performance as well as helping him establish his attitude to his own and other characters and to events.

(White, email)

The practice of editing texts was not the prime topic of the session, but Carroll's focus on it as a starting point indicates that editions are the most significant intersection where scholars and practitioners meet, making questions of different languages particularly visible. But it raises, Smith argued, and equally starkly, the relationship of other modes of critical intervention to performance and how they are best articulated and integrated:

Whereas footnotes in critical editions tend to be preoccupied with the explication of certain locutions or topical references in an attempt to bridge the gap between modern and early modern readers, much criticism has been concerned to lever open this space into a chasm, a site of consistent misunderstanding rather than communion across the centuries. It would be extremely difficult to articulate Orgel's densely sustained engagement with the connotations of Viola's chosen alias Cesario (in his *Impersonations*), or Greenblatt's discussion of the one-sex model (in his *Shakespearean Negotiations*) through performance in other than the most bookish, dare one say academic, dramatic style.

(Smith, email)[20]

In fact, Smith notes the negative connotations of 'academic' meaning, as the *Oxford English Dictionary* has it, 'not leading to a decision; unpractical; theoretical, formal, or conventional' did emerge during the workshop. One participant, a theatre director, described working with a social historian during rehearsals of the history plays:

[She] was able to explain in great detail to the company information that, in a sense, we would then throw away. We would take from it certain lessons and understanding about the relationships, which then became about characters not about history, to make it immediate for the production we were doing. When she then started to

… give line readings to the actors, I started to find myself getting irritated, even though I understood the motive was a pure one. And then when she started explaining lines that *had* to be, which I'd cut nine months before, but *had* to be there to make sense of something historical, that was a problem for me as well.

(Annabel Arden, 38)

This interesting image of the academic, providing background information just useful enough to be thrown away, irritating when questions of interpretation emerge, offers a more significantly frictive relationship behind the questions of communication than the idealised image of mutual collaboration to which we might all feel abstractly committed.

(Smith, email)

Carroll identified ways in which editorial approaches appear not always to address the kinds of questions that emerge very rapidly in the rehearsal room, such as if character A says 'x', in what way is that a response to what character B has just said? Carroll had recently directed *Twelfth Night* in an all-male production at The Globe and he chose examples from that play: at 2.4.80–1, Orsino says 'Once more, Cesario, / Get thee to yond same sovereign cruelty'. Carroll queried 'what has just happened to make Orsino suddenly decide that he doesn't want to moon about listening to music but wants action instead?', but was even more struck by why 'Orsino suddenly starts telling Viola that he does not love Olivia for her money' since that's never been mentioned. 'Has there been any trigger for it in what has just come?' He quoted line 257 in 5.1 ('So comes it, lady, you have been mistook') which 'requires no explication in terms of its meaning, but there is a great deal that could be said about its import':

In rehearsals we have to try to define the moment when it becomes clear to Sebastian what has been going on all this while – i.e., why this beautiful woman simply threw herself at him. If, as we are free to, we identify the split second before he says this line as that moment, we then have to think about the attitude with which it is spoken. If Sebastian is attending to the fact that Olivia could just as well have married a girl, he might be appalled, and need to say the next line ('But nature to her bias drew in that') to reassure himself that all is well; or he might be embarrassed in Olivia's presence, realising that he really was not the object of her desire so much as his sister, and fear that she will be furious at having been hood-winked – in which case the next lines could seek to reassure *her*.

(Carroll, email)

Carroll noted that these are, of course, not the only options, but argued that criticism that 'pointed out such incongruities might be very help-ful if only to reassure actors that they are not simply missing the whole point' and that these are the questions that he believed made for 'the most purposeful playing' (email). But what, responded Emma Smith, 'was the critical equivalent of purposeful playing?' Focusing on the example from Act 5 Scene 1, she suggested that line 257 is 'very impor-tant for the characterisation of Sebastian and for this marital rela-tionship which forms one of the play's concluding gestures'. She argued that many critics ignore Sebastian as 'essentially a cipher – someone whose main purpose is to look like someone else and therefore some-one who, of necessity, cannot be individually or uniquely characterised' (email). She raised the question, too, about critics:[21]

who argue that Olivia's love for Cesario and her subsequent mis-taken marriage is a humiliating punishment on her for being so hoity-toity earlier on. Does Sebastian's remark push home this humiliation? Or attempt, as Tim suggests, to ameliorate it, to re-assure himself or her? Does it depend on how truly impossible it is, in the world imagined between actors and audience, for a woman to marry a woman? And is this point differently made when Olivia has fallen in love with someone whose sex is more indistinct because of men in women's roles?

(Smith, email)

IN FOCUS: TWELFTH NIGHT

Following these email discussions we decided that in the workshop session we would concentrate initially on 2.1 of *Twelfth Night*, helped by two experienced actors who first presented the scene.[22] Two men enter the stage. With no programme, and no text to buy with it, the original audience had only what they saw and heard to go on. Invariably (and difficult always to bear in mind when reading a play) an Elizabethan actor's costume would have provided some clue about the character he played, given that spectators were alert to the social, hierarchical niceties of what people wore, their codes of behaviour, their weaponry, and so on. One of the men, we discover, is a sea-captain: what precisely he wore is a matter of conjecture, though presumably something similar to the other Captain (why did this boat have two captains?) whom we have seen with Viola in the second scene of the play. But there is little beyond that *in the text* to indicate specific social status until the man who is not the Captain informs his companion that he is not, in fact, Roderigo (which no one has called him, anyway) but 'Sebastian', and that his 'father was that Sebastian of Messaline whom I know you have heard of' (2.1.16–18). In tears, he tells Antonio (though we don't actually learn the character's name until line 34) that his sister is drowned. Antonio's subsequent line 'Pardon me, sir, your bad entertainment' (32) is, Carroll pointed out, 'a very curious response to the news that Sebastian's sister drowned', noting that the line that immediately precedes it, about Sebastian crying, 'doesn't appear to trigger the line'. Carroll suggested that the answer lies in one of the crucial, and usually unremarked, revelations of the scene: that the man whom Antonio rescued is not only not Roderigo, but is in fact 'a toff', the hint being 'that Sebastian of Messaline whom I know you have heard of', which indicates the father's fame and reputation. Simply explaining, Carroll argued, 'as the Arden 2 edition does, that bad entertainment means limited hospitality may be necessary but it is not sufficient' (email).

Carroll offered further examples. As a director, 'one of the first things we would do in rehearsal' would be to 'identify the turning points in the scene, and one of the things that strikes me very strongly is how jagged those turning points are' (Carroll, 6). For instance, before Sebastian has explained who he is, he says to Antonio that 'I perceive in you so excellent a touch of modesty, that you will not extort from me what I am willing to keep in: therefore it charges me in manners the rather to express myself' (2.1.11–14) and immediately goes on to say 'You must know of me then, Antonio, my name is Sebastian, which I called Roderigo' (14–16). Carroll identified this as a 'turning point', where 'for some reason, and it's very vague in the text, there is something implied about Antonio's manner: "I perceive in you such an excellent touch in modesty, you are not extorting from me what I want to keep in, so I must tell you …"'. It is, he argued, 'a rather mysterious moment':

I think it's interesting to work out what it is that Sebastian means by that, and why he suddenly tells Antonio. We know why

Sebastian tells Antonio *dramaturgically* – he tells him because the audience needs to know it – but again, that isn't our job, because in the rehearsal room we don't bother ourselves with dramaturgical things [such as] why the audience needs to know this. We have to find reasons why the actor has to say it, why Sebastian needs to say that to Antonio. So we might well be talking more about that particular line and what it implies for that relationship between the two of them and, for instance, the accumulated burden of guilt Sebastian has that he's been lying and pretending to be Roderigo for the last couple of months while Antonio has been attending him.

Sebastian now goes on to say that he is the son of 'that Sebastian of Messaline whom I know you have heard of'. You probably noticed that Michael very dutifully nodded at that point – 'Oh yes, hmm, Sebastian of Messaline'. And that's right: of course he has heard of him. But it's more significant than that because it implies that Sebastian is in fact way out of his class; that having assumed that the two of them might even be equals, he suddenly finds out that they can't actually ever be friends. Not in this world. Which in turn explains the rather extraordinary line later, 'let me be your servant'. Antonio couldn't have said that *before* that revelation, it seems to me. All the notes in the editions I've read simply explain that the line that I started with – 'Pardon me, sir, your bad entertainment' – means 'pardon me for the limited hospitality I have shown you', but none asked what kind of a response that is to someone who's just told him that his sister's died? But that's what we ask ourselves in rehearsal. It could be derived from the fact we've just mentioned, which is 'I didn't realise you were Sebastian of Messaline's son, in which case the way I've been putting you up in the past couple of months must seem like an insult. You must be really shocked at the way you've had to live.' Or it might be something more emotionally, psychologically founded. I don't necessarily think that an edition's job should be to speculate, and certainly not to state why this remark might be made at that point. But I've seen productions and been involved in productions as an assistant director where the *question* wasn't even noticed. And an editor could have quite usefully pointed out that it is, if you think about it, a rather curious thing.

(Carroll, 7–8)

Following Smith's response to 5.1 in which she discussed the importance of line 257 to the characterisation of Sebastian, White, in the email exchanges, offered a response to 2.1 from the point of view of a critic:

> In the editions [of *Twelfth Night*] I've looked at – apart from the performance-oriented Cambridge School Shakespeare[23] – no attempt is made to mark the 'turning points' in the scene that Tim notes. Clearly there are guides to Sebastian's mood from the outset: 'my stars shine darkly', 'malignancy of my fate', 'distemper', 'evils', etc. No edition I have remarks on the revelation of Sebastian's background despite, as Tim says, the enforcers of 'You must know' and 'whom I know you have heard of'. The New Cambridge editor's footnote is interested in the mention of the possible link with the 'Massilians' in Plautus's *Menaechmi* 'in the context of one twin searching for another'.[24] The Signet editor makes no reference to Messaline at all. Whether Shakespeare's audience had heard of Messaline (or needed to have) is not the point, presumably, as the *way* Sebastian gives the information informs us (as will Antonio's reaction, I assume) of its significance in helping us (and Antonio) 'place' Sebastian.
>
> My own sense of Antonio's response ('Pardon me, sir, your bad entertainment') is that it embraces *both* the speeches he hears – about Sebastian's status and his loss – *and* that he is regretting how inadequate his treatment of Sebastian has been in the light of these two circumstances he's only now become aware of. It's not always easy in real life to find the right thing to say when people tell you sad things, so while we might expect Shakespeare to know how to do it, it's more affecting that Antonio can't find what might seem the right words.
>
> Perhaps Sebastian's response to Antonio ('O good Antonio, forgive me your trouble') may help us read it that way, and his phrase 'my bosom is full of kindness' supports that interpretation too.
>
> (White, email)

But these turning points are not easy for an editor who is not focused on the questions of performance to recognise and so the example helps focus on the ways in which practice informs scholarship and, of course, vice versa.

We talk a lot now (as scholars/critics) about 'stage-centred' or 'performance-focused' approaches, but a single example like this illustrates how difficult it can be. An edition shouldn't be expected necessarily to offer a solution (there will be as many as there will be productions) but here the editors – apart from Gibson – failed to notice the question.

(White, email)

This practical demonstration of the scene and its issues prompted other suggestions about how one might 'get at' the scene. One participant suggested that practitioners might draw on a study of the social and political world of the two characters to suggest how separate they are in terms of status: that, somehow, the world that the actors create on stage has to make that look normal (Michael Gould, 10–11). Another drew attention to the criticism currently coming out of changes in the way people look at language, focusing on 'social interaction in language'. Instead of the categories of literary criticism ('words, sentence structures, rhetorical figures, puns/word play'), the development of 'discourse analysis and linguistic pragmatics has opened up a new field of how language works in social contexts, how interaction works in language, how social relationships are built up in language and inflected in language'. She suggested that this criticism speaks to the questions that Carroll claims are not being sufficiently addressed and that it 'will start seeping a bit more' into the dialogue between academic criticism and performance practice (Lynne Magnusson, 27). Another participant argued that the actors would need to fill in the 'back story' in order to 'build a biographical picture of the characters and the relationship they have established'. Yet he noted too that as an approach it presented 'all sorts of difficulties' and that it would be 'hard to build up a consistent logic throughout *Twelfth Night*' (Alan Cox, 10).

In response Smith observed that:

given Sebastian's function in the play is to substitute for somebody he looks like, one reading would be that in order to effect that substitution he mustn't have any complicating kind of 'back story', a biography of his own which makes that a more problematic speech at the end. And that seems the point actually where what's possible in a *critical* reading – the suspension of Sebastian's characterisation as a function of the text – seemed impossible in a theatrical one or one which was thinking about performance.

(Smith, 11)

So how far is it the job of criticism to support performance? Is that indeed its ultimate function? For Smith, the answer is no: 'criticism is not only validated by either its realisation in performance or its proximity to performance or its use-value in performance context' (Smith, 11–12). For White (using the critical edition as a model since it sits at the interface between scholar and practitioner) it was key that 'actors start with the text and critics come to the text' (White, 12). He wanted to introduce the word 'script' to underline the flexible relationship of the performer (and all the other agencies of performance) with the 'text', and argued that criticism should be as 'performance-centred' as possible: 'there's far too much "what" and not enough "how" in a lot of writing about early texts in performance' (White, 12). He suggested these different biases were in part located in institutional priorities – whether the particular critic came from a drama/theatre or a literary perspective. White identified his own perception of the difference between writing about plays following investigation through practice (one's own or other people's) and about those one has simply read. Citing remarks on the physicality of language and gesture in other workshops, the need to see the three-dimensional image and hear the sounds of the play, he noted the difficulty in 'reading plays quietly', even on one's own (White, 13). Smith challenged the implication she perceived here of 'the denigrated space of the library', raising the question,

> [whether] there aren't clearly avenues of thinking about words on the page which could never make it through into performance, because they're about words, they're about words visually, they're about … patterns and … aesthetics of print. In a way the theatre performance is the phantom here – that's what we don't have, and that's what we partly say is so wonderful about it, that it's transient. But I think we're reifying it in a curiously idealised way, by minimising the intrinsic interest of the text.
>
> (Smith, 14–15)

For Lynette Hunter,

> the production of the page involves just as much complexity in that loads of different people [editors, designers, printers, compositors, inkers, pressmen, paper folderers, and so on] are doing all sorts of different kinds of tasks, just as in a stage production … the space on the page is extraordinarily important to the physicality of my

reading, just as the space on the stage and how that's operating with me in the audience is also very important to how I'm going to react to that performance. If working in rehearsal is like going into a gym, as someone said yesterday, you go into a gym when you read, as well.

A scholar of rhetoric, Hunter argued that:

> the differences between the theatrical performance and the page performance are obviously huge in their material, [and] in their materiality, but they're not all that different for me in terms of rhetorical structure; and I think it's quite interesting that we've been talking about reading as though it is not a bodily experience, and I think reading *is* a bodily experience, it is embodied.
>
> (Hunter, 35–6).

To Smith, 'one of the material conditions that's operating in the construction of the play text is print. It's print that we've got in some form in front of us and I do think it's as important as the material conditions of the play' (16): the fact that the works were originally conceived as plays to be performed, as a participant put it, 'doesn't obviate the fact that they have a completely other history in our culture, that they are books for us too' (Smith, 22). But White argued that this is to ignore the nature and function of the 'script' in the original process: flexible, handwritten, altered by scribe, author and bookkeeper, and forming and responding to the actors' vocal and physical engagement with it, as the surviving manuscripts of *Believe as You List* (Massinger) and *The Second Maiden's Tragedy* (?Middleton) can demonstrate.[25] And perhaps because the surviving examples are so sparse, we may forget that this 'text' was complemented by its Plot – a document that set out the logistics of the performance itself (as the Plot of George Peele's *The Battle of Alcazar* shows).[26] Only later, and, indeed, usually once it had invariably ceased to have a specific practical purpose, was this script transformed into an ordering and fixing of the action, put into print, and bound. How might this intermediate stage influence our thinking about the 'text'?

HISTORICAL RESEARCH AND PRACTICES

Appropriately, given The Fifth Wall workshop venue, the final part of the session discussion moved to consider the ways in which scholarship in the areas of the history of theatre practices and performances might inform, and be informed by, current professional practice. Discussion concentrated on the context of The Globe's 'original practices' productions and on Tim Carroll's all-male production of *Twelfth Night.* 'Pretty much all' of Carroll's general research for his production was practical rather than critical. A main aim was to learn about Elizabethan life and customs 'in order to understand better Olivia's predicament, Toby's dependence, Andrew's status, etc.'. To help this exploration, Carroll and the actors worked, during rehearsals, with The Tudor Group ('who live as Tudors'), who introduced them to details of how Elizabethans bowed, doffed their hats or codified their weapons and other such 'calibrations of social interaction'. From being initially sceptical, Carroll had realised how this information had 'increasingly liberated the actors' (Carroll, 32). Smith noted that this value he placed on 'the authority of individual experience, that comes up over and over again' when talking of performance practice 'is not really a scholarly, academic language', and that Carroll's choice of those who had 'lived' an experience rather than studied it, suggested that for practitioners '*knowing* about something is not as valuable in theatrical, performance terms, as *doing* it' (Smith, 33). But how can – and, indeed, should – 'doing it' challenge and reshape critical opinion?

Focusing on the issue of male actors playing female roles, Carroll acknowledged the usefulness of much of the critical/historical work he'd read about 'male relationships and the much less demarcated sense of love and eroticism in the Renaissance compared to now', reading which had given him the 'confidence to think that one could really explore any version of love between the two men and wait for it to settle between the two actors what kind of relationship it was' (Carroll, 18). In terms of how men play (and might have played?) female roles, he had been reassured by reading White's work as it appeared to confirm (or 'authenticate', to use Dillon's term) his decision 'to have a 32-year-old playing Maria, and indeed a 40-year-old playing Olivia, and a 20-year-old playing Viola, when I had been told it would definitely have been a 14-year-old' (Carroll, 19). Some workshop participants challenged White's view, citing parallels with Guild practices and the age of their apprentices (Smith, 20). But White pointed out that there were contemporary references that seemed to suggest that older men, as well as young, had played female roles and wondered to what extent the experience at The Globe might encourage scholars to rethink their position.[27]

Referring to the range of criticism that deals with the issue of cross-dressed performance, White observed that, apparently, many of those who wrote such criticism 'were not applying the experience of actually seeing an all-male cast' (White, 20). He was not, of course (given the cultural and social differences between the periods) suggesting that seeing a modern production could answer all one's questions, but 'it is surely important for the critic in the audience at least to think what he or she can take from that performance that might make them pause a little, or rethink that aspect of early performance' (White, 20). Carroll thought there was a definite gain in having an all-male company:

> The fact is that the audience was able to imagine that the actor playing Viola was a girl, and was then frequently in danger of forgetting that he was supposed to be a girl because he was dressed as a boy. As a result, all the collisions that you get with Orsino nearly kissing Viola at one point, produce a much more charged and confusing moment than when it's an actress – looking terrifically sexy in a boy's costume and not like a boy at all – nearly being kissed by this man. In that situation you might just think, 'Oh go on then kiss her', because you barely remember what's supposed to be difficult in the onstage situation, and what a mess that might have caused.
>
> (Carroll, 21–2)

Bridget Escolme, who works on questions of the links between early modern and modern performance, observed that in her experience of watching women played by men at The Globe,

> you remain convinced for a while and then you're suddenly jolted into remembering it's a boy, and then you go back into being convinced; which is to do with the script, and it's to do with the decisions the director makes. But it seems a classic instance of where current performance could inform a not necessarily theatre-based criticism.
>
> (Escolme, 26–7)

Emma Smith was not convinced:

> I don't know whether I agree with that, because I think it's too functional to think of gender and queer criticism as some kind of historicised representation of the early modern theatre. This is criticism – doing cultural work in university departments and beyond – which is about different voices being heard, which is about having, say, a

queer or feminist stake in Shakespeare as a cultural icon. For example, when I read Pauline Kiernan's interesting book about the findings of the first season at The Globe,[28] and she talks about the way in which, after a few initial giggles, audiences accepted as a convention a male Katherine in *Henry V*, I felt hugely disappointed. Not, probably, for theatrical reasons but for critical-ideological ones, because that seemed to take us back to a pre-critical stage where the male acting tradition was seen simply as transparent. This seems not so much a clarification through the empirics of performance, as a loss, a retreat from interesting, politically engaged criticism about gender and sexuality and topics which matter now, and which we can get at and have a forum for via these plays.

(Smith, 21)

CONCLUSION

So, where had we arrived? Had we discovered answers to the questions we posed at the beginning of this chapter? Smith was properly cautious:

I don't necessarily think we are talking to each other just by picking up words that each of us uses and simply revisiting them within our own discourse. I think unless we set out some real differences we might just *think* we're talking to each other, and actually we're just having mostly the good grace not to start our talk until someone else has finished, and to pick up some of their language as a sort of narrative device.

(Smith, 34–5)

White agreed with Smith's point, but maintained that the key to having dialogue was for critics and practitioners:

to understand better what it is we *do* want from each other, and the ways that we can articulate that to each other and then achieve it. But no one could claim that at the moment that dialogue is as strong and active and eloquent as it should be.

(White, 39)

Carroll found some middle ground:

there's no kind of criticism that could not influence the way I do a production. It's absolutely vital that you shouldn't *necessarily* write criticism thinking of performance, because you can write it for what-ever reason and it could be the very thing that makes me think 'I know how to do that now'.

(Carroll, 25)

Despite our best efforts at presenting a polemic, the gaps between us were by no means unbridgeable: as one participant observed, 'there's not anything really *oppositional* about these positions' (Hendricks, 23). No, but there may still be some distance between them. We need to spend more time together, to see more scholars in the rehearsal room where their presence is valued and understood, and for the lessons of performance to be valued by and employed by the academy. Then, the dialogue between critic, historian and practitioner can strengthen knowledge *and* performance – purposeful playing through purpose-ful criticism, and vice versa. Maybe William Bagnall (if it was he) had a point about the interdependence of reading texts and watching performances when he wrote, in a preface aimed at the prospective purchaser of the quarto of Massinger's *The Bondman*:

> *'Tis granted for your twelve-pence you did sit,*
> *And See, and Hear, and Understand not yet.*
> *The AUTHOR (in a Christian pity) takes*
> *Care of your good, and Prints it for your sakes.*
> *That such as will but venture Six-pence more,*
> *May Know, what they but Saw, and Heard before.*[29]

NOTES

1 Emails exchanged between Tim Carroll, Emma Smith and Martin White prior to The Fifth Wall research workshop have been amalgamated in this paragraph.

2 Quoted by Tim Carroll during the workshop.

3 Martin White, the writer of Chapter 2, later refers to himself in the third person.

4 Quoted in Martin White, *Renaissance Drama in Action* (London: Routledge, 1998), 40.

5 In addition to the two plays mentioned, the season included *Edward III* (?William Shakespeare), *The Island Princess* (John Fletcher) and *Eastward Ho!* (Ben Jonson, George Chapman, John Marston). The season ran at the Swan Theatre in Stratford-upon-Avon before transferring to the Gielgud Theatre in Shaftesbury Avenue, London.

6 Antony Sher, *Guardian* (3 July 2002).

7   See Ben Jonson, *Timber: or, Discoveries Made upon Men and Matter*, in *Works*, vol. 8, ed. C.H. Herford, P. Simpson and E. Simpson (Oxford: Clarendon Press, 1947), 625.

8   The 2003 'Read Not Dead' season, for example, comprised staged readings, with high-quality professional casts, of *Philotas* (Samuel Daniel, 1604), *The Second Maiden's Tragedy* (?Thomas Middleton, 1611), *The Bondman* (Philip Massinger, 1623) and *Sir John van Olden Barnavelt* (Thomas Dekker and Philip Massinger, 1619).

9   'Winter Playing' aims to bring together scholars and practitioners to explore some aspect of staging identified by the scholars. In 2002 to 2003 the sessions have included work on *Romeo and Juliet*, *Richard II*, *A Game At Chess* (Middleton) and an exploration of clowning and comic performance.

10 Janette Dillon, 'Is There a Performance in this Text?', *Shakespeare Quarterly*, 45 (1994), 74–86.

11 *Ibid.*, 74–86.

12 To be published in the Revels Series, Manchester University Press.

13 Quotations from *The Roman Actor*, in *The Plays and Poems of Philip Massinger*, ed. Philip Edwards and Colin Gibson, vol. III (Oxford: Clarendon Press, 1976).

14 See, for example, Roberta E. Pearson, *Eloquent Gestures: the Transformation of Performance Style in the Griffith Biograph Films* (Berkeley, CA: University of California Press, 1992).

15 See Martin White, *op. cit.*, 68.

16 Nathan Field, *Amends For Ladies* (?1610–11), in *The Plays of Nathan Field*, ed. William Perry (Austin: University of Texas Press, 1950), 1.1.96–7.

17 Martin White, *op. cit.*, 73, citing E.K. Chambers, *The Elizabethan Stage*, vol. IV (Oxford: Clarendon Press, 1923), 255–7.

18 Martin White directed a staged reading at The Globe as part of the 'Read Not Dead' season, 2003.

19 Quotation from *The Bondman*, in *The Plays and Poems of Philip Massinger*, vol. I.

20 Stephen Orgel, *Impersonations: the Performance of Gender in Shakespeare's England* (Cambridge: Cambridge University Press, 1996); Stephen Greenblatt, *Shakespearean Negotiations* (Oxford: Clarendon Press, 1988).

21 Examples cited were Jean Howard's 'Crossdressing, the Theatre, and Gender Struggle in Early Modern England', in *Shakespeare Quarterly* 3, 4 (Winter 1998), 418–40, and Lisa Jardine's *Reading Shakespeare Historically* (London: Routledge, 1996).

22 Alan Cox and Michael Gould.

23 Edited by Rex Gibson (Cambridge: Cambridge University Press, 1993). Gibson notes that, 'Many people find it puzzling that Sebastian and Antonio apologise to each other in lines 24–5 … consider how you could make sense of the lines for the audience', 36.

24 See Elizabeth Story Donno, The New Cambridge Shakespeare edition (Cambridge: Cambridge University Press, 1985).

25 Both are held in the British Library.

26 See *The Dramatic Works of George Peele*, ed. John Yoklavich (New Haven: Yale University Press, 1961).

27 See Martin White, *op. cit.*, 82–8.

28 Pauline Kiernan, *Staging Shakespeare at the New Globe* (Basingstoke: Macmillan, 1999).

29 William Bagnall, 'The Author's Friend to the Reader', in *The Plays and Poems of Philip Massinger*, vol. 1, 17–22. This edition of *The Bondman* was published in 1624.

3

GESTURE, LANGUAGE
AND THE BODY

Annabel Arden (Théâtre de Complicité)
Margo Hendricks (University of California, Santa Cruz)
Lynette Hunter (University of California, Davis): respondent

Concerned with the relationships among gesture, language and the body, the essay explores the implications of the statements 'The body animates the text' and 'The text animates gesture'. While focused on what 'gesture' signifies to a critic, and a theatre practitioner, by developing an understanding of textual gesture and specific languages for stage gestures, the exploration investigates the way that each area is based in specific training. The essay brings together many contributions from the main participants and from other actors, directors, editors and critics to argue that both acting and reading are embodied practices.

Gesture and its interrelation with language and the body is an area of practice that at first sight relates more to the theatre than to criticism. The critical vocabulary for talking about how the actor's body works is in short supply, and when actors speak about their bodies they often retreat to a popular psychology version of explanation. The discussion between Margo Hendricks and Annabel Arden started off with this inbuilt difficulty of communication, not between the theatre practitioner and the reader-critic, but with the topic of gesture itself. But Arden, as with directors Calixto Bieito, Anne Bogart and Peter Lichtenfels, has developed a career investigating the expressive potential of the actor's body, and Margo Hendricks has elaborated specific concerns about the reader's body, especially in terms of race, gender and ethnicity. A good deal of the dialogue between them worked on building bridges to an understanding of the other's practice.

Initially Arden argued that 'the body animates the text', and Hendricks replied that if the body animates the text, 'the text animates gesture'. Much of the session circled around the implications of the different emphases, and the developing conversation led to a number of attempts to debate, to differentiate between and to integrate them.[1] Looking back on the session, it is clear to me (Lynette Hunter), the respondent writing this essay on behalf of all of us, that there was an unnoticed imbalance in the argument: the practitioners spent considerable time laying out the detail of their training to explain how they engaged the body and the text especially in acting, while the critics spent no time whatever on this element in their own training, and mentioned nothing about their education either in reading or about how their criticism was made public. My contribution to the discussion here will address this gap, but the primary function of this essay is to consider the differences between the approaches to gesture taken by theatre practitioners and by critics of theatre and performance. Not surprisingly, given the emphasis in each play on the gestures made by tongues, hands and bodies, the session focused on *Titus Andronicus* and *The Winter's Tale*.[2]

APPROACHES TO LANGUAGE, ACTING AND GESTURE

First, let us turn to the grounds laid down by the two primary participants, Annabel Arden and Margo Hendricks. The director Annabel Arden trained in the physical theatre tradition of Paris' Jacques Lecoq, in which gesture is specifically related to the body. Lecoq represents part of a western theatre tradition that focuses on the interaction between the physical body and theatre texts. Other crucial figures in the tradition include Vsevolod Meyerhold, whose early twentieth-century investigation of movement led him to develop highly choreographed texts for traditional plays.[3] Directors such as Jerzy Grotowski and Eugenio Barba worked from Asian theatre traditions and focused more on what the actor can get the body to do, how the actors' body can construct story in itself. Other theatre practitioners have worked with indigenous traditions, such as Tadeusz Kantor's work in Poland. Still others, such as Robert Lepage, have brought together visual and physical theatre, or those like Anne Bogart use physicality to collapse story into unfamiliar bodily structures.

Arden began her contribution to this session on gesture by talking about her training at Jacque Lecoq's school,[4] and how her acquisition of practical techniques had heightened her awareness of her body and its meaning:

It's the meaning of the body in space, that's what we learnt about. And so I learnt the word '*geste*', '*Les gestes de l'acteur*'. For me, it means something quite different than its connotations in English. Because I think when you talk about gestures in English – first of all you remember Hamlet's advice to the players, that they not 'saw the air' too much with their hands. But by *les gestes* it was always understood that whatever movement is made by the hand and the arm, comes from the centre [of the actor's body]. *Les gestes* are mysterious. They're the part of the actor's craft which is almost the most difficult to talk about. They're highly instinctive: they have the same kind of relationship to the body as, say, *timbre* does to the voice. So that a mark of a great actor is this sort of indefinable, surprising, inventive, eloquent quality of his gesture. I think that gesture is something quite different from action.

(2)

Actors work from their training in rehearsal, and the actor and workshop participant Alan Cox expanded on the kind of practical application that this kind of physicality encourages. He described the way that he had learned about his body through mask-work and improvisation. Mask-work involves developing skills with a variety of full mask, half-mask, *commedia dell'arte* mask and neutral mask, among others – neutral mask being the antithesis or epitome of the concept of mask based on the Japanese mask of 'calm', which is so contained that the most imperceptible tics of the body are revealed (Arden, 20). To carry this mask 'the body must be [simultaneously] at maximum neutrality and physical awareness' (Arden, 20). Japanese theatre traditions such as Noh or Kabuki treat the hands and face as the neutral mask and the body as gesturally expressive. Real masks hide the eyes, whether they cover the full face or only half the face allowing the jaw and lips to move freely, and this has the effect of enlarging the facial area and rendering it static.[5] If an actor cannot use their face then they have to work on body movement and gesture moment by moment, taking apart their physical actions in a manner that resists the conventional reliance on facial expression. This 'playing the moment behind the mask' increases the perception of body size. Because a western audience is trained to look at the face, masking has a twofold effect. First, the audience may be induced to read its own responses to the story more easily onto the mask, and it may look elsewhere for the physical embodiment from which it constructs significance.

The second training element, improvisation, allows interactions or energies in a production to be pulled out of a group of actors (Cox, 20) working collectively, and the director is there to fix that set of inter-relations in the actors' awareness. Again, it is the 'awareness' that is fixed or made coherent, not 'meaning' or 'verisimilitude' or exact 'truth to the text', and it is awareness on which the actor will draw in rehearsal and performance as a resource for action. Cox described awareness as 'an improvisatory quality that supports the formal nature of the language' (20): not what language does to the actor, but what the actor can do for language. Improvisation led to a central part of the rehearsal process, what Cox called 'making rituals' that went on 'all the time' (Cox, 21). When asked to elaborate on ritual in acting, the director and acting trainer Peter Lichtenfels described it as working on possibilities for action. If you are not sure what movement, or voicing, is going to be functional, you need to work through the action or speech, trying things out and retaining the elements that communicate, practising them again and again to find out if they can sustain a response. The moment of awareness or 'ritual' is incorporated into rehearsal so that it slowly becomes part of the actor's body memory, the muscles, bones and blood remember it as an action that is appropriate, a resource to draw on.

By implication, the actor works with the ability of their body, in inter-relation with the production – especially other actors and the director – to acquire or learn about the possibilities for and a recognition of that heightened movement, which, like heightened language (see Hytner, Reinelt, Thompson), can 'boost' awareness to the audience when performance begins. As an example Arden commented on watching Michael Gambon in Caryl Churchill's *A Number*, a play about family relations, breakdown and divorce (6). At one point Gambon simply glanced at the wedding ring on his hand and the audience thrilled to the suddenly charged air of that small detailed action. It was, said Arden, the 'perfect gesture' for that play. For the practitioner, the body itself is a gesture, and Arden developed this idea by talking about gesture in relation to music. Arden pointed out that 'melos', from which we get 'melody', means 'limb' in Greek, a connection that underlies most of her comments on gesture as musical, and on gesture as especially to do with the hand. Like musical gesture, bodily gesture is to do with phrasing, with creating time and space on stage. It indicates the distance travelled in space and time, and most importantly it allows one to hold the body in 'suspension'. Held in 'suspension', the actor's body is in imbalance, and the audience is maintained continuously in a state of high awareness because of the unpredictability that results (3).

For an opera singer, gesture is essential because the audience usually cannot see the singer's face or fully hear the words (3), and Arden notes that Maria Callas never moved until she had learned her part, only then did she use her hand as a 'prolongation' of her voice (3). Gestures of the hand carry enormous moral and ethical meaning, particularly for the actor. The critic David Bradby later reminded the workshop that while the poet Keats was represented by a death mask of his face, the actor Edmund Kean was represented by a cast of his hand (19). When meaning travels, asks Arden, 'does it travel from my body via my hand, out there?' (3). For example, she suggested we might think of the difference between greeting someone by shaking hands with them or by using that 'strange kissing movement' that is becoming increasingly familiar. When shaking hands one maintains a distance, possibly even a perspective on people (4).

My own work on gesture in the history of rhetoric has found that during the Renaissance, hand movement on stage, in parliament, in the pulpit, indeed in any public space, was highly coded, probably for the same reason that an opera singer's movements are often coded, if not melodramatic or clichéd. All these performers are working with large audiences from several hundred to several thousand. It is said that up to ten thousand people would go to hear John Donne deliver sermons at Old Saint Pauls in London. During the early part of the seventeenth century several books were published to help ministers of the church understand how to move their hands when taking services.[6] These books were essentially rewritings of Cicero's guides in *The Orator*, to hand and body movements for politicians speaking in public in the first century BCE. The movements formed the basis for actors training in the early modern period, and came into full flower during the eighteenth century when theatres became huge boxes with proscenium arches between the audience and the stage. They were used throughout the nineteenth century, and in the silent movies, only becoming more muted with the advent of naturalism in theatre, film and television, especially in the twentieth century.[7] In the western media the most pronounced use of traditional hand gesture is currently in promotional music videos.

Because of the longevity of these actions, they constitute a kind of physical language, and indeed in the seventeenth century John Bulwer who wrote on both hand and facial gesture, also wrote one of the first 'signing' languages for people without hearing or voice.[8] The longevity of these gestures gives the impression that they are as Arden initially noted 'instinctive' (2) to each actor's body. The body directs and uses energy in roughly the same biochemical and biophysical patterns, which affect a wide range of movement, so that the tensely knotted fist denotes anger in many cultures.[9] The arm horizontally outstretched in front of the body with a vertically upright palm (the back of the hand toward one's face) often denotes 'stop' because the open palm sends energy out from the body in the direction of the person in front of it, potentially repelling them or bringing them to a halt. The arms held out to the sides but slightly curved in a wide circular embrace with palms facing inward, denote the welcome and comfort of a closed circle (which is of course threatening if one does not want to enter). But as Arden later suggested, they cannot 'just be instinctive' (6) because we have to learn to share them with other people. Just so, the actor's rule of thumb about the relation of the hand to eye and heart (Arden, 6) – if the hand is extended higher than the eye it asks 'who am I seeking?' of someone or thing who exists only as a possibility (a wish, a deity, a prayer), or if the hand is extended below the heart it begs, clings, implores – is only as helpful as the actor's skill in bringing it to our awareness. Not all actors could say with Alec Guinness that 'one gesture above the head is worth a 1,000 words' (Cox, 21). If Hamlet's actors who 'saw the air too much' tell us that gesture was coded on the Renaissance stage, the complaint also tells us that stereotyped gesture was, as it still is, limiting.

At one point in the workshop, Alan Cox commented that handbooks of 'codes' of gestures were useless because they were inorganic, and cited Edwin Booth's early nineteenth-century *Richard II* with its detailed notes on Booth's gestures as an example. Russell Jackson responded that this publication was not something Booth 'followed' but that it had been put together and notated by someone else. Cox replied that it was like 'French's Acting Edition and I can't understand it[s purpose]'. Jackson again responded saying that the book was 'descriptive not prescriptive', to which Cox said, 'but is it practical for the actor?' The exchange was rather like watching trains on different and parallel lines trying to meet at some point. The actor was thinking about the detailed process of training and rehearsal in which coded 'answers' to gesture are meaningless, and Jackson was rightly pointing out that that was not the purpose of the book, that it was simply to record Booth's gestures.

However, it remains a legitimate question: why was anyone record-ing these gestures? Did someone think that actors *could* learn from this account? Was it intended to revive in the reader's mind a visual image of a performance they may have attended? or indeed to substitute for an actual performance? Was there something so 'aware' about the gestures that after the play finished the audience referred to them, much as Annabel Arden referred to Michael Gambon's glance, as the 'perfect gesture' for a particular play? In other words, the book would have made possible a social and cultural discourse about an interpretation of *Hamlet* important to the contemporary audience. All these books illus-trating gesture are also part of the tradition of rhetorical training, and are directly analogous to the handbooks of rhetorical devices that have been written in western culture for over two thousand years. No one is going to be effective simply by copying a device, it has to be re-embodied in a particular moment: this is of course the significance of the word *mimesis*.

Arden spoke at length about the importance of gesture being inte-grated with the text and shared with the audience – not that it should 'underline' the text, do the same thing as the text (an effect that she later referred to as 'telephoning'), but that it should be functional rather than a simple reproduction of a code. Once more she turned to a musi-cal analogy: the orchestra in front of the opera singer is engaged in a series of functional gestures that produce music from their instruments (5). The opera singer cannot afford to make a coded gesture that is not functional because the context in which it occurs will make it look in-effective. An actor is faced with similar issues in relation to the environ-ment of stage and theatre. Any gesture may have to work alongside the use of voice, and an example that was offered was the Get-out syndrome. If one extends the arm in a dismissive gesture and then says 'Get out', the action is effective. It is almost as effective to extend the arm while saying 'Get out'. But to say 'Get out' and follow the phrase with the action, is almost invariably funny (the workshop audience laughed). Why this is so is difficult to explain. The same effect occurs with 'I'm thinking', with the chin held in the hand and one finger extended up the cheek. Gesture in these cases may not be as strong as the words, or possibly it may be because it is stronger (Arden, 3). But the effect does not always happen, for if one says 'Fuck off' and fol-lows it with the gesture of the left hand slapping down firmly into the crook of the right arm bent at right angles, the gesture reinforces. Yet there is something in the ritual of following the word with the gesture that is often bathetic. Possibly, it is not shared with the audience and hence disrupts and makes a mockery of its own intentions.

It was at this point in Arden's introduction that she turned to *A Winter's Tale* to elaborate on the way that gesture integrates with text. She opened her comments on the play by talking about the certainty of physical gesture within the ambiguity of language. I will preface her comments with a brief close reading to provide context for her discussion, but would like to point out that Arden herself did not seem to think that her skill with reading was worth commenting on, despite the extensive description of acting and despite her evident subtlety of reading. In the second scene of the play, a field of significance builds around specific words, and focuses on the gestures made by hands and voices. Hermione speaks of 'prisoner' and 'guest' (1.2.51–60), playing at length on the ambivalence of the two words, while the text builds a connotative field around 'limber vows' (mere politeness), tongues and hands. Leontes challenges Hermione to persuade Polixenes to stay, saying: 'Tongue-tied our queen? speak you' (1.2.27), and later congratulates her on her success in getting him to stay by referring to her one previous good deed with words (1.2.89). Reluctant to tell her what this was, Leontes prompts Hermione to ask if she will die 'tongueless' (1.2.92) and without words to embody it. He then confesses that this good deed was when she said 'I am yours for ever' (1.2.105), although it took a long time 'Ere I could make thee open thy white hand, / And clap thyself my love' (103–4). But as Hermione leaves with Polixenes, the growing-jealous Leontes exclaims they are, 'to be paddling palms, and pinching fingers, / … and making practis'd smiles' (1.2.115–16), and later she is 'Still virginalling / Upon his palm!' (1.2.125–6). Is the apparent friendliness between Hermione and Polixenes evidence of a sexual relationship? The problem here for an audience is that no one knows who or what to believe, so the certainty of the gesture is undone by its context.

The focus of Arden's introduction was on the way an actor trains so that he or she can integrate gesture not only with the human body, but also with the elements around it such as props: for example when Paulina looks at the 'baby' and declares that it is Leontes' child, in 'ninety-nine point nine percent of productions there is no baby. But the gesture to that little object, whatever it is on stage … You gesture to a tiny object like that and the words do the rest' (5). Another way of saying this is that:

> The body has to support the text. The body is like a bow, and unless it is in tension, the textual arrow will not fly. …this unique relationship of gesture to text … should be in order that the text flies, … the body has not a decorative or an illustrative role, but it has a function.
>
> (5)

The analogy with the opera singer's gesture that is functional, foregrounds the element of time, because a singer's gesture is partly defined by the tempo set by the music, whereas the actor, and certainly the Shakespearean actor, creates tempo through their own gesture (6). Arden also argued that gesture creates space, and that one reason the hand is so important is that it is at a physical extremity of the body and in relation to the body it can build a 'largeness' and 'dimension'. There is a certainty in physical gesture that opens up space and controls time:

> when you create something which is not there with gesture, or indicate a space which is not there, or a time which has been, it is magical. It is potent … And it's not necessarily always possible to describe what it does in words – *you had to be there.*
>
> (5)

APPROACHES TO LANGUAGE, READING AND GESTURE

If for the theatre practitioners who spoke at the workshop the body itself was a gesture, that mysterious 'suspension of the body' on the edge of calling something into being that supports the text, for critics and readers the text itself is a gesture because the text is a kind of body. Textual gesture, in the introduction made by the literary critic Margo Hendricks, multiplied into the diversity that the word 'textual' signifies: from word to phrase to syntax, and from rhetoric to cultural and social topic. In response to Annabel Arden, Hendricks plunged straight into the text of *Titus Andronicus* without saying anything about her own training, in either reading, criticism or dramaturgy. However, in following correspondence and in response to my concern to fill this apparent gap in the workshop material, Hendricks elaborated briefly on a variety of factors that had led to her skills in reading and criticism. She described the context for her education in terms of the historical period in which she went through graduate school, a period in which there was a lot of genuinely exploratory thinking about feminism, and detailed research into Marx's writings (Hendricks, private communication). The result was a commitment to historical materialism, especially to issues of race, class and gender. But it was the *process* of training that was central for her development.

Hendricks pointed out that critics and skilled readers are trained 'not to let words mean what they might literally mean', and to 'read below the surface' of any literary text. This kind of training starts in primary school and is reinforced in secondary and further education. The specific elements in one's reading approaches will partly depend on the analytical and critical tools that one is taught at each of these levels, and Hendricks said that for her own part she was 'always [involved] with deciphering "image": what conventions are at work in this image, what can the writer be attempting in that image?' (Hendricks, letter). The process of asking questions about a text is fundamental to her methodology. It is the process of taking 'an assumption and turning it on its head', which means that often we do not know what the answer is, or even if there will be an 'answer', but that the action of asking the question is a material element, possibly the most important element, in the analysis. Reading groups were central to the way she learned her critical skills, because typically they involve a group of people who have chosen to read a text about which they all have questions, and to get together to discuss it.

I would add that classes of all kinds, seminars, tutorials and lectures, all have their own structures for training the process of reading, and instilling the ability to ask subtle and detailed questions about words. A reader has to ask themselves, and the text, what is the appropriate question? for me, here and now? They have to work on the particular task that any one word, phrase, sentence or scene, puts in front of them, and figure out (literally, by working through the figures or images of language) what they might signify. It may not be that we are reading 'below the surface' so much as recognising that the surface is simply a set of assumptions that apply generally, and that if we want to read so that the text makes sense specifically to us, we will have to read by working on those assumptions. For a text to 'make sense' it needs to become valuable to us, we need to be able to play it out within our own environments, a mimesis of reading if you like. This translation of the text through our own contexts, is not only a conceptual act. Most of us learn to read aloud before we read silently, and the physical vocalisation of words in our musculature and breathing patterns becomes part of the experience. Even when we begin to read silently, and of course silent reading was not common in the west until the last couple of centuries, that physical vocalisation is still going on. Reading is a physical performance that integrates with the conceptual, so that the body is reading the words as we make sense of texts, become aware of words with our senses.

Hendricks agreed that the body reads the text, for her own readings had to be 'literally embodied' to be realised for others. This workshop on 'gesture' focused on training from acute angles, because gesture is a category that describes performance and embodiment, and the topics that emerged in looking at *The Winter's Tale* and *Titus Andronicus* were thematically to do with bodies and parts of bodies. Yet it is the case that the text is a kind of body that defines Hendricks' reading, and it is the skilled engagement with reading that underlies her approach to language and gesture. She stated in the early correspondence that 'as someone who works with texts as historical documents as well as performative texts … what intrigues me (and keeps me deeply involved) is the fact that for the stage (and thus text) language is protean' (Hendricks, email). Her analysis of both textual and bodily gesture focused on working on and opening out the issues that could inform an actor's performance and its effects on the audience. And her process of analysis consisted of a series of questions with which she invited the participants of the workshop to engage.

Turning to *Titus Andronicus*, Hendricks began with the dominant theme of 'hands'. If Annabel Arden was interested in how 'the body animates the text', for Hendricks 'the text animates gestures'. *Titus Andronicus*, she claimed, engages 'that which is in ourselves with respect to a kind of disrespect for the human body – in times of war and in times of action and in times of revenge' (7). So many scenes in the play concern the act of dying, and use of the hands as gesture works with the text 'to give life to a body at the same time that life is being drained from that body'. This play in particular, with the loss of Lavinia's hands and of Titus' hand, relies on the text to animate the body, either mutilated or dying or dead. The animation of the text by the body is at least partly inspired by Hendricks' long-term commitment to dis-engage issues of race from the body, in order to re-engage them with the body in less predictable ideologically bound ways.[10]

Hendricks also shifted the perspective of the discussion to the responses of the audience, saying that the play 'forces you to … use your body to understand what's going on. The only way you can truly understand the impact of language on you psychically, on you intellectually, and on you physically is to pay attention to your own body' (7–8). She called attention to the moment in the opening scene when Tamora is told that her oldest son is about to be sacrificed, and asked 'What would it mean for us [the audience] to be at that moment …?' (8). Responding for the first time to this question, a question that surfaced repeatedly throughout the rest of the session, Hendricks said that her approach to working with practitioners as a dramaturge would be to raise questions about 'the possibilities for the actor in terms of the text animating the actors' bodies toward a certain relationship with the audience, with the [words of the] text, with the other characters or with the other persona on the stage' (*sic*) (9). This questioning of how the text forms relations between the actors on the stage, the language they are speaking, and the audience, calls forth a much larger signification of the word 'textuality', but also one that is rooted in language. She went on to say that for her gesture had been rooted in temporal issues, because language takes place in time, but that listening to Annabel Arden she had begun to think about gesture and space, and its construction of 'distance that takes you away from language but also takes you a little bit closer to it' (9). The spatial gesture adds significance and hence takes one away from the language alone, yet in setting up a dynamic tension with language it brings it out, draws one into an engagement with it. I would want to add that spatial gesture also involves time in the process of making the gesture that defines the space – gesture always takes place in time, it is not instantaneous. Just so verbal language, whether it is written/printed or spoken, has a spatial presence, on the page, in the air, within the body.

If she began with the hand as the most dominant thematic gesture in the play, Hendricks then added the 'eye', pointing out that *Titus Andronicus* is, if nothing else, interested in spectacle. The eye is intimately involved with many human interactions, yet when someone looks you straight in the eye, Hendricks argued,

> you're … struggling to remain focused [to] find something else
> to look at … What is it about looking each other in the eyes that
> itself gestures toward something and at the same time away from

something? It's as though it's a protective device and at the same time a kind of exploratory device.

(9)

In *Titus Andronicus* 'we are constantly being invited, … being positioned as voyeurs. We witness so much that we shouldn't have witnessed. Everything is laid out for us, and it's always done in relationship to the body' (10). Hence the way the text and the body interact 'builds into the way we are expected to see things', and 'sometimes our tendency to look away, look askance, prevents us from recognizing what it is that we are to see'. This poses real tasks for the actors, and she asked 'Can an actor guide us to [what] … we don't want to see?'

This central question released a multiplicity of ways of looking at text, the body and gesture. The first area for discussion was based on Hendricks' suggestion that skin colour is a gesture. She opened out a debate about the character Aaron, saying that depending on how we think about the racial tension between the Goths and the Romans, we will think about Aaron differently (7), adding that the audience must work out what it means that Aaron 'suddenly acquires an incredible amount of importance from … the second act of *Titus*. And then becomes … the way in which we understand all that takes place in this play'. Even in the first scene, in which he is silent, Aaron is there but not-there (Hunter, 12). Silence is also a kind of language, and in this scene it becomes a gesture toward all the unseen and unheard deaths that will occur in the play, specifically to the sacrifice of Tamora's son that takes place offstage at this point. And the fact that this gesture of silence comes from a character with black skin is going to animate the gesture in ways specific to the context of the audience. For the audience, Aaron's 'blackness surface[s] as a kind of gesture in this text: as something that animates the language associated with Aaron and the language associated with Titus and Tamora' (9). For example, Hendricks raised the possibility that for a contemporary audience in the United States, there can be no catharsis because the play does not allow us to walk away from it. Instead of ending with the deaths of Tamora and Titus, and implying that this long-standing conflict between the Romans and Goths was over, the play insists on returning to the remaining personae, including Aaron, who is then put to death even though he is not part of that conflict. This death is but one gesture that creates textual resistance to cathartic release.

Gregory Doran, who directed *Titus Andronicus* in South Africa with Tony Sher as Titus,[11] took up this question and talked about his production which cast the Goths as 'coloureds' and the Romans as Afrikaners, with Aaron and the Nurse as the only two black actors in the play. As a director acutely aware of the political and social contexts of producing *Titus Andronicus* in South Africa one year after the end of apartheid, he was particularly interested in how one black audience from the Anglican Church Society of Soweto responded to Aaron, who was in this context carrying 40 years of apartheid on his back, a very specific grudge. The actor playing the part was the hugely popular television soap star Sello Maake ka Ncube, and every action he took was interpreted as a significant gesture, for example, his silence at the beginning of the play. The audience even cheered him through the rape of Lavinia, but booed him when he chopped off Titus' hand, and cheered him again when he held his own child later in the play. Doran argued that the swings for and against Aaron did produce a cathartic experience for the black audience, themselves potentially locked into a cycle of violence, and that Marcus' words in the concluding scene, 'This scattered corn into one mutual sheaf, / These broken limbs again into one body' (5.3.70–1) were fully resonant with the newly formed Truth and Reconciliation Committee.

The gesture of Aaron's blackness also informs the textual gesture of fatherhood that runs throughout the play. How, for example, do the actors playing Titus and Aaron deal with the different attitudes to 'fatherhood' the text makes available to each of them (Hendricks, 11)? Aaron is initially portrayed as a 'better' father in a modern context because he spends time and energy trying to save his son, while Titus allows 'honour' to substitute for his children. Can the actor or the audience of today reconcile their social and cultural assumptions with those of Shakespeare's time? For example, the post-Victorian western concept of a parent 'willing to absolutely sacrifice for the child, everything' (Hendricks, 11) is an anomaly for the sixteenth century. Can an actor play the fact that Aaron's behaviour is something an 'uncivilised' person would do, that 'his actions are not appropriate to maintaining his honour? And could this be played in the opening scene: where you have maternity, paternity at odds with each other?' (Hendricks, 11). Aaron is further complicated as a character by his willingness to substitute his friend's white-skinned son for his own black-skinned child, in the Emperor's house (4.2.154–63). The action will prevent the discovery of his sexual relations with Tamora, and save his son's life. But Aaron immediately betrays Tamora and her whole family to the Romans, resulting finally in her death and theirs, and, possibly, her substituted son's. Hendricks suggests the skin colour of the two boys upsets any idea of absolute black or white, and asks 'how do we deal with that white moor who … could have been the Emperor's son' (Hendricks, 11).

Skin colour as a gesture that engages the audience into the text in ways specific to context, overlapped with another of Hendricks' concerns, gender, and provoked her to ask about 'the whole issue of whiteness in terms of the representations of female bodies' in Shakespearean texts (9). Specifically in the opening scene of *Titus Andronicus*, when Titus tells Tamora that he is going to sacrifice her son, there is the question of how we read gender in historical terms, by paying attention to that gesture of sacrifice. It points us toward thinking about primogeniture and the importance of fatherhood in the Renaissance. The gesture prompts the audience to engage with what it would mean for her son Alabarbus to live, especially with Tamora in a captive state. It also by subtle analogy prompts us to compare Titus, and the ensuing sacrifice of his children, to Tamora, and to consider what it means for him 'to be positioned as a mother in terms of his struggles' (9).

Hendricks subsequently added:

> If one thinks about the representations of 'mothers' and war, it is somewhat easy to view Titus' mourning of his sons as emblematic of images of stoic mothers whose sons have died to save the warring nation. More importantly, when we (as spectators) expect Titus to react with anger and seek revenge at the deaths of his two sons and the rape/mutilation of Lavinia, we are given a 'weeping' almost inconsolable, thus effeminate Titus. The question: given the general absence of mothers in Shakespeare's play-texts, is this the text where the horrific events necessitate a maternal figure and Titus becomes both, though not simultaneously? That is, the father who sacrifices his children for the state and the 'mother' who mourns the sacrifice? … it seems to me that there is a physical change, a gestural shift if you like, in Titus at the moment of his two sons' deaths and the rape/mutilation of Lavinia, and that shift is the physical and intellectual awareness that he (Titus) somehow gave birth to that which claimed the lives of his children. And, the critic

speaks here, perhaps Titus realizes if not understands Tamora's loss when he sacrifices her two sons.

(Hendricks, email)

Furthermore, Titus' statement to Tamora that they are going to sacrifice her son in a sense reduces her to a body that produces children who become soldiers in a war machine: the female body 'is a machine and loses any animation, and it's disconnected from the children' (9). And, again by analogy, Titus himself becomes reduced to a kind of war machine.

The intimacy of much of the play, and the way that it consistently forces large social and political issues into private, domestic space so that we cannot avoid their brutality and violence, is itself a gesture, Hendricks implied, to the irresolvable structure of the play and its never-ending conflict. Once the private world has internalised what society needs from it, it perpetuates that horror. For example, as critic and historian she knows that the Romans did not sacrifice people on return from battle; she also knows that this information was available to Shakespeare who has Tamora say 'O cruel, irreligious piety!' (1.1.133) when Titus has Tamora's son Alarbus taken away to be killed. Here the text is prompting the actor playing Tamora to ask what is to be done with this knowledge, for the words indicate that the character knows that this is gratuitous slaughter rather than potentially honourable ritual. This example also displays the potential overlap between vocal gesture and verbal gesture in a challenging manner. Margo Hendricks asked how the actor playing Tamora in *Titus Andronicus* could infuse 'O cruel, irreligious piety!' with a gesture to alert the audience to its fore-telling of all the other deaths in the play (Hendricks, email).

Margo Hendricks concluded her introduction with a comment that in working with actors, she has come across a perception that 'somehow the text circumscribes the body and that actors have to often go beyond the text in order to animate it' (11), they think that it is only a first step. Comparing a Shakespearean play with others that either explicitly or implicitly embed stage directions into the text, she suggested that actors need to establish a relationship that actively accepts that language will never be 'restrictive', it can only be 'liberating', and with that relationship in place 'text and body are almost one' (12). If we keep in mind what Hendricks says about her training as a critic, we could extend that relationship out to the reader, but with a different emphasis. Most skilled readers do treat language as if it will always release something more, be liberating in the sense of opening up significance, but readers could benefit from thinking about this process as one in which the text and body are almost one.

ACTORS AND CRITICS

Underlying all of Hendricks' introduction was a statement she made at the beginning: that she did not want to separate language from the body. From an earlier communication it is apparent that Arden would agree: her fascination 'lies in integrating a "physical text" with what I would call the vocal text in such a way that both action and gesture supply a level of meaning which is NOT POSSIBLE TO DESCRIBE IN WORDS' (Arden, email) – a fusion that ensures that 'movement is content', that there is no distinction between movement and text. What I find interesting about these statements is the word order. Hendricks worries about language and the body, and Arden about movement and text. It is as if each puts their primary training first, so that Arden focused on the actor and the body, and Hendricks on the audience and language. In the discussion that followed the opening introductions, the participants in the workshop moved to and fro between these different emphases, in a series of bridge-building exercises.

Arden picked up immediately on the difference between actor and audience, saying that, 'when you work on a play that you know you're going to perform with some kind of public, you have this time for rehearsal' (15), and in rehearsal although directors may have the audience in the back of their minds, they cannot encourage the actors to think too much about it. Actors 'have to experience, to gestate, in order to give birth' to a performance. She continued, 'There are certain things which in a rehearsal room are sublime, and never get seen because it becomes a reality of a different kind, because no-one's paying to see it' (15). The actors become spectators of their own work, 'It's very curious: you re-enact a drama for yourselves'. Although it was not mentioned during the workshop, I would suggest that the experience of reading groups is analogous. Just as people may have stereotyped views of how actors work, critics are similarly stereotyped as isolated individualists, whereas much of our work happens in communities of readers and writers and the final product occurs in the public space of a classroom, book, essay or conference.

For example, Gregory Doran noted that 'one of the differences between practitioners and, as it were, academics is that practitioners have to make a choice. Academics are lucky to be aware of several choices' (12). However, both critics and actors are aware of choices and can explore them with equal freedom until the public performance, typically in the critic's case, until the lecture, the conference paper, the written essay or book. During the performance both have to make final decisions about which elements they will choose, and for neither are these usually formal and rational decisions at all points, but often decisions that happen in the process, the moments of acting or writing or speaking. And readers or critics often also have their own rehearsal space – the classroom, the seminar, the reading group, or, like the actor, their partners and friends. What is different is that a primary rehearsal space for the reader is the physical activity of skilled reading which many of us do on our own, while engaging with a substantial body memory of previous texts, and that when we make public the mimesis of these readings, it is not always or even often recognisable to us or to others as a performance.

Shortly after the open discussion began, Patricia Parker began to address one of the ways in which critics and readers engage with the gesture of the text: through the families or relationships that words construct by the way they sound, or by their etymologies. Soon after *The Winter's Tale* begins, Hermione gives birth to her baby girl, and must be near the end of her pregnancy since she is 'something before her time, deliver'd' (2.2.25), a detail complicated by Polixenes' first words, that he has been in their house 'Nine changes of the watery star' (1.2.1) or nine lunar months. Her gestation must be quite evident, and in the workshop discussion Parker suggested that the floating play of the hand gestures and bodily gestation, with the word 'gest' (1.2.41) and near homonym 'guest' (1.2.53), is the language itself gesturing toward the ambiguity of Hermione's pregnant state, in which the baby is both guest and prisoner in the womb. At the same time, there is punning play on 'part' (1.2.10 and 1.2.18) and on 'parting' (1.2.42) as if there were some subliminal reference to 'parturition'. This kind of verbal sophistication and knottedness is to do with thoughts happening but not yet being worked out.

Another perspective on how readers and critics engage with this knottedness, was offered by Lynne Magnusson, a specialist in language and discourse. She pointed out the way that figuration becomes a gesture in itself, and offered as an example the scene in *Titus Andronicus* where Titus is drawing Saturninus into a debate about whether one should kill one's daughter if she has been raped (5.3.36–46). He performs an exact logical syllogism, asking the question 'Was it …' and receiving the answer 'It was …', then asking for the 'reason' and receiving the answer 'Because …', from which he concludes that he must kill her – and does so. The passion and tension infused into this dry syllogism provokes a verbal gesture of extraordinarily twisted contradiction that Magnusson suggested might be difficult for the actor to embody. What is the case is that the reader's analysis of the source of that contradiction in the rhetoric could become a tool for the actor's training. Rhetorical device directs the reader and actor to many textual gestures. A reader has to bring to bear all their training in an understanding of rhetorical device, syntax, poetics and punning on their working out of the interrelations between the words. Annabel Arden commented that actors too will bring all their rather different training to these 'seismic thought events' (16), and like the reader, will work on the relations during rehearsal. But she went on to note that the actor has only a moment to decide on how to perform the events, whereas a lecturer can plan in advance how they want to lay out the different elements of the signification.

When asked what kind of physical gesture the actor might make to indicate the pregnancy, Arden replied 'Well, she has to really play that tummy … awful prop. You know it's babies, pregnancies, money, daggers: they're all very difficult props' but in the end 'it's all about hands and sensuality' (17). The implication here is that the actor has to find a way of using the body to play the part; for example the prop has to be played as an extension of the body – but also that the subtle hand gesture may be more telling than the more obvious stage prop. At this point Martin White noted that often 'the unconscious gesture is more revealing', and the discussion moved on to the question of whether a theatre production could introduce a gesture new to an audience, and have them understand what is meant. The performance theorist Janelle Reinelt suggested that gestures always 'hover at the level of intelligibility' and that if they are powerful rather than clichéd, it is because they emerge into intelligibility when they are suited to the word in a novel way. In a subsequent communication Reinelt elaborated:

How do we ever keep from simply repeating or recycling previous representational strategies? This is the question. I believe that in rehearsal, working in creative/investigative, often improvisatory styles, we sometimes stumble on new, powerful images and metaphors or ways of gesturing, or expressions (verbal, for that matter) that then become refined and 'chanced' – risked in performance. If the fit between what is possible to be experienced in a given culture at a particular moment works with the new creative vocabulary of the piece, there is breakthrough and 'novelty' appears.

(Reinelt, email)

In effect the creativity of actors and directors is to 'bring into reception something newly intelligible' (Reinelt, 17). The training procedures of mask, improvisation and ritual, all encourage the repeated practice or rehearsal of body movements that realise significance in performance, that bring meaning into being during the process of acting, that bring gesture into intelligibility – or possibly intelligibility into gesture. A similar insight was offered by David Bradby, who prefaced his remarks with an anecdote about Diderot going to the theatre, watching a play with his fingers in his ears, and pronouncing that he could follow it perfectly because of the gestures (Bradby, 19). Hence, the language of gesture is 'deeply socialised communication' but practised like language with 'extremely individuated means' (Bradby, 19). A register of gestures could be one way into conceptual work with plays, but actors and audiences 'inhabit' plays today with styles of physicality unimaginable 50 years ago, let alone 400. At any particular moment in history the text becomes a formal ideological strategy that allows certain kinds of behaviour to the body which it defines as 'natural' for its time. Just so, the actor's body *because* it is behaving in a particular way naturalises and makes acceptable the text. The actor, faced with a piece of text that is 'difficult' or 'strange', rehearses to make it 'work', develops rituals or energies that make the text appropriate for the narrative action. Hence Bradby's claim that gesture 'naturalises the body of ideological structures' (19). This will happen in every time and place the play is produced. Gesture therefore becomes fundamental to situating the language in a specific context. In that context, gesture becomes a kind of physical proof, which, as Arden noted, is often the case in Shakespeare texts, for example the handkerchief in *Othello* (Arden, 4). But also, because gesture creates time and space, she continues, it can indicate a space that is not there and a time that has not been: you can create something that is not there (Arden, 5). Yet at the same time the certainty of gesture can be undone by its context, which is why with theatre performance, people so frequently say 'you had to be there' or 'you had to see it, you see' (Arden, 5).

My own contribution to the debate would be to emphasise the fact that the reader or critic is engaged in a very similar project. The textual gestures informing a skilled reading and making it valuable, are precisely those that 'hover at the level of intelligibility', not naturalised yet playing around the edges of the register of gestures that people will recognise. Textual gestures, the words, phrases and structures that prompt significance, are context specific and historically situated because they are by definition at the edge of naturalised communication. But what makes communication naturalised will depend on the cultural and social environment. Russell Jackson noted that *The Winter's Tale* is different from *Titus Andronicus* in that the former uses psychological gesture, while the latter in based is symbolic gesture. The symbolic gestures of *Titus Andronicus* were, he suggested, more readily accessible to people, such as a sixteenth-century audience, trained in symbolic ritual, while the psychological gestures of *The Winter's Tale*, raised problems of interpretation and misinterpretation which were more in tune with a modern sensibility (Jackson, 18). What needs to be added is that both plays have a huge range of rhetorical gesture, which will be more, or less, familiar to a reading audience today.

Yet a twenty-first-century audience has got a range of symbolic gesture, even if it is not the same as the range found within a Renaissance cultural context. The colour of skin, the body of the mother or father, are symbolic physical gestures that are animated by the text into larger rhetorical gestures toward cultural and social topics. Similarly, the limbs of the characters in *Titus Andronicus*, a play in which 'excruciating things happen to limbs' (Hendricks, 7), have a symbolic as well as psychological significance. Lavinia's hands are cut off, her tongue torn out, and she is raped. Literally there is no more gesture possible from hands or voice. The invisible gesture of her chastity as wife to Bassianus, toward her father's honour and family name, can, depending on the play's production context, become invested by others on the stage and in the audience with a symbolic weight of shame. Gestures cannot be 'aware' unless there is reciprocity, an answering gesture, so that actor and audience (or another actor on stage) engage in this process of 'bringing into intelligibility' at their particular location in space and time, their situatedness. With Lavinia the body itself becomes the gesture to the brutality that infests the narrative, to the excruciating implications of the loss of gesture, to the impossibility of depriving the body of gesture and communication even in death. But her body is also a narrative about the ingenuity of the human body in its need for gesture, when, for example, Lavinia uses the book of Ovid's *Metamorphoses* to reveal the invisible mutilations of the rape to her body, or when she uses a stick held in her mouth and guided by her feet to write the names of her two attackers. Deprived of its usual means of gesture the body finds others, such as tears.

Hendricks pursued the idea that we all learn gesture, all train ourselves in it by saying of Lavinia:

> How do you create something new and different in the gestures when you have no hands … You have symbolic hands on some level because you know what it means to have had hands and to have lost them. [But since Lavinia has lost her tongue as well she] has to invent a new way of using the language that people understand without the familiarity of familiar gestures.
>
> (18)

The director Peter Lichtenfels discussed a production he had seen with a cast of actors, some able-bodied and some with a variety of hearing and speaking disabilities.[12] Lawrence Till had received a special grant to develop a production at the Octagon Theatre in Bolton for a mixed-cast company of hearing-speaking and deaf-mute actors. The work provided the opportunity to bring issues of ability into the mainstream, integrating differently abled actors, so that hearing-speaking actors learned signing (as in sign language) in order to work alongside others. The text was spoken by those who could speak, and signed by all the actors. Lavinia was played by a deaf-mute actor and Lichtenfels noted that her mutilation became especially horrific to the audience. Their context and knowledge of the actual absence of her vocal and aural capacity, made the performative rendering of absent communication intensely painful (Lichtenfels, 18), probably because that separation between the acted character and the actual actor dissolved in the mind of the audience. At the same time the actor's manifest skill as an actor to develop other kinds of ability, invested Lavinia's subsequent communication with enormous empathy as the dramatic text became compounded with and involved in the larger political context for people with disabilities in the Anglo-European world today.

A register of genre is socially and culturally shaped and given material presence, and all of us learn how to work with the expectations and contradictions that it enables. Writers use genre as a kind of 'handshake' or introduction to a particular perspective or approach. Register is recognised as such by readers engaging with texts, but this procedure is also recognised by theatre practitioners. Annabel Arden noted that as a director she has to 'create a climate' for a production from the start of the play by helping the actors to realise their 'awareness' of gesture (Arden, 19) and create the detail on which that climate depends. This 'climate' is similar to the 'register' that marks a reader's reading, and is being self-consciously constructed here by the director. Returning to Michael Gambon's 'perfect gesture for the play', Arden explained that while there is no one formal code that will guarantee that the audience is made to look at the hand, a director can chart moments like these throughout the play 'that occur and re-occur with all their musical variations … like great symphonic writing' (19). The whole production has to support the actor's physical gesture for it to 'boost' meaning out to an audience.

With this observation the workshop concluded with one possible answer to Hendricks' question about the gesture that an actor would use to alert the audience to the significant foretelling of Tamora's 'O cruel, irreligious piety!' Arden described the moment from the perspective of a director:

> The son is taken away from her and so you've got – in musical terms – … twenty-five bars, and then a fabulous exit. And then the only people left in any kind of focus are her and Titus. And she's got all the time in the world and she's also got an 'O'. She's got an 'O' to start with. And so the whole function of that line must be, the whole production has to help that actress, to do as little as possible but for those words to buttonhole what it means.
>
> (21)

Explicit in this comment is the belief that the entire production must work toward the gesture of the single actor: for example, that Tamora does not 'do' any gesture, others do it for her, as in Deborah Warner's production of *Titus Andronicus* in which the young men return from the murder/sacrifice covered in blood.[13] Also implicit in this comment is an understanding that many practitioners have about the vocal density of 'O', its physical articulation coming from below the solar plexus region through the core of the body. The sound itself is a gesture, the word becomes a physical action as it moves through the body. In rhetorical terms, 'O' is an apostrophe, a reaching out to something that is not there – possibly questioning why this is happening yet knowing or sensing that no one will be able to tell her, possibly surprised by injustice, and possibly emptied by the sudden recognition of her son's death. But 'O' is a word difficult to carry off onstage, just as it is easy to skim past it in a reading. The register of the text, the climate of the production, has to set the audience toward a particular awareness of significance, so that it slows down and engages, participates in the gesture.

DISCUSSION

For the theatre practitioners, talking about gesture meant talking first about the body, about hands, eyes, voice, but also about props, costume and staging. Getting to grips with gesture and language meant talking about the actors' training in some detail, about their practices and physical preparation, about in this case masks and improvisation, about rehearsal and production. Part of this focus probably came about because the practitioners were not sure that the critics fully understood the kinds of skilled training that they have to do – after all to some extent everyone performs all the time. On the other hand, none of the practitioners present in the workshop felt it necessary to account for their ability to carry out subtle readings of the texts. For a literary critic, gesture is not only physical but part of the textuality. It works from words and phrases, to the larger structures of rhetoric and communication that invoke social, cultural and political topics. As skilled readers, the critics and performance theorists focused on the etymologies of words such as gest/gesture/gestate, on phrases such as the apostrophe 'O cruel, irreligious piety!', on syntax such as part and parting, on logic such as the effect of dry syllogism within a passionate declaration, on topics such as hands and eyes and the themes they generated around love, power, friendship and communication, and around the cultural issues of race, parenthood and ability, and the social structuring of our understanding of time and space.

As indicated at the beginning of this essay, there was however a curious imbalance because the critics and theorists never mentioned their training. They did not talk about their education or their practices, and probably took it for granted that the practitioners would understand what they did because after all everyone learns how to read in school. But just as many first-year undergraduates think that acting is a simple exercise, so many people can read but do not realise that there are different types of reading. This is one of the reasons that this essay includes the recounting of Margo Hendricks' training as a reader. What that recounting sharply puts into the foreground is another element missing from the description critics give of themselves, that highlighted the fact that critics did not account for their readings as types of physical performance. For a reader or critic gesture is mediated by the text, the translation from the body to the world is via the page or stage, and is not often or necessarily seen as located in one's own body. While for a theatre practitioner, although the translation from the body to the world is still via the text, the text is usually mediated by the actor's body. Readers often if not usually bypass their own bodies when thinking about textuality. Practitioners never do, but they can frequently bypass the diversity of textuality. Neither the practitioners nor the critics discussed how the process of engaging the text into the body and the body into the text has long-term effects on physicality. There was no discussion about how to control those effects, manipulate them, use them; nor any attempt to account, for example, for the pleasure and fear involved in the act of reading or for how the practitioner succeeds in preventing the internalisation of character-parts. There is, in fact, a substantial body of literature addressed to the latter discussion, but virtually nothing on the former that could begin to account for the physical satisfaction that reading can yield.

In this workshop there was a meeting ground of sorts, especially between the directors and the performance theorists, and I conjecture here that this may have been so because both of these kinds of practitioners are self-consciously concerned not only with the production of the gesture but with the reception of the gesture by audiences. Actors rehearse and then perform; skilled and trained readers read and then perform self-consciously as a critic of one kind or another. In fact criticism in western educational settings seems to offer strong evidence for the need for some readers to perform their readings in formal environments. But for gesture to be more than reductive (Magnusson), restrictive (Hendricks), obvious (Jackson) cliché (Arden, Reinelt), it needs an audience, and the kind of engagement with audience that goes on is what lifts gesture into the liberatory (Magnusson, Hendricks), the practical (Cox), inhabited (Bradby), awareness (Arden). Where the two groups began to talk to each other in positive terms was when they began to address that performative interaction, and the way that performers of any kind have to use gesture to 'bring into intelligibility' significance (Reinelt), for example the ethnic-specific casting in the South African production of *Titus Andronicus* (Doran) or the issues around ability foregrounded by the production in Bolton of the same play in which half of the cast were deaf-mute actors (Lichtenfels). To do so they have to 'inhabit' the language rather than simply rely on register (Bradby), they have to create a climate within which actor and audience can become 'aware' (Arden), or they have to read with their bodies (Hunter).

NOTES

1 An exchange of emails also took place before the workshop, with one email received each from Annabel Arden and Margo Hendricks. References to these communications, and to all other email communications with them and other participants which took place subsequent to the workshop, are cited as: (Writer, email).

2 Line references to the texts of these plays are to: *Titus Andronicus*, ed. J. Bate (London: The Arden Shakespeare, 1995, 3rd edition); and *The Winter's Tale*, ed. J.H.P. Pafford (London: Methuen & Co.; The Arden Shakespeare, 1963, 2nd edition).

3 Meyerhold's techniques have been used by later practitioners as an antidote to Stanislavski's acting methods that experimented with naturalism. However, he himself saw his work as a direct result of Stanislavskian observation rather than an act of contradiction.

4 Perhaps the best introduction to Lecoq's training comes from commentary contributed to the ongoing discussion that followed the workshop, from performance theorist David Bradby. He says, 'Arden explained that her understanding of gesture and movement in this sense derived from her training at Jacques Lecoq's *Ecole Internationale de Théâtre* in Paris, where she, Simon McBurney, and the other founder members of Théâtre de Complicité, had first begun to work together. It may prove helpful, in pursuing the aim of understanding what the actor can bring to the Shakespearean text, to dig deeper into what Lecoq understood by gesture. In the Lecoq School, a major part of the first year's work consists of what he called Movement Analysis, which is applied to the human body and to nature, charting the economy of physical actions. Lecoq says, "The things I had practised as an athlete naturally carried over into action mime. When I started, I used Georges Hébert's 'natural method', which analyses movement under eleven categories: *pulling, pushing, climbing, walking, running, jumping, lifting, carrying, attacking, defending, swimming*. These actions lay down circuits in the human body, through which emotions flow. Feelings, states and passions are expressed through gestures, attitudes and movements similar to those of physical actions. Young actors have to be aware of how the body can

'pull' or 'push' so that, when the need arises, they can express the different ways in which a character can 'pull' or 'push'. The analysis of a physical action does not mean expressing an opinion, but acquiring physical awareness, which will form an indispensable basis for acting".

Lecoq's method derives, not from character study, nor even from the search for a particular performance style, but from athletics. He believed that there are certain fundamental gestures and movements that every human being begins to make as a tiny baby, and that these all differ from one another in small ways, just as physical characteristics differ. Lecoq begins by working through very simple physical movements with the students, and then goes on to the analysis of what he calls "attitudes". By "attitude" he means a particular physical gesture that can be performed (and read) in a multitude of different ways. Through the interplay of such contradictions and variations, an extremely complex physical "score" may be built up, and give rise to a dramatic performance.

In the second year of the course in the Lecoq School, students are confronted with the concept of the "gestural language", characterised as different forms of mime, including what he terms *pantomime, figurative mime, cartoon mime* and the "*image*". He then moves on to the exploration of what he names the four great dramatic territories: *melodrama, commedia dell'arte, tragedy, bouffons* and *clowns*. For each of these, he emphasises the particular movements and gestures out of which they are constructed. In the case of *commedia*, for example, the actor must be able to develop movements and gestures that are acrobatic in the extreme. But although the starting point in the pedagogic method will always be the movement itself rather than its dramatic justification, the dramatic justification remains paramount.' See also Bradby's comments in Jacques Lecoq, *The Moving Body* (London: Methuen, 2002, 2nd edn), 74–5.

5   The technique was used very effectively in Maria Grazia Ciprani, *Romeo e Giulietta* (Teatro del Carretto, Riverside Studios, 1999).

6   Cressolio, L. (1620) *Vactiones Autumnales sive De Perfecta Oratoris Actione et Prounnunciatione* (Paris: Sebastioni Cramoisy,) and Vossius, G. (1633) *Commentariorum Rhetoricorum sive Oratariarum Institutionum* (Leiden: Joannis Maire).

7   See for example the work of Norma Shearer, playing Juliet in Georg Cukor's film of *Romeo and Juliet* in 1937, who uses her hands in what appear to us now as highly artificial movements. Two scenes from the film stand out in particular: the scene at the window (2.2) and the proepithalamium (3.2). Shearer was an actor who made the transition between the silent movie and the talkie.

8   Bulwer, J. (1644) *Chirologia and Chironomia*, ed J. Cleary, fore. D. Potter (Southern Illinois UP, 1974), and (1649) *Pathomyotania* (London: for Humphrey Mosely).

9   This gesture and others are found not only in Cicero's *Orator* but also in many other cultures, including Chinese physical cultures working with traditions dating from 3000BCE and outlined in early Daoist texts for practical exercise.

10 See for example her essay 'Civility, Barbarism, and Aphra Behn's *The Widow Ranter*', in eds M. Hendricks and P. Parker, *Women, 'Race,' and Writing in the Early Modern Period* (London, 1994), 225–39.

11 Gregory Doran's production opened at the Market Theatre, Johannesburg on 29 March 1995, and toured England later in the year.

12 *Titus Andronicus*, directed by Lawrence Till and Carole Tweedy, at the Octagon Theatre (25 March–10 April 1993).

13 Deborah Warner directed the Royal Shakespeare Company in *Titus Andronicus* at The Swan Theatre, Stratford-upon-Avon, opening 28 April 1987.

4

GESTURES THAT SPEAK: SPECTATORS WHO LISTEN

David Bradby (Royal Holloway, London): respondent
Greg Doran (Royal Shakespeare Company)
Russell Jackson (Shakespeare Institute, University of
Birmingham)

Given the difficulty of matching the verbal density of a Shakespearean text on stage and in film, this study explores 'How a performance can get the audience to listen' from the viewpoints of both criticism and performance. Starting with the concept that a bare stage encourages the audience to listen while a film employs visuals to create its world, the essay turns first to the many strategies used by film to encourage the audience to listen, and then to specific examples of theatre practice which have used the visual image to stimulate an engagement with the text. The discussion contributes to an understanding of the growing range and repertoire of gesture, both in the media and the body of the actor, that can match the textual vocabulary in flexibility and variety.

Following Annabel Arden's exploration of some gestures that are available to the actor, this workshop developed the theme of how Shakespeare's language may be staged, using both gesture and visual image. An underlying problem might be paraphrased as follows: since Shakespeare's text offers a verbal density and complexity that is endlessly satisfying, how can actors hope to match this power and depth in what they bring to their performance? It is one of the oldest critical debates, and it would not be possible to rehearse all the different stages that have been worked through over the centuries. Taking our lead from Greg Doran's contribution, we shall concentrate on his account of the precise character and function of the actors' vocal work, before considering Russell Jackson's analysis of the use of image in the film of *Richard III* with Ian McKellen in the title role, and then returning to the discussion of how image and gesture worked together in the Théâtre du Soleil's production of *Richard II*. In this way we shall hope to reveal something about methods that have been effective in bringing Shakespeare's plays to life for audiences of both theatre and film over the past 30 years.

Comparing his experience of working in both theatre and film, Doran maintained that the greatest challenge to a director was how to achieve the quality of 'live-ness'; in other words, how to present Shakespeare's text with the same freshness and vitality it would have if it were being performed for the first time. Doran made the point that this need for freshness faces a contemporary company in a way that it never did for Shakespeare's own players, not only because the plays now have the status of 'classics', but also because the original performances were never repeated more than a few times, whereas a successful production today may run for a number of years. It may even enjoy a further afterlife by being transferred to film (44).

Doran compared his experience of working in theatre and film in order to clarify what confers freshness on a text. At the Swan in Stratford, he maintained, the actors and audience feel they are part of a shared experience in which Shakespeare's words create a world conjured up by the collective imagination. In such performances, the audience must complete the experience by supplying the images that are provoked by Shakespeare's language, since the bare stage of the Swan has a quality described by Doran as neutral. It offers free play to the imagination without constraining it by providing fully formed visual images. As a result, it enables the audience to *listen*, hearing the text as if for the first time. With Shakespeare on film, however, it is the images that create the world for the audience, so that there is necessarily less room for the imagination and this, he said, 'is why, for me, Shakespeare rarely works as well on film as it does (or *can* do) in theatre' (11).

The key to making the audience listen in this way was, Doran explained, to develop the Shakespearean actor's *oracy*. Oracy, he said, meant getting actors to go beyond the meaning of the words and to feel their physical, visceral qualities:

> Oracy is your skill in self-expression. It's your ability to put words together, to use your mouth. When I work on Shakespeare with actors, I tend to talk not about how to do Shakespeare's *verse*, but

how to make the audience listen, because that is why he wrote the way he wrote: to reach an audience, *out there*, at the moment the words are uttered. Not to reach an audience that's just dead, like a film audience [i.e. an audience that is not part of the experience at the moment when the text is physically performed] … I think it is about the way the language engages the audience, and I suppose because it's live, and because the actual vowels resonate and the consonants clash against your eardrums in a way that is not cloaked with background music and all those other visual distractions.

(12, 13)

Doran went on to explain a particular exercise that he uses to develop the skills of oracy:

I do an exercise every time I do a Shakespeare play with a group of actors, some of whom may never have done Shakespeare before. I take the prologue to *Romeo and Juliet*. The first step … is that we just go round and make sure everybody knows what the lines mean, but then try and work on how *feeling* is implicit, in every word, in every clash of consonant, and how the emotional impact of the vowels works, that sort of thing, and it's brilliant. I mean, people become quite amazed by what Shakespeare has given you in that one prologue, how the rhythm of the iambic breaks against itself, and on crucial words Shakespeare's kind of saying, have you noticed this word? If you looked at what the rhythm is giving you on this word, wouldn't that be interesting?

(11–12)

In this exercise, and in others like it, Doran felt that his actors were able to discover the emotion of the lines in a way that was physical. It was, he added, an 'entirely poetical device':

In 'An Essay on Criticism', Pope says, 'True ease in writing comes from art, not chance, / As those move easiest who have learned to dance.' And then he says a very good thing that I often quote: 'When Ajax strives some rock's vast weight to throw, / The line too labours and the words move slow.' Actually, what he is saying is, by putting together those very difficult consonants you can't rush it, it's a complete technique: 'Soft is the strain, when the gentle Zephyr flows, / And the smooth stream in smoother number flows. / But when loud surges lash the sounding shore, / The line that thunders should like

the torrent roar.' What Pope is recognising there is that poets use vowels to give you an aural picture of what they are talking about.
(31)

Doran then applied these ideas to his recent stage production of *Macbeth*, focusing in particular on the question of which parts of the text are spoken directly to the audience. He pointed out the interesting differences between the monologues of Macbeth and those of Lady Macbeth: while Macbeth speaks directly to the audience, Lady Macbeth does not. In attempting to develop the skills of the actor so that s/he can make an audience *listen*, in the manner desired by Doran, the question of direct address is clearly very important.

In *Macbeth* a case in point is the role of the Porter. This is a character clearly intended to deliver much of his speech directly to his audience. But how is the modern actor to approach it when most of the comic references that would have had a direct appeal to the play's original audience are lost? In Doran's production the role was played by Steve Newman, an actor who exploited the opportunities for direct address to the full, sometimes adding extra lines of his own. When this production was on tour, it visited the Theatre Royal in Bath and Martin White (who had been in the audience at Bath) gave the following account of Newman's performance in the Porter's scene:

> He did a series of jokes about Harold Shipman, to an audience at Bath, which is a very elderly female audience. Harold Shipman was a celebrated doctor who killed more or less every old lady he treated. And if you sit in the Circle in the Theatre Royal in Bath, you look down, and the stalls are more or less grey-haired, mauve … and he did this quite relentlessly, and it was very interesting because there was a bit of fuss about it, locally. The point is that, it was interesting because here was an audience watching a play about killing an old person, which they were receiving as a great classic event and they were thrilling to these fabulous performances (quite properly). Yet when the porter intruded with a joke about real killing, in the newspaper, in what they had just had on the television, now, in the theatre, *that* was more difficult and I suppose it comes back to your point earlier about the element of the *now*.
>
> (27)

Doran agreed with the point being made and added another anecdote from the run of the same production:

One night in the Young Vic … Steve went down to one of the audience and said 'What are you?' which is in the text: 'What are you?' A woman on the front row replied 'Is this in the play?' and in a fantastically Pirandellian moment Steve said 'I'm in the play'. I suppose I'm talking about complicity, and about it being live, now, in the present moment, but it can be taken too far. I mean he did once ask Nigel Lawson [a British politician] who was in the audience what he'd do, and that was a completely blank response. I mean the live-ness of that was fascinating because it did shake you out of the play for a moment. I think directors sometimes try and weave the porter into the play, rather than let him crash out through the play.

(28)

FILMING SHAKESPEARE

Macbeth

Doran went on to discuss the difficulties he had when filming this production of *Macbeth* (made in 1999, with Antony Sher as Macbeth and Harriet Walter as Lady Macbeth), explaining some of the challenges and opportunities involved in the switch to a different medium. In the first place, he encountered the difference of pace: even though film versions invariably leave out vast swathes of Shakespeare's text, they need more time to tell their story because it takes longer to recreate a convincing visualisation than it does to evoke something through the power of language: 'When we did it in the theatre it lasted one hour 59 minutes. Trying to get the thing on film, it took at least two hours and twenty minutes' (21–2).

He had been determined to find a way of preserving the immediacy and urgency that the production had acquired on stage. The original staging had been directed for the Swan Theatre at Stratford-upon-Avon, which has a thrust stage, with its audience seated on three sides, an arrangement that enhances the sense that the actors are speaking directly to the audience. Doran was acutely conscious of the danger of losing this vital relationship with the audience as soon as the production was transferred to film. So rather than filming in the theatre itself, or in a studio, with cameramen used to making art films, he chose to shoot it in the cellars of the Roundhouse, using only one camera, and a cameraman who was used to making documentary films (in fact he had just returned from covering the war in Bosnia):

> The Roundhouse is the most glorious brick extravagant building, built on a turntable for trains, so that underneath there are these great concrete spokes, forming a kind of wheel, supporting the turntable, and they have removed all the rubble from between these spokes, so you have all these wonderful receding rooms, in this strange non-specific place. The camera followed Macbeth around so that Macbeth could talk to the camera at times and talk to himself if need be.
>
> (16)

The challenge that Doran and the cast set themselves was 'to make the experience of watching it in the theatre as live on film' (22). Many of the scenes were shot in a single take with no interruptions or cross-cutting, and the use of the single camera and the rough brick walls in the background gave the whole work a documentary feel. Because the setting and the style of filming carried associations of urgency and relevancy, Doran was able to present the language in a fresh and un-expected manner. He made use of his insight into Lady Macbeth's lack of direct address to the audience by having the cameraman follow her around, filming her from behind as he had followed people running around in the rubble of their ruined homes in Bosnia. In the discussion that followed the screening of a section of Doran's *Macbeth*, the workshop participants agreed that it had captured a sense of the danger of the live moment.

Richard III

Russell Jackson, in his presentation, began by explaining that he wanted to consider what happens when one sets out to transfer a complex rhetorical text to the medium of film; what are the problems that arise through a mismatch between the language of Shakespeare's plays and the demands of cinema? In film, language is merely one of a multitude of signifiers, not privileged as it is in the kind of theatre for which Shakespeare wrote. This is not just a matter of the way so many directors of Shakespeare on film have sought to bring the events depicted up to date; it also reflects the expectations of naturalist setting and performances that the commercial cinematic medium itself tends to create. Various strategies had been tried out by different performers and directors to resolve these problems. In the case of Laurence Olivier's films of *Henry V* and *Richard III*, for example, deliberately stagy settings helped the audiences to accept the unnatural rhetorical complexity, the old-fashioned vocabulary and the stylised delivery of the lines. Orson Welles, on the other hand, subsumed Shakespeare's lines into a much more impressionistic sound-mix and, when faced with particularly difficult passages, was not above speaking them in a barely audible whisper, so that they passed almost unnoticed. The spectators felt as if they were overhearing Welles, whereas Olivier addressed them quite directly. What, Jackson wanted to know, are the differences between the balance that must be achieved between text and *mise-en-scène* in the theatre, where only the actors, stage and settings rival the words as bearers of meaning, and the cinema, where the images are so much more powerful than the words?

In order to explore these differences, Jackson chose a scene from the 1995 film version of *Richard III*, directed by Richard Loncraine from the stage production by Richard Eyre, with Ian McKellen in the title role. This scene (the wooing of Lady Anne over the dead body of her uncle) was deliberately chosen for its length and its 'wordiness'. One of the difficulties frequently evoked when this scene is discussed in terms of theatrical performance has to do with the relationship between rhetorical patterning and psychological realism. That is, to put it very simply, the question of how much Lady Anne falls for Richard, and how the actress can deal with that. In the film, this is dealt with in a heightened way and also by very careful cutting of the text. A great many alterations have been made, both to text and to *con*text. In the first place, words that are spoken publicly in the play, in front of a number of coffin bearers and other bystanders, are here spoken privately: even the mortuary attendants have the good grace to leave, so the only witnesses to the scene are a few dead bodies. Moreover, the whole situation has been altered, so that the corpse in question is not the corpse of her prospective father-in-law Henry VI, but that of her husband, and her behaviour displays an intimacy that is appropriate to this situation. When Richard appears on the scene, the various patterned stages of Shakespeare's dialogue (especially the stichomythia and the language of cursing) somehow have to be delivered in a way that is appropriate to an intimate situation. Moreover, the actress (Kristin Scott Thomas) has far fewer words to speak than in the play and much of what she is feeling is conveyed by close-ups on her face (in one, for example, we see tears in her eyes).

Just like the stage production on which it was based, the film was set in costumes and settings that evoked a fascist state of the 1930s. This meant that the gestural language, and the way language is used, had to accommodate themselves not only to the question of working in another medium, but also to the fact that all the signals about the period in which the action is set would normally carry their own gestural language and way of using language with them. Jackson offered a key example of this difficulty:

> the moment when she suddenly says, 'Dost grant me, hedgehog!', in a slightly snappy Noël Cowardish way, provoking a sharp disjunction between the way we respond to the situation as written by Shakespeare, on the one hand, and the memories we may have of films from the 1930s on the other. Another point of similar friction occurs in the way the lines are delivered at the beginning, where she's talking to the dead body, and the change that then follows in the way the language is being used when she's talking to Richard. Another change that makes it easier for the text to fit into the cinematic convention, and lessens the emotional difficulty of playing the scene, is the way certain phrases, e.g. 'Your bed-chamber' are spoken directly to the camera not to her. Since Kristin Scott Thomas appears not to hear this remark, she doesn't have to face the difficult problem of how to react to it – something that she could not avoid on stage. Because of the way the scene has been cut, many of the difficulties it poses are reduced. In the first place, Scott Thomas has *less to do*, everybody has less to do, but she has a *lot* less to do verbally than she would normally. Whether she's doing more in other respects (she the actress is doing more), is an open question. The moment when, for example, Ian McKellen salutes her, or the moment of acknowledgement when he's turning to go, seem to be things that are ideally picked up by a camera, they are very subtle, very simple. But whereas there are things in the acting that gain enormously from using this medium, there are things in the use of the text that are more problematic; the camera makes much of the language into a 'problem'.

(6)

In the end Jackson wondered whether, if you are determined to film this scene, it might not be better to re-write it in a different language.

In fact, it seems as though there are two sets of problems here at once. One has to do with the medium, the premium it sets on intimacy, its tendency to domesticate all speech and its hostility to expansive public address. The other, which is related to what we expect of behaviour familiar in films made during the period represented, has to do with social inhibitions that get in the way of rhetorical address. The actress in this scene may have her task lightened – slightly – by not having to respond to Richard's 'Your bed-chamber', but her life is made more difficult by the social constraints associated with such points of reference as Celia Johnson in *Brief Encounter*, that exemplar of ladylike restraint in a sensible suit. The way Kristin Scott Thomas is seen, especially in the last moments of the sequence when (from Richard's point of view) we look from a distance at her doll-like figure standing helplessly by the morgue tables, seems to position her as the kind of disempowered female we remember from films of the *Brief Encounter* period. The attenuated script has robbed her of her more flamboyant attacks on Richard, and reduced them to laconic insults uttered through decorously gritted teeth. Moreover, the removal of all onlookers from the scene may offer a heightened personal intensity, but it also removes a performative dimension. Lady Anne simply does not get her day in court with Richard. In the full version of the play she may capitulate eventually, but he has a much harder struggle as she holds forth to an onstage audience of pall-bearers and guards. In his film Olivier compromised by cutting the sequence in half, and having the final section, with Richard prevailing, as a 'private' conversation. Loncraine and McKellen make this a taut, anxious scene, but they still take away much of Lady Anne's opportunity to dominate. She is positioned as a victim, both visually and in terms of the dialogue itself and the way it has to be delivered.

The following sequence, with Richard jubilantly soliloquising in the hospital corridor, apparently careless of whether the assembled extras can hear him or not, seemed to Jackson to demonstrate exactly the kind of outspoken ebullient showmanship denied to Scott Thomas' Lady Anne. Richard is almost like one of those happy characters in a musical of the 1930s or 1940s (and the soundtrack music supports this), who can sing and dance unselfconsciously while passers-by pass by. It is one of the liberating elements of the musical genre that its characters can sing and dance not only with a technical accomplishment not possessed by the audience, but also with an insouciance that they can only dream of. Here the scene is ironically set in a grubby hospital corridor, with some bad stretcher cases and a good number of fairly miserable lower orders to perform to. In fact, McKellen doesn't sing and dance *for* them, but he does acknowledge their presence, stopping to lay a reassuring hand on a patient receiving a blood transfusion, and chucking a raw-kneed little boy under the chin before he whirls up the staircase past the bemused gaze of a group of young women. Have these people become an audience for Richard? If they have, they are aligned with us, the cinema or video audience. Like the great Warner Brothers' musicals of the 1930s, the film plays off one mode against another: gritty realism and un-gritty exhilaration in performing skill – here with the added irony of a murderous monarch as the entertainer. McKellen's gesture at the top of the staircase – one arm raised jubilantly in silhouette – even looks a little like one of John Travolta's postures in *Saturday Night Fever* (which, by the way, is a musical without being a 'musical' – all the singing and dancing has a credible diegetic pretext).

Russell Jackson's conclusion was to ask the question:

Where does this leave the language? In this part of the film, pretty much where it found it: McKellen has an 'audience', can play to us and to 'them' and can evince the same degree and kind of self-conscious oral skill as he would in a stage performance of the play. It's just what Kristin Scott Thomas has been denied. Maybe the lesson is that 'updating' in the film medium (which has prevailed in recent Shakespeare films with varying degrees of postmodern intention) entails shifting the social contexts and modes of discourse according to the time depicted, but also brings with it the versions of these as we are used to seeing them in old movies. As it happens, when we update to the 19th century, as Branagh did in his *Hamlet,* we are stalked by the way that period has been depicted in the movies. In that film, when Branagh was directing Charlton Heston and Rosemary Harris as the Player King and Queen in *The Murder of Gonzago (The Mousetrap)* – dressed as medieval monarchs on a pseudo-Elizabethan platform stage in a Ruritanian court theatre – I remember him asking them to play it 'as if it were Chekhov'. So here were several different performing modes and their attendant cultural contexts all firing at once, and that in the most rhetorically mannered section of the play! And then most of the scene was shot in close-up, and the actors spoke at a level that, in crude realistic terms, would have prevented any of the court 'audience' (let alone the distant royal box) from hearing them. We had established, though, that they were part of a rather old-fashioned Victorian travelling troupe, so anything was acceptable. Branagh also knew that 'epic' is a button you never press with Heston, unless you really want the works.

(private communication)

Ultimately, Jackson felt that realisms (note the plural) in film are so malleable – or perhaps their boundaries are so permeable – that Shakespeare's rhetorically designed language always moves in and out of register with the prevailing mode: from one part of McKellen's 'mortuary' sequence to another; from one kind of character (and one gender and social position) to another; and with varying intensity according to the degree to which the original theatrical mode is conjured up. The most important task for anyone who works with actors on text in these circumstances is to find the way for them to present their character effectively in this particular situation, and in accord with the way the medium is used in a certain sequence.

Moving a staged play into a different historical or geographical context sets up expectations of a number of different social and behavioural codes. Transferring this play to film complicates matters by bringing into play *also* the expectations associated with the cinema of different epochs and cultures. And the way that Shakespeare's language is perceived as relating to those behavioural and gestural codes is in a constant state of instability. Different actors and directors have exploited this instability to achieve the qualities of freshness and surprise that provide their audience with a sense of discovering something for the first time, making them sit up and *listen*.

THE THEATRE DU SOLEIL

Towards the end of the discussions in this workshop, the French production of *Richard II* (Théâtre du Soleil, 1981, directed by Ariane Mnouchkine) was evoked. Reflection on this production made it possible for the workshop to circle back to questions of gesture and meaning, and to build on the insights that had emerged in the presentations by Greg Doran and Russell Jackson, and so we shall conclude this chapter by exploring further the techniques it employed. For her production, Ariane Mnouchkine was determined to face the challenge of staging Shakespeare's language by discovering a form of physical embodiment strong enough to speak on its own terms, not pale into insignificance beside the richness of the language. Of additional interest, given the reflections on film and theatre that featured in this session, was the fact that this *Richard II* drew inspiration from the Japanese Samurai film tradition. This was not the first Shakespeare play that Mnouchkine had directed. In 1968 the Théâtre du Soleil had performed *A Midsummer Night's Dream* at the Cirque Médrano in a production that began to explore the elements of ritual and of 'rough' popular theatre in the play. This was one of Mnouchkine's first productions following her training at the Lecoq School, and it served as a practical application of some of the things she had learned. Each of the characters was identified by particular bodily gestures, and the roles of Titania and Oberon were performed by dancers from the Béjart Company, lending a further dimension to the research into physical means of expression. These researches were brought to a halt by the events of 1968; the company developed in quite a different direction for the next few years, attempting to make sense of what had happened to France in 1968 through devising three productions that confronted history and politics directly: *1789, 1793* and *L'Age d'or.*

When Mnouchkine returned to Shakespeare in 1980, it was, in her own words, 'in the way that one embarks on an apprenticeship with a master craftsman'.[1] She had been struggling with a play on recent political events in South East Asia and, finding that she was making no progress, decided to turn back to Shakespeare. The South East Asian figure who had caught her imagination was Norodom Sihanouk, King of Cambodia, who had been forced to abdicate. *Richard II* was probably suggested to her by the Shakespearean scholar and writer, Hélène Cixous, who was her partner, as a classic drama of the problems confronting a king stripped of his power.[2] In early rehearsal work the actors performed wearing masks, which obliged them to rely on gesture and movement rather than on facial expression. Each of them was encouraged by Mnouchkine to depict, through gesture and movement, their character's fundamental emotion or passion, which she named *un état* (a state), and which corresponds roughly to what Lecoq named an 'attitude'.[3] The word *état* was used to indicate the primary passion inhabiting the actor and motivating his approach to the other characters in the play. Through this primary *état*, a number of secondary emotions could be demonstrated, just as Lecoq's nine basic attitudes are each subject to a number of variations. The reference points with which the actors worked in rehearsal were related to Lecoq's 'territories': Philippe Hottier (a leading actor in the company) explained how he understood the notion of *état* as follows:

> There are two things: the character's base state, and then the successive states he traverses. I would say that the base state is the attitude to life. Arlequin doesn't have the same base state as Pantalone. An actor will only begin to animate the character of Arlequin when he's found Arlequin's attitude to life – his perpetual jumps in perception, the state of curiosity and alertness that characterises him [...] the base state is modified through the secondary states.[4]

Hottier's use of *commedia* characters as illustration shows the debt owed by Mnouchkine to the categorisation she had absorbed at the Lecoq School. Like Lecoq, she begins from work with the mask: 'At the Théâtre du Soleil, ... mask work constitutes the *essential training* of the actor. As soon as an actor "finds" his mask, he is close to possession, he can let himself be possessed by the character, like oracles'.[5] The reason for the importance of the mask is that it facilitates what is the 'core discipline' of the actor for Mnouchkine:

> An actor produces a kind of writing in the air, he writes with his body, he is a writer in space ... I believe that theatre is a back-and-forth between what exists at the deepest, least known levels inside us and its projection, its maximal externalisation towards an audience. The mask requires precisely this maximal internalisation and externalisation.[6]

Mnouchkine's aim for her actors was to achieve the maximum physical externalisation of the most intense inner emotional state, and, in fact, she declared in the same interview that 'the entire body [of the actor] is a mask',[7] demonstrating her belief that the gestures and movements of the actor could compel the audience's attention and reward its concentration.

The resulting production was described in the following terms by Colette Godard, drama critic of *Le Monde*:

These 'English cavaliers' wear wide, dark skirts shot through with reflective brocade, which swirl around speckled felt leggings. Embroidered head-dresses frame faces, some masked, some paint-ed white. Beneath Tudor ruffs, doublets are criss-crossed with obis and the flapping scarves of kimonos draped over shoulders; they resemble glittering scarabs. Cousins to the samurai in *Kagemusha*, these theatrical warriors flank their young king Richard, enveloped in the white drapes of his robes like a tiny bird.[8]

Gilles Sandier described the actors as 'a dream-like cavalcade of Elizabethan samurai'.[9] The costumes evoked by Godard, the live accom-panying music of Jean-Jacques Lemêtre, the acrobatic vigour of Mnouchkine's young company all combined to extraordinary effect in the dazzling entrances and exits, made along a runway leading off the stage at right-angles. The stage itself was bare, about 18 metres square, covered with light brown coconut matting divided into sections by broad black strips running from back to front. Each entrance was heralded by loud percussion, then the actors entered in a group, run-ning at breakneck speed, leaping and capering as if on horseback. They wheeled around the whole expanse of the stage before taking up posi-tion in a long line, facing front. This grouping was a reminder of the rigid, hierarchical nature of feudal society. Each lord stood with knees splayed, palms on thighs, remaining within the limits of the lists, or paths defined by the black strips on the stage floor.

In the powerful alternation of their galloping entrances followed by motionless hieratic poses, most commentators saw a strong Japanese reference. But Mnouchkine's response to questions about Japanese influence was to insist that the Samurai warrior was only one of a num-ber of inspirations behind the production's visual imagery: 'As the basis for our work we took Asian *theatres*, Japanese theatre (Noh, Kabuki), but also Balinese theatre, Kathakali, etc.'[10] Godard confirmed this, from the point of view of the spectator: 'it's not a question of borrowing a vocabulary from the Japanese theatre, but of saying everything through gesture; even the naked face becomes a mask'.[11] The positioning of the Lords, ranged on either side of their youthful king, supporting but also threatening him, corresponds precisely to Lecoq's practice of 'balan-cing' the tragic stage and of demonstrating, through movement and arrangement, the hero who emerges from, and stands out against, a chorus. The text was spoken by the actors facing directly out to the audience. Mnouchkine discouraged them from speaking to one another, seeing this as fundamentally hostile to the kind of text Shakespeare had written, and resulting from the 'venomous' influence of popular television and film psychology:

> I said to them, 'Tell it to *the audience*.' … When the 'state', the passion that he [i.e. the actor] must express in relation to the character is not sufficiently clear, there's always a tendency to take refuge in a psychological relationship with one's partner on stage. The psychological venom has been injected deep inside us – by cinema and television – and the actors have been deformed by it.[12]

As the tragedy unfolded, the production moved through a sequence of powerfully seductive images. King Richard was gradually stripped of his dazzling white robes, he was imprisoned in a cage, he was attached by ropes coming from all four corners of the stage; the final image was of his near-naked corpse stretched over Bolingbroke's knees, deliberately recalling images of the dead Christ. The back wall, behind the stage, was hung with enormous drapes of coloured silk, which fluttered down to suggest a change of location at the end of each scene. The dynamic use of colour, rich fabrics, space and movement, exerted a strong sensuous appeal and managed to offer visual images that did not pale into insignificance beside the richness of Shakespeare's verbal imagery. By rejecting all elements of mimetic-realistic acting, and by drawing on visual associations with the films of Kurosawa, Mnouchkine had succeeded in finding a fresh way of representing the political struggles of Shakespeare's nobility, without making them seem dusty or irrelevant. Her demonstration of what could be achieved by focusing purely on the actors, their movements, gestures, costumes and groupings, was hailed as setting her in the tradition of Jacques Copeau. And like Copeau, she was insistent that everything in the production came from the text, nothing was 'bolted on'. The programme note contained these words:

> They [Shakespeare's kings and nobles] look closely at themselves, analyse themselves: they give breath to a flood of images – raw, sumptuous, bloody, extreme – at every moment bringing their destiny and their mortality to the surface, as in a vivisection of the soul. Confronted with this text, we have worked from word to word, as if we were at the foot of a giant mountain, attentive to each word

pronounced by these great visionary primitives, trying to see what they see, in order for us in turn to be able to show it, to place it in space, in bright light.[13]

The production's ambition was clearly stated as attempting to bring out on stage all the rich variety of Shakespeare's text, to find motivation only in his words, not to load them down with extraneous ideas or references. There were no allusions to contemporary events, no suggestions of parallels with contemporary wars or political events; nothing was gratuitous. Jean-Michel Déprats, a respected translator of Shakespeare into French, made the following comment:

> Certain kinds of Shakespearean productions are characterised by a simplistic determination to transform everything into gesture, scenic images. In [Mnouchkine's] *Richard II*, even though there is a constant and very strong theatricality, the production gives the text an autonomy. It enables images within the text to be inscribed in the spectator's imagination, and encourages a theatre of listening.[14]

The experience of the Théâtre du Soleil with *Richard II* sums up the challenge facing any company planning a Shakespeare production: how to ensure that the audience will listen. How to exploit as fully as possible the expressive powers of the actor, using all the means of expression available, both physical and vocal, in order to present the text on stage with the freshness and vitality demanded by Greg Doran? The answer for Mnouchkine lies in a special approach to actor training and the purpose of this training is to provide the actor with a range and repertoire of gestural movement that can match the playwright's vocabulary in its flexibility and its variety of modulations. It is obvious that, just like words, gestures 'speak' in particular ways that are far from being limited to the theatre. Milan Kundera, in his novel *Immortality*, bases the narrator's whole relationship with the central character on a gesture: the gesture of a woman who turns and waves goodbye. Kundera's narrator seems slightly surprised at himself for being able to attach such significance to a single (simple) gesture: he reflects on the fact that the number of gestures available to an individual human being is limited, and decides that, however many people there may be on Earth, their gestures are few. He goes so far as to sum this up in an aphorism: 'Many people, few gestures'.[15] But the same comment might also be made about language. Most of us use a relatively restricted vocabulary in our everyday lives, and it might just as easily be said of us: 'Many people, few words'. A recurrent complaint of Beckett's narrators, for example, is the difficulty of feeling that the words we use are really our own: the narrator in *Molloy, Malone Dies, The Unnameable* complains that: 'I'm in words, made of words, others' words'.[16]

But although we may occasionally be overcome by such feelings, most of us, in the course of our ordinary, everyday lives, accept the limitations imposed by language. We enjoy and respond to the variety of games that people play with the restricted verbal resources available to them. It is these variations and permutations of known words that go to build up what we call personality. The same is true of gestures and of movements. For when Arden spoke of 'gesture' she was not separating a gesture made to be understood by someone else from all physical movement, whether it be made in private or in public. Her understanding of gesture included all aspects of a person's bodily movement including the most personal and the most instinctive.[17] Gestures, for her, 'have the same kind of relationship as, say, *timbre* does to the voice. So that a mark of a great actor is this sort of indefinable, surprising, inventive, eloquent quality of his gesture' (Arden, 2). In performing Shakespeare, whether on stage or on film, the challenge faced by actors and directors alike is to discover a physical, embodied repertoire of voice, gesture and image that can match the richness of the original text. As Russell Jackson pointed out, 'My favourite filmed Shakespeare is *Throne of Blood* by Kurosawa, which has no lines of Shakespeare in it at all, but is one of the great films since it finds its own language and could only have done this starting from Shakespeare' (44).

NOTES

1 'Performance as Autopsy', programme note for the Théâtre du Soleil's production of *Richard II* in 1981, in *Collaborative Theatre: The Théâtre du Soleil Sourcebook*, ed. David Williams (London: Routledge, 1999), 89.

2 Cixous' own epic play about Sihanouk, *L'histoire terrible mais inachevée de Norodom Sihanouk, Roi du Cambodge*, was produced by Mnouchkine. It opened on 11 September 1985 and ran until the end of 1986 at the Cartoucherie de Vincennes, as well as going on tour.

3 Lecoq's method derives, not from character study, nor even from the search for a particular performance style, but from athletics. He believed that there are certain fundamental gestures and movements that every human being begins to make as a tiny baby, and that these all differ from one another in small ways, just as physical

characteristics differ. The reason for asking acting students to analyse and practise movement in the same way that an athlete does, is so that they can understand how these actions lay down circuits through which emotions flow. By analysing and understanding their own physical movements, Lecoq believed that his acting students would acquire the 'physical awareness, which will form an indispensable basis for acting'.

His analysis, as set out in the book that explains his pedagogic method, *The Moving Body* (London: Methuen 2002, 2nd edn), is complex and moves through a series of stages. Actions are broken down into very precise component parts, not unlike the taxonomy of different movements devised by Rudolf Laban, on which much actor training in England is based. Lecoq begins by working through very simple physical movements with the students, and then goes on to the analysis of what he calls 'attitudes'. By 'attitude' he means a particular physical gesture that can be performed (and read) in a multitude of different ways. The first example he gives of this is of waving goodbye.

As this implies, a movement or a gesture can be analysed from the purely mechanical point of view, or it can be placed within a narrative context, where it has a dramatic justification, and such justifications can be highly complex. Each will result in a slight variation of the same 'attitude'. Lecoq's training method located the sources of all human movement in nine basic attitudes, each of which has its own precise physical and mechanical explanation. But each of these nine fundamental attitudes is subject to variations or can be combined with others. He explains that: 'The nine attitudes and their dramatic justifications are interesting because of their contradictions. "The great Harlequin", a movement pulling the pelvis back, may equally well suggest reverence, fear, or stomach-ache. There is never one single justification: its opposite is often equally possible. All the main attitudes bring multiple possibilities, and this makes them eminently dramatic, as well as being very valuable in a pedagogic perspective' (82).

4 Jean-Michel Déprats, 'Shakespeare is a Masked Text', an interview with Georges Bigot and Philippe Hottier, in Williams, *op. cit.*, 106.

5 Odette Aslan, 'The Entire Body is a Mask', an interview with Ariane Mnouchkine, in Williams, *ibid.*, 109.

6 *Ibid.*, 109.

7 *Ibid.*, 109.

8 Colette Godard, 'Shakespeare's Samurai', in Williams, *ibid.*, 91–2.

9 Gilles Sandier, *Le Matin* (19 Dec 1981).

10 Jean-Michel Déprats, 'Shakespeare is not our Contemporary', an interview with Ariane Mnouchkine, in Williams, *op. cit.*, 93.

11 Colette Godard, 'Shakespeare's Samurai', in Williams, *ibid.*, 92.

12 *Ibid.*, 94.

13 'Performance as Autopsy', in Williams, *ibid.*, 89–90.

14 Jean-Michel Déprats, 'Shakespeare is not our Contemporary', an interview with Ariane Mnouchkine, in Williams, *ibid.*, 95.

15 Milan Kundera, *Immortality* (London: Faber and Faber, 1991), 8.

16 Samuel Beckett, *Molloy, Malone Dies, The Unnameable* (London: Calder and Boyars, 1959), 390.

17 For a more extended discussion of Annabel Arden's notion of 'gesture' in the context of acting, see Chapter 3, 'Gesture, Language and the Body', 63, 65–6.

5

RESISTANT READINGS, MULTILINGUALISM AND MARGINALITY

Calixto Bieito (Romea Teatre, Barcelona)
Maria M. Delgado (Queen Mary, University of London):
respondent
Patricia Parker (Stanford University)

For both the critic and theatre practitioner contributing to this essay, translation is a key concept in engaging with Shakespeare's plays. The translator, like the director and the editor, uses language to open up the text and foreground the work of the dramaturge, which questions past versions and other languages of the play, and initiates new conversations with it. Translation can effectively resituate a play in completely new settings, not only opening up into a different language but, as the play is physically reshaped, also into new structures. Translation can also be exceptionally helpful when it occurs within the English language, recognising its historical connections with many other languages. The point of any translation, they argue, is to engender resistant political readings that prise apart given conventions.

> The movements to deconstruct Shakespeare's plays, or revise their representation by radical visual methods, have been located chiefly in Europe. The traditions of performance in English, dominated and continually reinforced by the two Stratfords, have normally maintained that Shakespearean interpretation and Shakespearean acting should be centered in textual analysis and linguistic interpretation.
>
> Dennis Kennedy[1]

MARGINS

This chapter seeks to interrogate some questions around directing, translating and the excavation of language for alterior/ulterior meanings, which emerged during the workshop I, Maria M. Delgado, chaired between United States' academic Patricia Parker and Catalan director Calixto Bieito. If I begin this discussion of the encounter between Parker and Bieito, which probed analogies between dramaturgy and editing, and questions of linguistic play and the staging of it, with Dennis Kennedy's observation on trends in Shakespearean staging, it is perhaps because such a view seems indicative of a particular Anglophone approach not only to production but also to criticism.

The Bard's enduring greatness is often located in the majesty of his language and, as Indian academic Laxmi Chandrashsekhar indicated to Peter Holland in 1993, 'there is always this illusion that a British director understands Shakespeare better than an outsider can'.[2] Such a myth has also permeated Shakespearean criticism, which is noticeably dominated by an Anglo-American pantheon of critics. The work of these critics around historical materialist, post-structuralist and post-colonialist discourses, while opening out various productive avenues for Shakespearean studies which have impacted on production practices, has engaged only marginally with the multilingual textures of Shakespeare's plays. There is no denying that deconstruction has offered challenges and openings to Shakespearean scholars. The 'de-centring' of our universe, questioning of the stability of the sign and the possibility of any stable centre of meaning has brought about recognition that any search for a single, fixed truth or meaning in a text is pointless. Rather than a unified entity, texts are fragmented and capable of providing conflicting meanings. As such all that can be relied on are interpretations, but it is effectively the interpretations of certain, I would argue, Anglo-American readers that have been 'privileged' over others who, working within other languages that lack the (post-) colonialist hegemony of English, have languished in the margins.

It is the repositioning of these margins that unites both the work of Bieito and Parker. Both are involved in the process of excavation, re-positioning texts that have accumulated layers of meaning through editorial and staging mediations over the past 400 years. While Parker's approach may be summarised as etymological, it is also, as both Bieito and Annabel Arden noted during The Fifth Wall research workshop, a valuable resource in locating oral/aural significance on the stage. Parker's approach is perhaps best exemplified in her key 1996 monograph, *Shakespeare from the Margins: Language, Culture, Context*, where an exploration of resonances of Shakespearean wordplay concerns itself with what 'in Shakespeare has been marginalized or overlooked, and the edification from the margins (to borrow from *Hamlet*) that can be gained by attending to what might appear the simply inconsequential'.[3] For Parker,

> the terms of this wordplay make possible glimpses into the relation between the plays and their contemporary culture, in a period when English was not yet standardized into a fixed orthography, obscuring on the printed page the homophonic networks possible before such boundaries were solidified.[4]

Janelle Day Jenstad's contribution to this volume (Chapter 1) lucidly details the forms in which the first printed texts of Shakespeare's works reached us; tainted by the scribes and typesetters who were responsible for putting together the quarto and folio editions that are frequently positioned as the point of 'origin' against which subsequent performances are measured. If we recognise that our access to both the quarto and folio editions can only ever be mediated by the unknowable nature of the punctuation, lineation and spelling imposed by those who were responsible for first bringing the plays into print, then the implications of resistant readings that negate the possibility of an authoritative artefact offer a more expansive framework for the interrogation of Shakespeare's plays.

For the critic Paul de Man 'a deconstruction always has for its target to reveal the existence of hidden articulations and fragmentations within assumedly monolithic totalities'.[5] It is this search for 'fault lines', gaps or fissures, disunities and paradoxes within the text, that roots Parker, and, as I will later argue, Bieito's approach. In a world where we can never be exactly sure what language means or how it controls us, Parker's etymological approach facilitates a process of 'disentanglement' that asks pertinent questions about the multicultural society that engendered these works.

The United States' director Peter Sellars has drawn attention to the implications of Shakespeare having named his playhouse 'The Globe'; 'a sense of what slice of the world are we able to present in theatre?'[6] The ethnicity of Shakespeare's worlds is self-evident. At The Globe, English actors played foreign characters in plays that transported the audience from Venice to Rome, Arden to Dunsinane. In a dramaturgical climate all too dominated by the domestic frames of naturalism, how much more limited have our theatrical norms become? The steady erasure of the ensemble and its celebration of a performance style which casts against type and where you might play a young gigolo in one production and an ageing father in another, has resulted in a theatrical landscape where casting is emphatically based on as close a correlation as possible between actor and role. As the gaps have closed up and homogeneity has, contrary to cultural protests, displaced heterogeneity, we are reminded of Parker's articulation of what is

> too readily forgotten about a cultural icon as central as William Shakespeare. This includes what Jean Howard, Louis Montrose, Steven Mullaney and others have described as the marginal or liminal position of the Shakespearean theatre itself, located in a so-called Liberty (outside and inside the City at once) and featuring players who if upwardly mobile came from the socially or geographically marginal, elevated (in cases like Shakespeare's) to the position of gentlemen forged or made but also ranged among 'mechanics' and cited in the statute that included vagabonds and other placeless men. The popular theatre in particular – as the last decade of scholarship has taught us – was a threateningly liminal space, whose 'mingling of kings and clowns' (in the famous phrase of Sidney) blurred a whole range of distinctions, evoking the specter of adulterating, crossbreeding, and hybridity.[7]

Calixto Bieito is artistic director of Barcelona's Teatre Romea, located off the Ramblas on the Carrer del Hospital in the city's Barri Xinè's. The Romea was built in 1863 on the site of the convent of Saint Agustín and through the association of dramatist Frederic Soler (known as Serafí Pitarra) and subsequent Catalan playwrights like Santiago Rusiñol, Ignasi Iglésies and Adrià Gual, soon assumed the status as the home of Catalan-language dramaturgy. Like the Principal and Liceu, it forms part of a triptych of theatres that map out the city's theatrical heritage over the twentieth century. For Hermann Bonnin, one of Bieito's predecessors at the helm of the Romea, writing in 1989, the theatre embodies 'quasi totes les accidentades i, tanmateix, simptomàtiques peripècies del teatre català dels darrers 125 anys – de la "renaixença" a la "institucionalització", de l'empresa privada de Frederic Soler a l'oficial del "Centre Dramàtic de la Generalitat" – es manifesten a través del Romea' (Almost all the eventful and at the same time symptomatic vicissitudes of Catalan theatre during the last 125 years from the *Renaixença* to the developments of theatrical structures, from the private company of Frederic Soler to the official company of the Generalitat's Dramatic Centre, are shown through the Romea).[8]

The history of Catalonia is irrevocably bound up with the struggle against the unionist imperative of the Spanish state. Catalonia (and in particular its capital, Barcelona) has often stood as a potent symbol of 'otherness'; seeking to forge a national identity in opposition to that imposed by centralist Castile. Cultural production in Catalonia has been irrevocably linked to nationalist struggles; indeed for John Hooper it is the cultural movements of the *Renaixença*, and the successive *Modernisme* and *Noucentisme* that offered both 'the raw material and the driving force for the political movement known as Catalanism'.[9] I have written elsewhere of more contemporary theatrical embodiments of a nationalist struggle which has interrogated the city's marginalised status of 'other' against the supposed capital centre, Madrid.[10] The establishment of a Catalan National Theatre in the late 1990s and the plethora of Catalan-language theatres that now litter Barcelona have necessitated a rethink of the Romea's mandate and, since 1999, under Bieito's directorship, the theatre has negotiated a bilingual policy which has seen both Catalan- and Castilian-language stagings produced by what is increasingly viewed as an ensemble company. Against a cultural policy promoted by the Generalitat de Catalunya's president Jordi Pujol, which has sought an absolute displacement of Castilian by Catalan as the 'official' language of the Catalan nation, Bieito has sought to promote a policy that recognises the multilingual landscape of contemporary Catalonia without replacing one linguistic hierarchy with another.

His own trajectory with Shakespeare has negotiated the Catalan/ Castilian axis. His have been resistant readings that have not always assuaged critical anxieties. His approach, like Parker's, has often result-ed in taking a particular line or lines that may have been previously overlooked as a central pivot or motif around which to construct part of the edifice of the *mise-en-scène*. With his 1997 Catalan- and Castilian-language staging of *The Tempest*, this line was, according to critic Marcos Ordóñez, Gonzalo's final few lines 'all of us ourselves, / When no man was his own' (5.1.213–14),[11] grounding a series of permuta-tions, duplicities and transformations that characterised Bieito's visualisation of the play. For Bieito, as with Peter Sellars, this vision is never a question of eradicating or ignoring that which is not easily understood. Sellars has often stated that the process of engaging with

Shakespeare in the present always involves a recognition that 'there are parallels, there are correspondences, but there are also differences. I try to leave those differences there on stage staring at you, rather than lop off everything that didn't fit'.[12]

As early as 1989 when he staged a Catalan-language *Two Gentlemen of Verona*, Bieito acknowledged that his attraction to the play was based, in no small part, on its imperfect dramaturgy, a dramaturgy that he did not aim to mask but rather to expose.[13] His choice of a costume design that offered signifiers from different historical eras from Shakespeare's time to our own, recognised the layers of interpretation present when any cultural artefact from an earlier era is restaged in contemporary times. With *Measure for Measure*, presented in 1999, Bieito articulated once again a directorial tendency to veer towards the most problematic works in the canon. Patricia Parker, too, has been drawn towards what she terms 'critically marginalized works'[14] – *Love's Labour's Lost*, *The Comedy of Errors*, *Henry IV Part 2*, and *The Merry Wives of Windsor*. But even when approaching works that have a more prominent role within the canon, both have begun with 'elements that have been slighted or marginalized in the tradition of Shakespeare editing … criticism' and production.[15]

In Bieito's staging of *Macbeth*, first presented at the Salzburg Festival in 2001 and then restaged in both Catalan and Castilian in 2002 to 2003, he began by exploring the Macbeths' childlessness and how this played out in terms of the family structures set up within the body of the text. For Bieito, the process of staging a play always necessitates an engagement with language and context, beginning with historical and historicist exploration that then 'needs to be *translated* into what it means for the audience now'(1). The use of the word translation is key here, for translation involves not only the linguistic relocation and dislocation of the work, but its translation into what one Fifth Wall contributor termed 'a socio-political context that gives you some kind of psychological underpinning for the action' (41). It should always be, to quote Bieito, 'for the audience, about watching a play as if for the first time and, for me, like I have a new friend with me'.[16]

The socio-political context in Bieito's *Macbeth* established for the audience a family prised apart by civil war, which he relates to the experience of living and working in Spain, a country scarred by the fratricidal conflict of 1936–39. The action took place within a close-knit family unit with an initial mafia-world landscape providing the staging with a brilliant metaphor for the divisive loyalties of the domestic. Bieito's approach always involves the building in of conceptual links between the social structures and allusions of the play and reference points for present-day audiences. For *Macbeth*, Alfons Flores' set provided a lurid, tawdry world of disposable consumables: wipe-clean white plastic sofas from which traces of blood could be easily erased, garish carpets, a giant porcelain tiger that growled from the back of the stage and the detritus of a community at war – espousing loyalty and honour but brutally chasing the material. Roser Camí's Lady Macbeth and Santi Pons' Duncan were the monarchs of this contemporary landscape, defined by the director as 'a hedonistic, drug- and drink-fuelled culture with no bounds'[17] where protagonists prowl, bounce and charge across the stage in ruthless pursuit of power and the prestige it brings.

While his early Shakespeare productions relied on the 'canonical' translations undertaken by Josep Maria de Sagarra in the 1940s, more recently Bieito has turned to living poets and translators to work with him on Castilian- or Catalan-language versions of the plays. His has been a process of excavation – his 1995 staging of *King John* was the Catalan-language premiere of the play which visibly acknowledged anachronisms Shakespeare places in the text by referencing the time of composition; anachronisms that found an echo in Mercè Paloma's costume design. Interestingly, while this production was viewed as the premiere of a play without a production history in Catalonia, Bieito chose to prune it by cutting the character of Lady Falconbridge. For Bieito, the staging of Shakespeare has never been about reverence but, rather, active dissection of the language, nuances and textures of the plays. When discussing the impact of filmic reinventions of the Bard's work, Margo Hendricks articulated 'the level of engagement, of anticipation, of loss of predictability' that film has taken out of stage productions of Shakespeare 'that are pretty much the same from their [the audience's] point of view: we come in, we worship the Bard and then we move on' (Bradby, Doran, Jackson, 38). If, as Peter Lichtenfels has indicated, part of the trouble people have with Shakespeare is that they can think faster than the actors speak the language, then the achievement of films such as Baz Luhrmann's *William Shakespeare's Romeo and Juliet* (1996) and Kenneth Branagh's *Much Ado About Nothing* (1993) lies in the pacing of the language. Indeed Peter Brook reminds us that the 'appeal of Shakespeare lay originally in the tremendously exciting, fast-moving dramatic quality of the plays. But – let us confess it – how-

ever faithful to the text may have been the productions of the last century, Shakespeare has become for the ordinary playgoer, a bit of a bore'.[18]

His desire to challenge such a view has led Bieito to appropriate the
pacier rhythms of cinema and montage, twinned with a visceral
approach to acting that has proved key in many of his productions. The
language may be ostensibly Catalan or Castilian, but the visual references and rhythms are often those of popular and art house cinema.
For *King John* in 1995, there were clear references to Orson Welles'
Chimes at Midnight (1966) and Chéreau's *La Reine Margot* (1993).[19]
His *Macbeth* contained visual nods towards *Blue Velvet* (1986), *The Big
Heat* (1953), *Nosferatu* (1922), *Perdita Durango* (1997), *The Godfather*
trilogy (1972/1974/1990) and *Henry: Portrait of a Serial Killer* (1990),
further reinforcing the distinctive registers of Bieito's overtly intertextual
reading, his productions set against the simulacra of representations
past and present. If Parker's approach involves an interrogation and
questioning of the textual interventions of past scribes, editors and
critics, Bieito's eschews an evening out of irregularities in favour of the
over-articulation of fissures, fractures and paradoxes. In his Castilian-
language staging of *The Tempest* at Barcelona's Grec theatre in 1997,
later presented in Catalan, the play's dissonances were embodied by
actors from a range of forms that did not easily fit within a harmonious
performance aesthetic. Classically trained performers like Fermí Reixach,
an early associate of Barcelona's Teatre Lliure cooperative, performed
alongside veteran music-hall performer Pirondello and singer Rosa
Galindo, both of whom personified facets of the disembodied Ariel.

Margo Hendricks' interventions in The Fifth Wall engaged with issues
around 'the construction of distance that takes you away from the
language but also takes you a little bit closer to it' (Arden, Hendricks,
Hunter, 9). In a 1990 essay, Erica Fischer-Lichte details how Ariane
Mnouchkine's work with *Richard II* in 1981 overlays the kinetic gestural
vocabularies of Kabuki on her reading of the codes of Shakespeare's
text. For Fischer-Lichte this produces a distance that overtly announces
that Shakespeare is *not* our contemporary.[20] For Bieito the task is always
one of balancing distance with the proximity of certain concerns the
text may articulate about the anxieties of the age. This distance is always
enunciated through the prism of translation. If Peter Brook has repeatedly extolled the process of exploration and dissection that accompanies
his collaborations with translator Jean-Claude Carrière on French-
language Shakespeare ventures,[21] Bieito, too, acknowledges that the

actual process of linguistic translation necessitates a close examination of the text's ambiguities, flaws and patterns. If Shakespearean production in the UK has perhaps been overly anchored to issues of fidelity to the 'language' of the plays, foreign Shakespeares have always had the choice of releasing the language by rendering it in a more accessible, immediate or contemporary idiom. For Bieito, as with his first staging of Pedro Calderón de la Barca's *Life is a Dream* in 1998 through the filter of an English-language translation, this is a liberating process, that serves to free you 'from the tyranny of the words. You can see how alien the pieces are as well as what remains close or proximate to us'.[22]

Increasingly, for him, the linguistic transposition of the play has been irrevocably linked to the dramaturgical rewriting he has undertaken on the works he has staged. Miquel Desclot's version of *The Tempest* was accused of being a 'rewrite' by Catalan critics because it openly acknowledged refashioning the play, as if Sagarra's consecrated translations are not 'rewrites' because of the authority with which they are now invested. Bieito's rehearsal of *The Tempest* involved Desclot 'changing the text all the time' (5). With *Macbeth*, too, there was a working association with a translator – Desclot is credited with the Catalan version, and Bieito rendered the Castilian translation with his directorial assistant Josep Galindo. The director is, for Bieito, always a co-translator of the piece, whether formally acknowledged as such or not. Indeed, the modernisation that occurs through the modification of language via translation necessitates a process of compensation by means of the visual elements of production.

It is often said that there are parallels between directors and translators in that both are communicators; both are involved in making choices about how to bring a text to a certain audience. Both are intermediaries, although in production the audience is more likely to take note of the director's work than the translator's. The visibility of the director may well render the translator, like the editor, largely invisible, 'hidden' in what is perceived to be 'the service of' the text.

Theatre translation at its best is perhaps much like direction: not an individual pursuit, but part of the creative process of ensuring a play works on stage. Both processes, like that of editing, involve making choices and imposing a reading on a text as it is negotiated in rehearsal or prepared for publication. All three concern themselves with the re-creation of works, often with particular performance spaces or 'readers' in mind. All must juggle an awareness of how source-text conventions may function in what may be a very different receiving culture. Certainly Bieito, in recognising his negotiation of the director-translator-dramaturge axis, and Parker, in acknowledging the shaping that editors carry out, position themselves as part-authors of the work they help to render in production or print. While Janelle Day Jenstad may have used as a starting point for her 'Text and Voice' session the assertion that, 'for a theatre practitioner the text is the starting point and for the literary critic who's working in an editorial capacity, the text is the final product' (Jenstad, Lichtenfels, Magnusson, 14), for Parker there is no possibility of a definitive text. Likewise, for Bieito, there is no possibility of a definitive production, only the opening up of further questions and debates about the ways these texts have been constructed by previous generations of scholars, scribes and directors.

Some of the most provocative parallels that emerge in Bieito's and Parker's approaches come through the issue of multilingualism, although this functions in different ways in each of their working processes. For Bieito, there are performative implications in the language in which you choose to interpret the play.

> With Spanish actors it's good because they are very emotional. They go to the scene head on, like a bull, and just do it. It's [Spanish] a wordier language than Catalan which is closer to the English, more monosyllabic and very light … [Catalan is] softer to listen to because the language is less guttural than Spanish. I actually think it's lighter even than much English, it's very soft. German – and I must say I'm talking about emotions, impressions – is terrifying. When a German actor is shouting at you, it's frightening. But the work they are doing with the language is very intense and fierce, like the anguished release of breath. Spanish is very harsh. For my actors, they are alternating presentations of *Macbeth* in both Catalan and Spanish; but they are more exhausted when they do it in the Spanish than the Catalan. The sound is harder in Spanish and it's longer …; it's longer in German too, which is also less monosyllabic.[23]

Indeed Mingo Ràfols, who took the role of Macbeth in Bieito's production, has mentioned the slippage that occurs when you are performing the plays in two different languages. 'The pace is so hard and fast that there is sometimes a moment when you skip from Spanish to Catalan and you're not entirely sure it's happened until after you've said it'.[24] Roser Camí, when discussing the challenges of performing the play in the two language stagings, confirmed Ràfols' view but also mentioned the greater physical exertion necessitated by the Castilian-language performance, which placed a weightier demand on the voice. The rhythms of Shakespeare's prose certainly sound more distant within the linguistic parameters of a more rhetorical language like Castilian. Bieito has described actors as his 'indispensable associates' in the crafting of any of his stagings and they are always involved in what he terms a 'battering of the text' (email). While he is sure that you:

> lose something always in the translation, you can win a lot of things with the actors. I insist it is with the actors, always a journey with them. They are a tool, a way into the play. There is a story of Montserrat Caballé rehearsing a Verdi piece at Covent Garden and the conductor said 'Miss Montserrat, the tempo is this'. And she replied: 'Who said that to you? Verdi?' I think it's the same for me. You have to find some rules but ensure that they're not limiting. (7)

The process of engagement with the play always involves a fight: 'hitting each other with the text, coming to blows with it to see what's still standing when that process is over'.[25] It is the aggressive nature of this process that critics have found difficult to stomach. Margo Hendricks has probed the possibilities for the body to animate the text in the process of staging, delineating how it 'builds into the way we are expected to see things: sometimes our tendency to look away prevents us from recognising what it is that we are to see' (Arden, Hendricks, Hunter, 10). In asking whether an actor can guide us to that which we don't want to see, she touches on one of the pivots of Bieito's aesthetic: the unadorned centrality of the performers who reveal themselves as the central makers of the tale, unable to dissimulate themselves behind the display and construction of the theatrical illusion. His is an approach closer to the heightened incongruity and varied acting styles of theatre company Cheek by Jowl than the masterful artfulness of Giorgio Strehler. And while the metaphor of performance and performativity may be present in the work, it is in the corporeal realisation of the dilemmas and dynamics of the piece that the work is based.

MULTITEXTUAL, MULTILINGUAL SHAKESPEARES

'My Shakespeares always have traces of my cultural home', Bieito asserted during his Fifth Wall interventions. Buñuel's black humour has provided a tangible grounding for much of his work but his 'cultural home' also encompasses what he refers to as 'a big tradition of literature, cinema, painting, photography that comes between the first production or publication of the text and now' (6).[26] This is never effaced by Bieito but consciously exposed as a way of further enforcing the intertextual and interlingual resonances that would have been very present during the first production of the play.

Multilingualism is a tangible point of entry to these texts for Patricia Parker. Bieito has spoken at length of the multilingual strands that ground his own persona: Galician roots, an upbringing in Castile, a relocation to Catalonia, the bilingualism of negotiating both Catalan and Castilian, and linguistic fluency in English, French and Italian as well as an elemental knowledge of German. For Parker, too, her own multilingualism – in a world dominated by a particular hegemony of English – provides a valuable tool in the reading of Shakespeare's English.

> I grew up in Canada (in Saskatchewan and Manitoba), with an Irish father who came over from Ireland when he was 20 years old. I remember being terribly embarrassed by the fact that I was the only kid at school who had a father who pronounced the word 'ache' and the letter 'h' in the same way. It was only many years later that I realised that the pronunciation of 'ache' as 'h' was crucial to a pun in *Antony and Cleopatra*. I was also originally taught French in Saskatchewan, where I grew up hearing the sound of many different languages. My school had no one to teach French at the time except the football coach whose name was Philpot. He drilled us in French like the good coach he was, training us to pronounce all the syllables and consonants. I learned to pronounce the 's' and 'ent' in 'ils donnent', with no notion of what was to remain silent (until my family moved a year later to Manitoba, originally a French province). But I was grateful to him years later, when I realized that 16th-century French did not sound like modern French either, and learned how little we really know about 16th-century sounds, in English as well.
>
> My first real introduction to Shakespeare did not happen until I went to work (after completing my MA at Toronto) for Julius Nyerere, the President of Tanzania, who was translating *Julius Caesar* and *The Merchant of Venice* into Kiswahili … In Tanzania, I was

teaching a curriculum that was in the process of changing from the older colonial model (similar to the one in which I had also been raised) to one that incorporated the writing of African authors such as Soyinka and Achebe. My Tanzanian students were trilingual: with English as their third language, after Kiswahili and the languages of their own regions. Like the bilingual and multilingual contexts in Canada and the ones that I would come to know from Spanish-speaking students in the US, this experience introduced me to a different perspective on Shakespeare (through Nyerere's translations and a performance tradition that was as much oral as written). It also led me to think for the first time about the complex inter-relationships between language, rhetoric, and power.

(12–14 and email)

If Parker was to frame her intervention within such a stark auto-biographical preface, it was precisely because of a strong conviction based on these multilingual experiences that:

the language of Shakespeare's plays has to be approached as a multi-lingual experience, rather than the more narrow (or 'English only') approach that may itself be the product of viewing Shakespeare backwards, from the perspective of the later Empire that made him the 'English' icon par excellence

(email)

Teaching now at Stanford University in California, she is surrounded by students who come into her lectures with Spanish as their first language, thus immediately grasping:

that 'Iago' in *Othello* is a Spanish name – even without the benefit of reading the criticism of recent years that points out that Shakespeare chose for its villain the name of the 'Saint' (Iago or James) under whose ensign the Moors were driven out of Spain. The exclusively English-speaking students who come from San Diego are surprised to learn that their city's own name is another version of 'Iago' (though they have usually studied *Othello* there in their high school careers). My Spanish-speaking students also understand immediately why 'Mercatio' in *Two Gentlemen of Verona* is the name of its wealthy merchant, and even why 'Mercutio' in *Romeo and Juliet* is called a 'saucy merchant': scholarship tells us that Mercury (one of the resonances of Mercutio's name) was the god of market places as well as of crossroads of various kinds, but the students who hear the Spanish word for 'market' in Mercatio, Mercutio, or the Marcade of *Love's Labour's Lost* are hearing Shakespeare in the more macaronic or multilingual register that was Elizabethan and Jacobean English, which is much less available to modern-day English-only speakers.

(email)

Bieito too acknowledges that his own multilingualism offers an approach to the language that often permeates both the process of translation and staging. Indeed, while he was preparing his production of Verdi's *A Masked Ball* for English National Opera in 2002, Bieito studied the score with the close attention to linguistic permutations that Parker employs. The score indicates that King Gustavus pays a visit to the seer in the disguise of a fisherman or *pescator*, teasing out the slang associations of the Italian word – etymologically close to the Spanish *pescador* – which in translation refers to someone who is 'on the pull'. He chose not to place Gustavus in the habitual fisherman's attire but rather dressed him in an outlandish outfit described by the singer taking the role of Gustavus as 'a cross between Elvis and ABBA'.[27] As such, linguistic probings can have a hugely relevant impact on staging decisions.

As Parker reminded participants at The Fifth Wall workshop:

Shakespeare's plays are filled with multilingual and interlingual puns. The hilarious mispronunciation of 'Ninus' as 'ninny' in *A Midsummer Night's Dream* not only transforms this Babylonian ruler into a 'ninny' or 'fool'; it reminds us that in Ovid's Pyramus and Thisbe story – which Shakespeare was more than capable of reading in Latin as well as in Golding's English translation – the lovers are to meet *ad busta Nini*, or (we might say, already sliding between languages) at 'Ninny's tomb'. That kind of interlingual wordplay went on all the time in plays contemporary with Shakespeare. The assumption of an English-only Shakespeare (or London), if it exists, is a back-formation from a much later (or perhaps chimerical) history. Hearing such wordplay depends not only on a greater linguistic flexibility than most of us have, but also on surrendering the eye to the ear, print-based habits of reading (which we often take into the theater itself) to an aural (as well as oral) mode. In the famously mixed-up speech of Bottom in this play, when he awakens from his dream, it appears that he simply gets it wrong when he says that the 'ear' hath not 'seen'. But the plays of Shakespeare (and his contemporaries) demand that we learn, so to speak, to see with the 'ear' what is not available to the eye (as Hermia says that she found Lysander by hearing rather than by sight). Perhaps we need to start *learning to see all kinds of things in Shakespeare with our ears* [writer's emphasis].

(email)

In a reminder that 'multilingual networks [of sounds] were literally commonplace in the period of Shakespeare's plays' (5–6 and email), Parker delineates an argument that perhaps holds too little sway in a climate that while recognising the existence of a multicultural landscape, is dominated by the pre-eminence of an English language that increasingly negates its links to the 'other' languages of Europe. Parker's example of the case of 'Iago' in *Othello* has already been referred to. In delineating other instances of such multilingual practices she gives insights into a rich climate of wordplay whose resonances have largely been lost to us:

In approaching Shakespeare, we often need the assistance of our continental colleagues and students who come to our classes with a multitude of other languages. It was a student whose first language is Spanish who first pointed out to me, for example, that the English term 'ingle' (about which so much has been written, in relation to transvestite theater) came from the Spanish word for a bodily cavity. The *Oxford English Dictionary* tells us (under 'ingle', which it defines as a 'boy-favourite' or 'catamite') that it is 'of no known origin'. But if we consult an early modern multilingual dictionary – such as John Minsheu's *A Guide Unto the Tongues* (1617) – it tells us (under 'Ingle' or 'a Boy kept for Sodomie') that it comes from the Spanish (and is related to Latin *Inguen*, or 'the groine of man or woman'). The Spanish link here may extend to 'English' itself (which was written in Spanish as *inglés*, and hence available for puns on 'ingles' as lovers of both sexes). In *The Merry Wives of Windsor*, when Pistol says of Falstaff's pursuit of Ford's wife that he has 'translated her will – out of honesty into English', even the old New Cambridge editors Arthur Quiller-Couch and John Dover Wilson speculate that 'English' may be playing on 'ingles' as well as Spanish *inglés*. And precisely that kind of interlingual or multilingual wordplay may also be behind some potentially subversive puns in Shakespeare's *Henry V*. The play is filled with reminders that the 'English' were originally 'Angles', where 'ingle' itself (in the 'catamite' sense) may be suggested in the scene where Henry's former 'bedfellow' Scroop is described as an easily entered 'Englishman' ('Inglishman', or 'Inglesman', in its other familiar Elizabeth spellings). In a play in which England itself is called a 'nook-shotten isle', Henry is called the 'Roi d'Angleterre', and attention is called to 'breaches' of all kinds, such interlingual connections are far from out of the question. But they operate (like Welsh 'leeks' and 'leaks') at the aural rather than the visual level, and like Welsh Fluellen's notorious comparison of Henry himself to 'Alexander the Pig' (an apparent slip of the lip for Great or Big), they may escape the censorship of the eye.

(17 and email)

In her editing of *A Midsummer Night's Dream*, such multilingual networks have been crucial in considering both the name (and, by association, the sound) of Peter 'Quince':

the real revelation about the implications of Shakespeare's choice of 'Quince' did not come to me until I explored its other multilingual equivalents, and discovered (once again in Minsheu's indispensable *Guide*) that the familiar name for a 'Quince' in Spanish was 'Membrillo' (or 'little member'), which Minsheu informs his English readers came from the Latin for the sexual *membrum* and was used for the 'quince' because of its suggestive similarity to the genital members of both men and women. I subsequently came to learn from colleagues in Spanish that the quince was not only a well-known aphrodisiac or love potion in the period (evoked in contemporary Spanish writing by Gongora and Cervantes), but that it was the wedding-fruit par excellence, associated at the time of Shakespeare's *Dream* … with weddings in Athens in particular. Without the initial introduction to the Spanish form of English 'quince', I would not have had any idea of the riches behind the 'Quince' who comically appears in this play's own Athenian wedding. In this case, it was not just a 'French connection' (natural given England's Norman history) but the 'Spanish connection' that was the crucial one.

(17–18 and email)

Bieito and I may have jokingly referred to Patricia's works as 'music to our ears', because – as with James Tyrone in *Long Day's Journey into Night*, who believes that 'Shakespeare was an Irish Catholic. The proof is in his plays'[28] – we both subscribe to the belief that Shakespeare was Spanish! In an essay on *Macbeth* first published in 1970, Jorge Luis Borges writes of English as firstly a Germanic language, which, from the fourteenth century onwards, became contaminated by Latin. For Borges, Shakespeare alternates these two registers constantly in his work but never with the effect that they appear synonymous. In giving the example from the play of 'The multitudinous seas incarnadine, / Making the green one red' (2.2.61–2), Borges indicates how in the first line the Latin voice is dominant and in the second the sharp, direct Saxon inflections take over. For Borges, Shakespeare is the least English of all the English poets, almost a foreigner when compared with Wordsworth, Chaucer or Johnson.[29]

For Bieito, Parker's approach allows the reinscription through translation and then staging, of the implications of such linguistic wordplay. In this way, possible networks of associations – increasingly lost to generations for whom contemporary English seems painfully distant from Shakespeare's language – can be established anew. In Parker's case, her print-based training as a critic had not encouraged the saying-out-loud of the words. Parker may write about Shakespeare but for Bieito, as for Parker's daughter who is fluent in Spanish, he is 'Shak-es-pe-a-re'. In merely restressing the alternative pronunciation of the Bard's name through the filter of another language, Parker acknowledges the 'different perspective – including that "Shakespeare is Spanish"' – which is introduced when the Spanish counterpoint is raised as something that might 'crucially matter for us as interpreters of Shakespeare's "English"' (email). If, for Bieito, English is a tool which facilitates a fiercer engagement with the text in the process of reworking for translation and production, then Spanish – and by association other Romance languages – offers Parker the means to dismantle Shakespeare's language.

If director Leon Rubin was to understand the implications of Parker's etymological approach as relevant predominantly to the cultural transposition and translation of Shakespeare's work, this view was largely dismissed by Arden and Bieito who grasped its implications for staging. For Arden, it's too easy to say that the etymological implications should simply be present in translations. This, in effect, perpetuates an ideology where they ('foreigners') should engage with the nitty-gritty of such linguistic displacements while 'we' (the Anglo-Americans) are allowed to stage the Bard uninterrogated.

> I had an experience where I had an Italian actor from Bergamo, Marcello Magni, who was extremely funny, cast as Autolycus in *The Winter's Tale* [in 1991] and when he came on doing Autolycus in English he was not at all funny or interesting. So we decided he should do it in Italian – the whole part of Autolycus in Italian. What we lacked was having someone like Patricia [Parker], because then we could have done some really sophisticated wordplays to do with Italian and English, and we could have been faithful on both counts to that incredible text, and to our Italian actor. He really was an Autolycus, a trickster and a thief: he stole the handbags of the entire front row every night and although he gave them all back, he got into a lot of trouble. When he played here (in another show) at The Globe, he got into big trouble for throwing ice cream at people. I also remember him playing the Fool in *King Lear*, and in that production he was not allowed to appropriate the language, and I suffered for him. Because he did sound awkward; the language is not in him, it's not his language. The Fool's language is difficult enough when you hear it, and I felt he was diminished as an actor and the role was diminished. He needed to be freer with that allusive wordplay, as we [had] allowed him to be when playing Autolycus. So what we really need is the playfulness with which Patricia describes language, so that we can become multilingual stand-up comics.
>
> (Arden, 27 and email)

Turning her thoughts to a forthcoming staging of *A Midsummer Night's Dream*, in San Jose, etymological awareness raises for Anne Bogart the question of whether there are characters or a section of the play that could be done in Mexican Spanish. Bieito's own approach uses different dialects and speech patterns to articulate the 'difference' among the characters that populate Shakespeare's plays. Boris Ruiz's Lenox, with his languid, croaky delivery, stood in marked contrast to the brusque Catalan inflection of Mingo Ràfols' Macbeth, and the Venezuelan intonation – refracted through the characterisation of a Russian mafioso – of Carles Canut's Rosse; Javier Gamazo (Cawdor) and Daniel Klamburg (Malcolm) are musicians: the former largely known for his work in musical theatre, the latter a composer and member of the pop group Cactus Vapor. The extended family of the Macbeths and their coterie effectively saw difference played out vocally. Indeed, for Parker, 'experimentation with different languages or dialects on stage seems to me a potentially interesting way of exploring other kinds of social and political disjunction' (29 and email).

As Bieito prepared to make his English-language Shakespeare debut with *Hamlet*, the scenic and gestural possibilities opened out by *staging* such linguistic playfulness also served to displace a concurrent theory referred to by Bill Worthen during The Fifth Wall workshop. This theory, that 'the text tells us how to do itself and is a kind of instruction manual and this really is a deeply held understanding by editors' – and, I would suggest, directors – 'of Shakespeare, which is why they helpfully do things like put in asides, which is as if to say "Look, Shakespeare really knew what he was doing here"' (Bogart, Escolme, Worthen, 4). For Bieito and Parker, the process is always rooted in detailed investigation, interrogation and dissection, so that sound and gesture can be both unleashed and controlled. As Parker indicates:

> The attempt to 'govern' sound was … just beginning for English itself in Shakespeare's day – through the new disciplines in England of grammar and punctuation and the beginnings of the standardising of spellings, that would yield (only much later) different accepted spellings for words whose meanings were different, though their sounds were the same. It seems to me that *A Midsummer Night's Dream* stages some of these contemporary tensions between the new (elite) humanist disciplines of grammar and rhetoric and more oral (and less literate) modes – in the snide and often pedantic remarks of the aristocrats [when they ridicule] the artisans in the final scene (on matters of punctuation and the proper 'partition' of speech). We're seeing there the beginnings of the kind of neo-classicism, whose triumph by the 18th century would produce the prejudice against certain kinds of wordplay and punning that was expressed in Dr Johnson's remarks about Shakespeare's inability to resist such fatal Cleopatras. When Hippolyta remarks in response to Quince's mis-punctuated Prologue (the Prologue that turns an ostensibly intended compliment to the play's aristocrats into a series of insults) that it is 'sound', but not 'in government', I think that the line itself gives us an insight into the connections in the period between governing sounds and other kinds of sound government.

Because governing sounds, regional accents, and other elements of language were inseparable from other kinds of standardisation and government.

(23, 29 and email)

This is not to say that we can impose a blanket pronunciation on the language – as is all too often the case with Received Pronunciation and its hegemony over English-language Shakespeare production. As with so much around Shakespeare, the governing rule appears to be un-knowability. There is so much that we cannot be sure of, the process of editing and staging for Parker and Bieito alike is essentially one of playful investigation, the findings of which are shared with the reader/audience.

With regard to [Peter] Quince, we really don't know how his name was pronounced in the play – for example, in 1.2, where his name is repeated again and again, in the roll-call of the players. If, as I have suggested elsewhere in mentioning that English 'quince' may have been pronounced with the hard 'c' or 'k' sound of its contemporary English spelling as 'coynes' (the spelling that reflected the French 'coings' or 'coingz' from which it came), that sound might be much more sexually suggestive … than the modern English 'quince', since 'coint' was already part of commonplace sexual double entendres. This would bring the name of 'Quince' closer to the kind of sexual double meanings we associate with 'Nick Bottom' or the 'Joiner' called 'Snug'. With regard to other things, I feel that as an editor my job can at least be to underscore that '*Exit Philostrate*' might be a question, rather than an already foregone conclusion; or to draw attention to the fact that in the quarto, Helena appears silently on stage. Instead of erasing all those possibilities from the text, or obscuring them in the small print, it seems to me that an editor can at least put them out there and invite the readers of the edition to participate in rethinking them.

There is a lot about punning that we assume, which may not be true even in modern English. For example, scholars know that Thomas More's name was endlessly exploited for its similarity in sound to 'Moor' and even wall or 'mur'. In researching the folio's 'Now is the morall downe', when Wall departs, I came across the whole network of contemporary homophones and puns of which 'morall' (and 'mural' or wall) were a part in the Elizabethan period.

But I have always assumed that this homophone or pun could never be heard by modern audiences. Then, recently, I saw the remake of the film *Sabrina* (1995), where the Harrison Ford character is told by Sabrina that people think his idea of 'morals' is paintings on 'walls'. Even more recently, I've been coming across puns where I live in Silicon Valley on Moore's Law as 'Moron's Law', as well as on 'moore' or 'less'. Perhaps the exploitation of sound that produced Shakespeare's notorious punning is not as far away from us as we might think.

(Parker, 17–18 and email)

My experience of this [playful investigation] is with Calderón's *Life is a Dream* where we have Clarín the clown. And his text just no longer seemed funny, so we dissected what he was saying and then reformulated it both in the English and the Spanish versions. I don't know if this is right, or not right. But it worked perfectly well with the audience. It is always about exploring what the text is saying and then trying to present that on stage.

(Bieito, 31)

DRAMATURGY AND TRANSLATION

In preparing his English-language staging of *Hamlet*, the challenge for Bieito lay in finding ways of *theatricalising* the tensions and wordplay that Parker locates within what Dennis Kennedy views as a protectionist Anglophone tradition, one which is bound to 'modernist high culture and the entrenched position of the Shakespeare industry as with the inherent superiority of the originals'.[31] This has effectively prevented the transfer of the plays into a more contemporary English. Shakespeare in translation may sound like a new play. Shakespeare in English rarely does. This *difference* is crucial. Indeed, as Kennedy astutely reminds us, 'to seek fidelity to Shakespeare's "intentions", with regard to meaning or to performance style, is to ignore the vast distance the text has traveled to reach us, and to become, at least in one sense, traitors to our time'.[32] Just as Patricia Parker's work involves the repositioning of phrases and words to create different associations or patterns of meaning, so Bieito refashions the text to create a new dramaturgical shape. For Bieito it is a process analogous to that of Picasso reimaging Velázquez's '*Las Meninas*/The Ladies in Waiting' for a new age.

What Bieito terms dramaturgy – the pruning, cutting, reshaping of a play – is a strategy that he has increasingly employed in his work with Shakespeare. It is part of his need to 'question' the absolutes of past translations/productions, but it is also about 'having a conversation with the text'. Too often productions are considered against an imagined preceding play-text; the authoritative standard against which the staging is measured. While critics may loudly protest at Bieito's dismemberment of *Macbeth*,[33] his is not a novel approach. Bertolt Brecht's dramaturgical work has been immortalised in print through the published editions of his reshaping of Marlowe's *Edward II*. Federico García Lorca, too, spent a number of years in the early 1930s refashioning the dramatic canon of the Spanish Golden Age with the touring theatre company, La Barraca. According to Bieito:

> There is more of a tradition on the continent of doing quite radical dramaturgical work on Shakespeare. The classics are not seen as sacred or held up against what is understood to be 'the original'. When Federico García Lorca staged *The Knight from Olmedo*, he cut the end of the play. He was a Republican working at a politically charged time, he didn't want a scene of thanks to the king at the end of the play. He's manipulating the verse, manipulating the text, manipulating the rhythms of the words. This is the tradition within which I'm working.

> (8 and email)

If Bieito's approach has been subject to such a vitriolic response from British critics it is perhaps because he does not, in their view, accord the Bard sufficient reverence.

Only ten days before Bieito's *Macbeth* opened at the Barbican Centre, in London, in April 2003, the National Theatre hosted Yukio Ninagawa's reading of *Pericles*. I was struck by the largely rapturous critical reception it received. Ninagawa framed his reading of the play with a prologue and epilogue where a battered company of war-torn performers unite from the different corners of the cavernous auditorium, on to the jutting orchestra stage of the Olivier theatre. His was a theatrical world marked by the soothing sounds of fountains, acoustic music and Japanese iconography. For the *Guardian's* Michael Billington, this was the enactment of 'an ancient folk tale about death and rebirth … Even the sound of aerial bombardment and the pinspot lighting of Tamotsu Harada emerging through the bullet-pocked holes of the cavernous set suggest that, in times of crisis, man has need of resurrection myths'.[34] Ninagawa's interventions included the reconception of narrator Gower as a choric double act armed with a lute and percussive rattle, and the silent entry of black-attired performers (*kurokos*) animating puppets who enacted Pericles' Mediterranean odyssey. Nevertheless, for the *Observer's* Susannah Clapp, 'the strange watery beauty of Shakespeare's *Pericles*' was 'apparent in each trance-like gesture, each bubbling, musical note of Yukio Ninagawa's enchanting production' where, she confidently asserts, 'the different twists and moods of the play are transmitted *undamaged*' (my emphasis).

The reverent, holistic tampering of Ninagawa's approach replete with soothing trickles of water and potent iconography of rebirth and resurrection, provided what Dennis Kennedy labels an alluring *japonisme* where political and social commentary are avoided 'in favour of an aestheticist balance'.[36] Bieito's dramaturgical interventions are far more grounded in an engagement with the social and moral conditions of our existence, what Kennedy terms 'the movement to contemporize the plays': not through 'a view of the world … that privileges the anguish of the individual over the destiny of the social group' (as have Brook, Konrad Swinarski and Roman Polanski), but rather through the prompting 'of an awareness of the spectator's position within the political and economic construct' (as have Strehler, Patrice Chéreau, Roger Planchon and Benno Besson).[37]

And it is the former approach, rooted in what Kennedy terms 'Kottian fatalism',[38] of which Anglophone critics have been most tolerant. As such, Brook's bold dramaturgical work on *Hamlet*, evident both in his staged essay on the play, *Qui est là?* (1998), and his French- and English-language versions of *Hamlet* in 2000 and 2001 where he dispensed with the plot of Fortinbras, has not been subject to anything like the same degree of critical vehemence as Bieito's *Macbeth*. For while the majority of Brook's recent Shakespearean dismemberments have taken place within the remove of the French language, the muted critical responses to his refashioning may have been partly due to the reverence in which he is held – a reverence due perhaps to age and to the 'weighty' body of work he has produced over the past fifty-something years – partly to do with his Englishness; an articulated assumption that if you're going to dismember the Bard you ought to have the right credentials; and partly to do with a performance aesthetic that emphasises individual angst over political reasonings.

Bieito's dramaturgical rationale is rooted in a reading of the play where its 'foreignness' is never obliterated, what he terms 'dismantling the text to recreate the same play and not the same play' (9 and email). As such, with *Macbeth* he shifted the order of certain scenes (his adaptation opened with 1.2, with only a few lines of 1.1 resituated in 1.3, his second scene). Characters were reconfigured with certain roles condensed and others enhanced. There was no porter, no witches, no Siward, no messengers or murderers and their lines were redistributed. Lenox took the porter's lines, becoming much more of a wry observer on the action, giving a running commentary on certain actions and gaining a speech from Guy Ritchie's film *Snatch* (2000) on the easy dismembering of a body at the end of Act 3, which replaced the witches meeting Hecate in 3.5. Rosse, significantly a cousin to Macduff, here takes the role of the murderers in Act 3 and the messenger and murderers in Act 4. He is Macbeth's henchman, a man of few words who prowls around the stage in ominous silence. Bieito provides a Thane of Cawdor – cutting early references to him in 1.2 and envisaging him as 'a traitor among us' – who is killed on the orders of Duncan at the end of the scene. Seyton (a woman in this production) is conceived as an aide to Macbeth, seeking to usurp Lady Macbeth. *She* is allocated select lines from the witches in the early acts and the doctor and the gentlewoman in Act 5, and it is she who is positioned as being responsible for Lady Macbeth's death as she plies her with drink and drugs. Perhaps most significantly Macbeth is not killed at the end but rather remains alone onstage, deserted by any remaining lieutenants who exit indifferently following his murder of Malcolm.

If Bieito's dismembering and reimagining of the play led *El País* columnist Marcos Ordóñez to retitle the staging '*Macbieito*', this is in part recognition of multiple authors of any performative event and also evidence of what Ordóñez termed the removal of flesh from the play to leave a skeletal structure, where the characters have been plunged in boiling water to leave just the bones in place.[39] Bones which the performers rattle in bold characterisations that ground the staging in an atmosphere of male camaraderie, where institutional machismo masks a multitude of abuses and where a descent into social chaos is always anticipated in the debris that increasingly litters the stage. The clan is increasingly a family at war, destroyed by ambition, fear, paranoia and greed. The reading gravitates around domestic politics with the toys and paddling pool of the Macduff children used as icons to point to the central feature that separates their parents from the Macbeths; the former often appear with their children draped over and around them. It is through childlessness that Bieito locates the destructive anguish that fuels the Macbeths' avarice and orchestrates some of the production's most exquisitely choreographed sequences: the murder of the Macduff children, realised almost as a silent movie with a scalding pot of coffee, a Coke bottle, and the cord of an iron. The murder of Banquo, too, takes place above the wild partying of the barbecue as Rosse, in the clown disguise of a children's entertainer, suffocates the former with a plastic bag.

It is the ferocious energy permitted by such a textual dismemberment that provides the pace and impetus of the production. It allows Bieito to supply concrete reasons for the madness of Lady Macbeth in her necessary disposal of the three corpses of the Macduff children. Moments that are often hurried over or handled clumsily in more orthodox productions are given here a more central role. Lady Macbeth's supposed fainting in 2.3 is here a mock epilepsy, which returns to haunt her with devastating results in the final act. In a world of macho camaraderie, father–son relationships are – as indicated by Banquo's abuse of Fleance – grounded in fear and intimidation. The Law of the Father is gruesomely played out to indicate that the politics of fear and paranoia can invade the domestic to the point where, in Bieito's words:

> you suspect that everyone around you is out to kill you. I think that I read somewhere that in Shakespeare's time it was forbidden to show children killed on stage. Now this production is, in part, about informing the audience about domestic violence, which is a huge problem in Spain and elsewhere. There is a strong sexual drive that joins the Macbeths, why can't I show that? The text seems to indicate this very clearly. For me the key concept of my reading was the family, everybody is part of an extended family of friends, cousins and brothers. And the witch is someone who is part of this family: Seyton. It's a climate of fear that produces the witches, so here, in scenically imagining this atmosphere of fear, I have made all the 'outsiders' what they effectively are, 'insiders'.

(9–10 and email)

While critics bemoaned his 'lack of respect for the text',[40] – one critic titled his review 'How to murder Macbeth'[41] – Bieito justified his approach as a process of investigating what the text means, and as a veritable antidote to those productions where:

> you watch *Macbeth* and think this is where the witches come in and they'll be three old ladies. I always find the morality around what you can actually produce in Shakespeare perplexing. In *Hamlet*, the actors are referred to as the 'chronicles of the time' and this is what I'm trying to do in all my work: engage with the conditions in which I live and work.[42]

Parker's dismemberment may not involve such a wholescale revision, but she too is concerned with the implications of re-situating phrases, sections or characters that may have been erroneously 'canonised' in a particular way, to see what readings emerge when the section is configured anew.

> Take the opening lines of *A Midsummer Night's Dream*, for example. Shakespeare's *Dream* is so familiar … that we may not be aware that some of the lines that we read (or expect to hear in production) are the creation of earlier editors, that they do not appear in the earliest texts of the play (in either the folio or the quarto versions). One of the challenges I face as an editor, therefore, is whether to restore the lines that are shared by the folio and quarto, even though the later editors' emendations are more familiar to audiences and readers. Hippolyta's opening speech in the play, for example, refers to the moon, in lines that appear in virtually all modern editions as 'Four nights will quickly dream away the time; / And then the moon, like to a silver bow / New bent in heaven, shall behold the night / Of our solemnities'. But in both the folio and the quarto versions, what she says is not 'New bent' but 'Now bent'. Editors usually reject 'Now' for 'New' because of an argument related to the time scheme of the play, and figuring when the 'New' moon will appear: but that is famously complicated in this play. Since 'Now bent' here modifies not 'moon' but the 'bow', it may be that what is most important is the gesture of bending the bow itself, a gesture that might well accompany Hippolyta's line as it is spoken on stage. The bending and shooting of a bow is often a masculine image in Shakespeare (think of Lear's 'The bow is bent and drawn; make from the shaft', of Henry's 'bend up every spirit / To his full height!' in *Henry V*, or 'Cupid's fiery shaft' in *A Midsummer Night's Dream* itself) …

Whatever the implications of this 'bent' bow in the opening lines of Hippolyta the Amazon of Shakespeare's *Dream*, there is no reason that I can see why 'Now' should not be restored. As a more open vowel sound and 'present' term, it may even work better in performance than 'New'. The question here is whether to change – not just for students but for actors and directors who may use the edition – what audiences are used to hearing, even if 'New bent' appears nowhere in the early texts of the play itself.

A similar decision faces me at other points in the play. In the folio and quarto versions of this same opening scene, Hermia says to Helena (in modernised form, which the edition will have to do): 'Emptying our bosoms of their counsel swelled, / There my Lysander and myself shall meet, / And thence from Athens turn away our eyes, / To seek new friends and strange companions.' In the 18th century, Theobald changed these lines to make them perfectly rhyming couplets (like the rest of Hermia's speech here): 'swelled' was changed to 'sweet' and 'strange companions' was changed to 'stranger companies'. But the concern to make everything rhyme was a more 18th-century preoccupation than a 16th-century one. It is possible that a sophisticated poet like Shakespeare is intentionally breaking the rhyme scheme of perfect couplets here, in a play in which disjoining or un-coupling is as prominent in the plot itself as any perfectly harmonious coupling or joining. Faced with the possibility that the broken rhyme might not be an 'error' (made, for example, by the compositor) but something that has as much authority as an 18th-century emendation, I find myself leaning towards unrhyming Theobald's perfectly rhyming couplets.

Editors routinely make other changes to the early texts of the folio and quarto … the entrance of Egeus [in 1.1] presents a problem for the editor (and an interesting possibility for staging). The folio text has him enter with Hermia, Lysander and Demetrius – the usual trio who appear at this point in performances of the play. But the quarto has Helena enter along with Egeus, the two young men, and Hermia her childhood friend – even though she remains silent as they speak. The quarto opens up possibilities for performance that make for a different kind of atmosphere in this opening scene. If the stage direction that has Helena entering were the first to appear in the scene itself, it might be argued that it was simply an omnibus stage entry, announcing all of the actors who would appear on stage as the scene progressed. But as the second stage direction, its inclusion of Helena cannot so easily be dismissed.

(20–3 and email)

While listening to Parker's interventions, I was struck by how little of this careful deliberation reaches us; sometimes in a printed edition, we may be aware of it as a note, but often not even that reaches the viewer. Bieito is given the chance to *stage* his discussions, debates, insights, critical and audience responses, to produce a debate of sorts on the 'merits' or otherwise of such an approach. Harry Berger Jr confidently argues that:

> The ease with which we can breach the conventions of inert typographic space and sequence gives us a control over meaning which performance in the theatrical space time denies us. Performance does not allow us the leisure to interrupt, challenge or question … we are prevented as spectators from carrying out central interpretative operations that presuppose our ability to decelerate the text, to ignore sequence while accumulating synchronic or paradigmatic clusters of imagery.

Certainly what Berger calls 'the shadow of textuality' is present in all stagings of the work, but this textuality does not stand in opposition to the ephemerality of the stage moment. There is no complete understanding possible of what Berger terms the 'figurative acrobatics executed by Shakespeare's language',[43] the approaches of Parker and Bieito merely indicate that both stage and page provide strategies for resistant (political) readings that prise apart (mis)conceptions and givens around the cultural and linguistic worlds of the plays. And it is perhaps this that Brook is referring to when he states that, 'It is only when we forget Shakespeare that we can begin to find him'.[44]

NOTES

1 Dennis Kennedy, *Looking at Shakespeare: A Visual History of Twentieth-Century Performance* (Cambridge: Cambridge University Press, 2001, 2nd edn), 288–9.

2 Cited in Peter Holland, *English Shakespeares: Shakespeare on the English Stage in the 1990s* (Cambridge: Cambridge University Press, 1997), 9.

3 Patricia Parker, *Shakespeare from the Margins: Language, Culture, Context* (Chicago and London: University of Chicago Press, 1996), 1.

4 *Ibid.*, 1.

5 Cited in Jonathan Culler, *On Deconstruction: Theory and Criticism After Structuralism* (Ithaca: Cornell University Press, 1982), 247.

6 'Peter Sellars in conversation with Michael Billington at the Royal Exchange Theatre, Manchester, 18 November 1994', in Maria M. Delgado and Paul Heritage (eds), *In Contact with the Gods?: Directors Talk Theatre* (Manchester: Manchester University Press, 1996), 225.

7 Patricia Parker, *op. cit.*, 15.

8 Hermann Bonnin, 'Romea, 125 anys', in Enric Gallén (ed.), *Romea, 125 anys* (Barcelona: Generalitat de Catalunya, 1989), 9.

9 John Hooper, *The New Spaniards* (London: Penguin, 1995), 411.

10 See Maria M. Delgado, *'Other' Spanish Theatres: Erasure and Inscription on the Twentieth-Century Spanish Stage* (Manchester and New York: Manchester University Press, 2003).

11 'La isla de las mutaciones', *Avui* (18 August 1997), 29.

12 'Peter Sellars in conversation with Michael Billington at the Royal Exchange Theatre, Manchester, 18 November 1994', in Delgado and Heritage, *op. cit.*, 226–7.

13 C.S., 'Els cavallers de Verona, un Shakespeare joven, estrenado en el Mercat de les Flors', *El País* (25 July 1989), 27.

14 Patricia Parker, *op. cit.*, 15.

15 *Ibid.*, 16.

16 Calixto Bieito, interview with Maria M. Delgado, London (11 April 2003).

17 *Ibid.*

18 Peter Brook, *The Shifting Point. Forty Years of Theatrical Exploration: 1946–87* (London: Methuen, 1988), 71.

19 Marcos Ordóñez, 'El Rei Joan', *Avui* (10 July 1995), B4. Pablo Ley, 'Un Shakespeare sencillamente vivo', *El País* (2 July 1995), 32.

20 Erica Fischer-Lichte, 'Staging the foreign as cultural transformation', in Erica Fischer Lichte, Josephine Riley and Michael Gissenwehrer (eds), *The Dramatic Touch of Difference: Theatre, Own and Foreign* (Tübingen, Germany: Gunter Narr, 1990), 277–87.

21 Peter Brook, *op. cit.*, 94.

22 Calixto Bieito, interview with Maria M. Delgado, *op.cit.*

23 Transcript, 2–3; elaborated in interview with Maria M. Delgado, *op.cit.*, and in an email.

24 Mingo Ràfols, conversation with Maria M. Delgado, Barbican Theatre (8 April 2003).

25 Bieito, email; elaborated in interview with Maria M. Delgado, *op.cit.*

26 Both transcript quotations from p. 6 were adapted by Bieito in a subsequent conversation with Maria M. Delgado to clarify meaning.

27 Charlotte Higgins, 'Verdi with knobs on', *Guardian* (Review) (21 February 2002), 8–9.

28 Eugene O'Neill, *Long Day's Journey into Night* (London: Jonathan Cape, 1984), 110.

29 Jorge Luis Borges, 'Prologo', in William Shakespeare, *Macbeth* (Buenos Aires: Editorial Sudamericana, Colección Obras Maestras, Fondo Nacional de las Artes, 1970). Reproduced in the press pack for *Macbeth*, Teatre Romea, 2002.

30 Transcript quotation adapted by Bieito to clarify meaning.

31 Dennis Kennedy, 'Introduction: Shakespeare without his language', in *Foreign Shakespeare: Contemporary Performance*, ed. Dennis Kennedy (Cambridge: Cambridge University Press, 1993), 5–6.

32 Dennis Kennedy, *Looking at Shakespeare*, 207.

33 Joan-Anton Benach of the conservative Catalan daily *La Vanguardia* referred to this as 'sabotage' (Joan-Anton Benach, 'Interesante y radical sabotaje', [27 February 2002], 42). This was a line of argument followed by a significant proportion of the critics that reviewed the production when it was staged at the Barbican Centre, London, in April 2003. See *'Macbeth', Theatre Record* 23: 7 (29 April 2003), 445–7.

34 Reproduced in *Theatre Record* 23: 7 (29 April 2003), 412.

35 *Ibid.*, 410.

36 Dennis Kennedy, *Looking at Shakespeare*, 320.

37 Dennis Kennedy, 'Introduction: Shakespeare without his language', 10, 12–13.

38 *Ibid.*, 10.

39 Marcos Ordóñez, *'Macbieito', El País* (Babelia) (9 March 2002), 21.

40 Kate Bassett, 'Theatre', *Independent on Sunday* (ArtsEtc.) (13 April 2003), 10.

41 Charles Spencer, 'How to murder Macbeth', *Daily Telegraph* (10 April 2003). Reproduced in *Theatre Record* 23: 7 (29 April 2003), 447.

42 Email; elaborated in interview with Maria M. Delgado.

43 Harry Berger Jr, 'Text against performance in Shakespeare: The example of *Macbeth*', in Stephen Greenblatt (ed.), *The Power of Forms in the English Renaissance* (Norman, Oklahoma: Pilgrim Books, 1982), 50–1.

44 Peter Brook, *Evoking (and Forgetting!) Shakespeare* (London: Nick Hern Books, 2002), 47.

6

MAKING THINGS DIFFICULT

Anne Bogart (SITI, New York)
Bridget Escolme (University of Leeds): respondent
W.B. Worthen (University of California, Berkeley)

Resistance is central to the work of both critic and theatre practitioner, as it becomes a way to explore the energy of the text. The three contributors to this essay argue the need for an imagination for body, place and time, which has the political power to effect transformation and the willingness to embrace the potential failure that is a part of any resistant interpretation. At the same time, the essay analyses the potential misunderstandings between the two disciplines, discussing various cruxes in signification around the body and the arbitrary, 'sourcework' and authenticity, and originality and social and cultural meaning.

I will begin with an encounter between the theatre and the academy very different from that enabled by The Fifth Wall workshop. At a conference on Shakespeare in performance, an actor speaks to a room full of literature and theatre academics about her experience of playing Cleopatra. She is animated, engaging, passionate – and benevolently patronising towards an audience whose work she perceives to be the study of Shakespeare's plays rather than the 'doing' of them. She has discovered Shakespeare's Cleopatra in action, and not only that, through Shakespeare's creation, she has discovered Cleopatra herself, a historic but accessible Cleopatra: animated, engaging, passionate too. It is suggested that poring myopically over the first folio is not going to deliver similar truths about the play. She becomes most animated when speaking of the moment in *Antony and Cleopatra* in 4.15 when Cleopatra faints. Cleopatra doesn't faint, the actor has found on her journey towards performance. She is too strong a woman to faint, the actor declares, whatever these modern editors may put in their square brackets.

As a member of this academic audience, I expect palpable irritation. The actor's address contains much of the rhetoric lately eschewed by the kinds of people listening to her. To speak of the Cleopatra of *Antony and Cleopatra* as though she were a 'real' historical figure, to whose psychology the genius Shakespeare had privileged access, is to make assumptions about history, psychology, genius and Shakespeare that many academics like to consider have been thoroughly debunked. Here are theatre academics, who rather than spending their time considering textual cruxes, work with students on Shakespeare texts in practice; here are editors who might have taken the exclamations of Cleopatra's servants Charmian and Iras ('O quietness, lady! / She's dead too, our sovereign. / Lady! / Madam! / O madam, madam, madam!', 4.15.70–4) as justifying the direction 'She faints' (70); there are lecturers, of whom I am one, who might see Cleopatra as a figure constituted in stage and political history, inextricable from boy players and film stars that have made and remade her since the historical figure ruled Egypt. But there is dissent only among a few of us. The talk goes down a storm. The audience loves being patronised by a witty and passionate theatre practitioner. She appears to criticise our practice, but somehow to justify it too. It is reassuring that Shakespeare stirs such passion outside the academy. Isn't she lovely? Of course actors need their essentialist fantasies of psychological coherence and timeless truths (the patronising works both ways). And aren't we really rather dry old sticks, pretensions to 'Practice as Research'[1] notwithstanding? Time out was taken from the business of historical analysis, cultural criticism and editorial decision-making to listen to someone whose reputation as an actor and charm as a speaker silenced the criticism a student might receive for speaking in similar terms.

The Fifth Wall research workshop at The Globe promised a more direct encounter between academic and theatre practice. It had been created for that purpose, whereas the above anecdote comes from an academic conference with an actor as guest speaker. Fifth Wall would be an opportunity, perhaps, for theatre practitioners and academics to correct some assumptions about the kinds of activities that actually take place in the theatre, classroom or library. Having been present at the event just described, I was particularly keen to discuss the nature of the theatre academy in Britain, and to find out what actors and directors actually thought of their work being held up as an object for academic analysis. I wanted to find out about the practice that led to some of the more self-consciously theatrical work I'd seen recently at the Royal Shakespeare Company (RSC), whose results in performance suggested very different rehearsal methodologies from the almost parodic 'Method' process that could lead to the assertion: 'Cleopatra *did not faint*'. I will admit to hoping, in addition, that some sparks would fly, and that the interrogations of theatre practice and training that have come out of the academy lately would not dissolve in the mix of excitement and respectful politeness that coloured the encounter described above. If anyone was going to be claiming a direct line to Shakespeare's intended meaning through vocal training or Stanislavskian character study, I would be there, ideological and historicist objections at the ready.

During The Fifth Wall, productive debate rather than benevolent live-and-let-live *bonhomie*, was the dominant mode of the event. These academics and theatre practitioners appeared to find more points of agreement than dissent, and the pairing of theatre director Anne Bogart and academic theatre critic W.B. (Bill) Worthen was a particularly felici-tous one. They offered examples of the productive uses of difficulty and resistance in the theatre that it would be possible to consider quite seam-lessly in an essay such as this. Indeed, in what follows I will be draw-ing parallels between the writing and practice of the two, that suggest we are at a moment in theatre and academic history when theatre prac-tice and academic writing about it are genuinely close and potentially in dialogue. Nevertheless, the ways in which actors and directors on the one hand, and theatre academics on the other, speak about Shakespeare are different, and these different discourses make mean-ings that will, I hope, rub productively against one another rather than merge into a seamless whole.

A situated response

Before exploring the contributions of Bogart and Worthen to Fifth Wall, I would like, as I did at the workshop, to situate my own contribution within the *theatre* academy. Although theatre and performance studies departments in British universities do not train their students for jobs in the performance industries[2] – students graduating from them often take a postgraduate diploma in an accredited drama school if they want to join 'the profession' – teachers and students in these departments learn about theatre by engaging in theatre practice. The BA in English and Theatre Studies on which I teach at the University of Leeds, for example, assesses students through the performances they create, the performances of plays they produce and the participatory theatre workshops they facilitate, as well as through the essays they write about theatre. These teaching and assessment methods are derived from, and fed by, the research in which the staff of the department is engaged: research into current and historical theatre practice, and conclusions derived from practice in which staff members themselves are actively involved. That is to say, the divide between theatre as an object of *study* and theatre *practice* is not a clear one in these departments, certainly not as clear as the actor in my opening anecdote suggested when she exhorted us to 'Get up and *do* the plays'. In American universities, the potential for mutual understanding between theatre and academy is perhaps even greater, as many universities offer students both actor training and academic theatre courses – though speaking to American colleagues it seems the physical cohabitation is not always as productive as it might be.

This is not to say that there are not potential difficulties in an encounter between theatre academics and practitioners working in the industry; my own experience has sometimes been of unease or irritation on the part of actors at academic encroachment on their business. From the academic there is sometimes a tendency to shy away from rigorous critique when faced with those involved in 'getting up and doing it' for a living. Theatre academics regard not only theatre texts but theatre practice as an object for critique; but their own theatre practice – with students, as research – is not held up to public scrutiny in the same way as the professional actor's. Their books may be reviewed like an actor's performance; their students' multimedia deconstruction of *Hamlet* very probably will not be. Academics sometimes appear to actors, I think, as arrogantly overconfident in their articulations of 'knowledge' about Shakespeare, much of which may appear to be of little use to the company working on the staging of a play, and little of which will be put to any kind of economic test.

Paradoxically, this may appear to be especially the case when that knowledge is not of a historical or etymological nature but consists in an understanding, so the academic thinks, of performance. My experience as dramaturgical advisor on the West Yorkshire Playhouse's 2002 production of *Hamlet* is a case in point. Here, my own interest was in communicating to the actors theories I had developed about the actor's relationship with the audience and ways in which this was or was not encoded in Shakespeare's text, whereas the actors' interest was primarily in having someone in rehearsal who could explain what words and concepts meant. Moreover, the actors were very good at understanding what the words meant themselves – points of difficulty were often those on which there was ongoing textual debate, so that my answer to 'what does this mean?' tended ultimately to be 'we don't know'. However, my experience working on *Hamlet* was far from a negative one. There were strong points of communication between us, particularly where conversations happened that concerned the use of theatrical space, and it is perhaps in this area that the most productive dialogues can happen between the theatre and the theatre academy today.

I have chosen 'Making Things Difficult' as the title for this response to Anne Bogart and Bill Worthen's work on Shakespeare, language and space, because it was their mutual interest in difficulty and resistance in the theatre that, paradoxically, made their encounter seem so easy. Another potential area of mutual misunderstanding between theatre practitioners and academics is the economic and cultural imperative on the academic to make texts difficult, to point out that things – words, settings, character, the very notion of 'character' – are not as they seem to modern ears and eyes. The writer on Shakespeare and poststructuralism finds Shakespearean 'characters' fragmented, historically distant constructions. The actor's job, on the other hand, may often appear to be that of making texts accessible, finding out the ways in which Shakespearean characters are really just like us: otherwise, they argue, how will the audience understand the plays? Practitioner Anne Bogart's work appears to me to be a shift away from this notion of the importance of accessibility; she wants to play with, stage, embrace difficulty and resistance. It is perhaps for this reason that her contribution to Fifth Wall chimes so well with Bill Worthen's.

I am also going to suggest that the notion of productive difficulty in the live theatre event has infiltrated 'traditional' British theatre practice. In this chapter I also make substantial reference to a spring 2000 production of *Richard II* by the RSC. The RSC was represented at Fifth Wall by director Greg Doran, whose *Macbeth* was playing in the Swan Theatre, Stratford-upon-Avon, while *Richard II* played the Other Place, the company's studio space. *Richard II* is a production that continually invaded my thoughts on Bogart and Worthen's work, despite the apparent awkwardness of introducing a history play into a discussion that centred around *A Midsummer Night's Dream*. Steven Pimlott's 2000 production appears deliberately to have used the awkward resistance of its environment to produce uncomfortable but oddly compelling moments in the theatre, and its seeming determination to jar us into noticing the world outside the fiction appeared to me to infect and inflect Doran's *Macbeth*. Both were productions that provoked further questions about the resistance of space in Shakespeare performance, and I'd like to suggest that the productive resistance of space and place – as opposed to the transformative power of the set designer's imagination – has touched the 'traditional' world of British Shakespeare production as well as Anne Bogart's more consciously experimental practice.

A GYM FOR THE MIND

These are the titles of the meditations on theatre directing that make up Anne Bogart's book *A Director Prepares: Seven Essays on Art and Theatre*.

- Violence
- Memory
- Terror
- Eroticism
- Stereotype
- Embarrassment
- Resistance

One might tend to think of the first four as powerful themes or creative forces in rehearsal and performance, the second three as difficulties to overcome. However, the editor's note to the book suggests that Anne Bogart has identified each element in the list as 'both potential partner and potential obstacle to art-making.'[3] When Anne Bogart talks about theatre-making, notions of difficulty and disorientation as productive forces keep recurring. She opens both her Fifth Wall workshop address and *A Director Prepares* with an account of the first play she ever saw when she was 15 – a production of *Macbeth* – which she found terrifying, wonderful and incomprehensible. She speaks of having to *reach* to relate to it, and of its having taught her first lesson about directing, 'which is, don't patronise the audience: it's not about

making something easy – it's actually about making a gym for the mind'
(9). She speaks warmly of Peter Sellars, who approaches the cutting of
difficult texts by choosing 'the section he understands the least and
bas[ing] the entire production on that' (9). Tackling issues of interpretation, she describes her continuing struggle to 'open up multiple
meanings rather than close down on one' (10). Her wish is to stage
difficulty, to offer ways in for audiences to engage with it rather than
to overcome or smooth it over.

Bill Worthen's contribution to The Fifth Wall panel on 'Shakespeare,
Language and Space' draws on Anne's uses of resistance in the theatre
in his account of a Finnish production of *A Midsummer Night's Dream*,
whose outdoor setting appears productively to resist notions of the
transformative power of the imagination often seen as central to this
play. He interrogates the speech act theory of J.L. Austin as it might
pertain to speech in the theatre and challenges a 'perlocutionary' view
of drama, whereby performance is a direct result of text and thus 'it
should be easy to know which theatrical choices are wrong'.[4] Bill's
account of the Finnish *A Midsummer Night's Dream*, to which I will
return, suggests that seemingly 'wrong' choices, choices that appear to
resist the text or to foreground the ways in which it resists interpretation, can produce exciting and meaningful difficulty.

Viewpoints

The systems of rehearsal Anne Bogart has developed with the SITI
company, founded in 1992 with Tadashi Suzuki, can be understood
in the light of her delight in difficulty. The playwright Charles Mee,
who worked with her on *Another Person is a Foreign Country*, describes
her methodology as 'working without pre-existing rules' – then
qualifies himself with, 'or it is making up the rules as you go along'.[5]
The 'Viewpoints' that she works with in rehearsal, particularly the
'Viewpoints of Space', appear to be more about letting the material
world make up the rules as she goes along, as we will see. The
Viewpoints of Space offer the performer ways of describing and working with their relationship to the shapes bodies make in space
('Viewpoint of Shape'), to their gestures ('Viewpoint of Gesture'), to
their physical environment ('Viewpoint of Architecture'), to the
distance between bodies and objects on stage ('Viewpoint of Spatial
Relationship') and to the floor pattern created through movement on

stage ('Viewpoint of Topography').[6] Tina Landau, who has worked with Anne on a variety of projects since 1988, defines the Viewpoints as 'a philosophy of movement translated into a technique for training performers and creating movement on stage … a set of names given to certain basic principles of movement', and as 'points of awareness that a performer or creator has while working'.[7]

The Viewpoints have not been created specifically to make things difficult; indeed, Landau's account of Anne's methodology exhibits some of the concerns with spontaneity and the elimination of certain kinds of resistance common to much writing on principles of actor training. For instance, she describes how by using the Viewpoints in rehearsal, 'the actor exercises … the ability to listen with the whole body, and a sense of spontaneity', and how 'we give up on our own heady decisions and judgements'.[8] Here, one might think, lies fertile ground for dissent between theatre practitioner and academic, the former suggesting that decisions about performance come naturally and spontaneously from the body of the actor, the latter entirely engrossed in those 'heady decisions and judgements'. However, Landau suggests that attention to these concrete, material aspects of the theatre-making process also offers 'contradiction and unpredictability'.[9] The Viewpoints provide a structure within which to work, or rather an acknowledgement of material structures that already exist and that may contradict, resist and clash with the performer's efforts to produce work. Though Landau describes them as liberating – and no doubt it is liberating to work in this way – the Viewpoints are a set of deliberate restrictions upon the performer. They make the work difficult and they make difficult work.

Sourcework

The intensive period of research that begins the rehearsal process and which Anne terms 'Sourcework', encourages company members not only to discover things about a text or historical and cultural moment that they did not know before, but to reiterate what they know already in the context of production. Her performers are encouraged to 'lean into' the stereotypes and clichéd conceptions of the material they are about to tackle, to find out about them rather than to avoid them. She speaks in terms of finding freedom *within* 'the formidable cultural baggage' that a production of a well-known Shakespeare play carries with it, rather than 'pretend[ing] the baggage doesn't exist', and emphasises that 'the whole history of the play is part of it, the way audiences … and their expectations, are part of it' (14). Sourcework appears not to spring from the desire to find some historical or psychological detail that no one knew before – although that might happen. The process enables the company to find the ways in which the present moment in history and culture produces the meanings of a text or a historical period.

It is interesting to consider this approach in the light of The Fifth Wall workshop, taking place as it did in The Globe reconstruction. Bill Worthen argues in his essay 'Shakespearean Performativity' that:

> [I]n its meticulous reconstruction of building practices and ongoing research into the use of period costumes and staging, The Globe reflects a desire to see performance releasing original 'Shakespearean' meanings; The Globe is a monument to an understanding of dramatic performance as the embodiment of a textualised 'past', expectantly (or inertly) awaiting the chance to speak.[10]

Anne Bogart's work, as described by Landau, suggests that instead we make the past speak, and that the ways *we* do it are not entirely free and spontaneous but produced by all kinds of historical and cultural baggage. We impose our own versions of the past on a historical text when we work on it, and even those versions are not fully our own. Bogart does not attempt to strip away these impositions, as though they somehow contaminated a past which we are trying to recover in a pure form. Instead, she acknowledges and works with them in rehearsal; they are woven into the fabric of the piece she is creating.

To pay attention to the physical and cultural environment in which one is working is to acknowledge that the material conditions of production impinge upon the work, shaping it, forcing it into places outside the performer's agency. The vocabulary that goes to make up the world of a theatre piece is one that already exists in the lived world, in the cultural histories of the performers, the histories of the texts they are working on, the physical space in which they make the work. It has struck me while talking to actors about their work, particularly on Shakespeare, that two contradictory imperatives are at work as they rehearse: to be 'original' and to be 'true to the text'. Anne Bogart's Sourcework recognises the impossibility of the first ambition, while paradoxically producing work that critics and audiences have found to be startlingly 'original'. The fact that all kinds of pre-existing clichés and stereotypes emerged when the performers of Bogart's *Miss Julie* piece thought of Strindberg, is described by Landau as an artistic advantage. The work of the company is to transform the world through the arrangement – and 'arrangement' is a central concern of Anne's – of elements *found* in it. Of course, it will seem obvious to all but the most committed believer in Romantic genius that this is all any artist can ever do. What is exciting about listening to Anne Bogart, her audiences and her co-workers describe this work, is their active acknowledgement of the material and cultural world that circumscribes and produces it.

Bill Worthen describes the 'relationship between spoken language, narrative structure, movement and gestural structure' in Bogart's piece *Going, Going, Gone* as 'setting those things into a kind of constellation rather than the relationship of subordination they are so often in' (1). It is a piece about the laws of physics, laws that are spoken as dialogue by four characters who interact within the dramatic structure of Edward Albee's *Who's Afraid of Virginia Woolf?* Robert Hurwitt notes that:

> The entire structure of *Going* [*Going, Gone*] – the interactions, the flirting, the rise and fall of emotional heat, the intense game-playing, the rhythm of the dialogue, the vast quantities of alcohol consumed – is that of Albee's oh-so-familiar play, [while the dialogue consists of] quotations from Einstein, Heisenberg, Stephen Hawking … and from conversations between scientists that Bogart downloaded from the Internet … long and short snatches of Lewis Carroll, Poe, T.S. Eliot, Goethe, Robert Frost … [11]

Here, the physical world is a dramatic theme as well as a Viewpoint to work from in rehearsal, and it both resists and informs the emotional relationships between the characters in Albee's play.

THEATRES OF RESISTANCE

In his contribution to The Fifth Wall, Bill Worthen describes the resistances produced by the physical world of the island of Vasikkasaari, Finland, to Ralf Langbacka's production of *A Midsummer Night's Dream* for the Viirus company. His experience as an audience member illuminates Anne's use of resistance in the theatre:

> the production struck me as generating a remarkably productive 'resistance' to the text. I'm not sure that the directors of outdoor

theater always recognize how interesting, or how troubling, the 'natural' setting can be. Performing in an abandoned railway station, a public plaza, or other built space often transforms one register of habitation into another – these spaces become theater, or at least theatricalized. I'm not sure that trees work the same way: like dogs or children on-stage, they seem to stand outside or beyond the artifice, to refuse to become fully absorbed into it, a constant reminder of the theater's double. The environmental design framed the play in a certain kind of 'realism': everything in the play, Athens included, rested on, or in, a resolutely recalcitrant 'nature'. Although Viirus has now performed there on a few occasions, this island is not an 'outdoor theater' venue; it's simply a small, un-inhabited island, the kind of place you might go for a picnic. To my mind, the production insisted on the inability of the apparatus of theater to transform the world around it, even to carve out a little corner of it – up there, on-stage – where its magic could work.[12]

The setting of this production, Bill argues, makes it difficult to suppose 'a bush ... a bear' (*MND* 5.1.22); it works against 'one of the elements we usually take to be central to the meaning of *A Midsummer Night's Dream*: the necessity to understand the power of the imagination, to lend it its due, its space' (11). 'This production', he concludes, 'seemed to reinforce the quotidian reality of the world we shared with it, and so to question whether that materiality can, or should be, transcended' (15).

The RSC's production of *Richard II*, that began its life in Stratford-upon-Avon in 2000, takes place in what reviewers variously described as: a 'lethal debating chamber';[13] a 'white-walled squash court or science lab';[14] an 'anti-septic laboratory';[15] a 'mental institution or art gallery'.[16] The production became inextricably bound up with my thoughts about Anne Bogart and Bill Worthen's work as it appears to me to speak of an acknowledgement, within the mainstream of British Shakespeare production, of the multiple resistances that constitute the live theatrical encounter. The company's studio space, the Other Place, was painted entirely white, and lit so that the audience was fully visible. It is a space that the reviews quoted above struggled to name; the white walls, chairs and grave-shaped pile of earth do not suggest a 'setting', but the decor is none the less startling, it makes itself felt. A space has been created in which issues of kingship in the play can be debated, and it suggests a particular kind of examination: minute and clinical; none of the figures to be presented here will escape it. At two points in the performance, a stage-left door in an outside wall is opened – for Bolingbroke to leave for exile and for Richard to be taken to be imprisoned in the tower. The effect of this glimpse of the world outside the theatre is sudden and startling. We can just see some tarmac and the chrome bumper of a car parked outside the theatre. It is an aesthetically and semantically awkward sight; this outdoor space is impossible to read as part of the fiction, but is just as impossible to ignore. It is an odd scene to have to look at when we are otherwise engaged with the narrative of a medieval magnate leaving for exile, or a deposed king being escorted to prison. The lit auditorium, the largely bare, white stage, the use of direct address throughout, provoke some reviewers to comment on the 'Brechtian' nature of this production;[17] but this feels, perhaps, like an alienation effect too far.

This moment of meta-theatricality at the RSC was startling almost to the point of embarrassment, and appeared to refuse absorption into the fiction of *Richard II* in ways that went beyond the conventional soliloquy to the audience or interaction with the clown, that even the most naturalistically designed Shakespeare production often permits. *Richard II* is a play about a coup or an abdication, depending on how one regards Bolingbroke's return from exile to claim the lands and title Richard has stripped from him and Richard's seeming capitulation to him. This production demanded we examine not only its action, but our own attitudes to it. As Richard and Bolingbroke addressed us in turn and demanded loyalty that could not be given to both, the glimpses of outdoors reminded us, startlingly, that we were in a theatre building, obliged to be loyal to neither.

The debate as to how far the Elizabethan theatre ever demanded or even permitted the spectator's absorption into the fiction is an old one. As theatre academics have engaged in this debate, fashions in *mise-en-scène* and acting style have drawn us in to Shakespearean fictions set, variously, in nineteenth-century drawing rooms, Bosnian battlefields, the Weimar Republic – or presented us with stark, or comic, or celebratory reminders that we are in none of those places but in a theatre, where actors can slip from acting to commentary, and from seemingly naturalistic dialogue to overtly theatrical Bergomask dance at the drop of a blatant disguise. Meanwhile, much current performance practice outside the realm of the dramatic production of literary texts suggests that we can, in Willem Dafoe's words, 'get [our] cake and eat it too'[18] in respect of emotional absorption and critical distanciation.

Dafoe refers to his work with New York performance company The Wooster Group and a moment in *LSD (… Just the High Points)* when he puts glycerine in his eyes to 's(t)imulate tears (a motif of many Wooster Group performances)'.[19] Dafoe is a film actor as well as a member of the Woosters, very capable of naturalistic acting and emotional virtuosity. In *LSD (… Just the High Points)* he offers both the virtuoso performance and its deconstruction: 'You see the picture of the crying man, you hear the text, you see the whole thing before you'.[20] In Wuppertal, Germany, Pina Bausch's dance-theatre stages throng with figures desperately performing social and gender roles, repeating routines that are sometimes abstract 'dances', sometimes recognisable 'acts' and social rituals. The dancers run round the stage getting tired and announcing 'I'm tired', or swing by the arms from trapezes in ball-gowns, seducing us with their images of desire and despair, simultaneously demanding that we critique them. The music, the people, the costumes, the fragments of narrative can be emotive, tragic, romantic; the constant foregrounding of all these things as performance, offers them up for examination. In Cesena, Italy, the Socìetas Raffaello Sanzio has offered us a *Giulio Cesare* that might seem not to permit the least identification with character, or absorption into a fictional world. The first actor to speak, utters the lines of all the characters in 1.1 of *Julius Caesar* with an endoscope inserted into his throat and his visibly working vocal chords projected on a screen above him. Brutus addresses the people wearing a vibrating metal collar in one scene, sucking helium for an absurd Donald-Duck effect in another. The performance is a dissection of voice production, rhetoric and subjectivity. Yet when Mark Anthony, played by an actor who has had a laryndectomy, takes up one of the rough white curtains that frame the performance as if it were Caesar's robe, his soft, choked oration for his dead leader, enabled by a man-made voice box visible beneath the hole in his throat, is utterly convincing in its sincerity. We are convinced and at the same time, the elements that have convinced us are held up for examination: actor, curtain, voice box.

Much current performance practice seems concerned with the *work* that an audience must undertake in order to suppose 'a bush … a bear' (*MND* 5.1.22), and all the moments just described strive to lay bare the work the performer must undertake to persuade the audience into that state of imagining. Like Anne Bogart and Bill Worthen, these moments speak of the meanings produced by resistance and difficulty in the theatre. They play with our desire to be absorbed, to believe, and foreground those things that resist absorption.

PLAY-TEXT AS BLUEPRINT FOR ACTION?

In both his contribution to The Fifth Wall workshop and in his book, *Shakespeare and the Authority of Performance,* Worthen resists the notion that encoded in the texts of Shakespeare's plays are the writer's instructions for what to do with them in production. His example of the *Hamlet* editor who inserts the stage direction '[*aside*]' at Hamlet's line in 1.2, 'A little more than kin, and less than kind' [65], demonstrates that to assume that a particular line demands a particular action or mode of address proscribes another range of possible meanings. Mark Rylance speaks the line straight at Claudius in The Globe's 2000 production, and a defiant, politically dangerous prince is staged, one that has now to some extent replaced the introspective character who might mutter the line to himself or the audience. It is, argues Worthen, the ritual structure within which the lines of a play occur that determines their particular force; 'you can't read from the text to the performance, because it is the performance that is going to instruct the meanings that the text can have' (5). We have come to think of *A Midsummer Night's Dream* as a play which 'validate[s] the power of the imagination' (6) – but the physical discomfort of following the Finnish actors 'Thorough bush, thorough briar' (2.1.3) appeared to be resisting these claims of the text.

To use the speech-act theory terminology Bill Worthen interrogates, the circumstances are infelicitous for a particular kind of meaning-making that takes text as a blueprint for action. In *How to Do Things with Words*, J.L. Austin points to the fact that in order for speech to perform action, the social and cultural circumstances in which the words are spoken must permit them to do so – they must be felicitous. Saying 'I do' will only marry someone to someone else if the law or church sanctions the speech act. Worthen notes that although Austin dismisses stage performance from his analysis, his account of 'illocutionary' and 'perlocutionary' speech acts can be productively applied to language in play-texts:

> Austin famously excluded theatrical performance from his discussion of 'performativity' (a creature of print, he tended to see the

meaning of plays to arise in the text, and so to be infelicitously falsified, betrayed, or weakened – 'etiolated' is his word – in stage performance). But it strikes me that Austin's 'performative' is a powerful instrument for rethinking the relationship between dramatic language and stage performance now, in what Michael Joyce has called the 'late age of print'.[21] How does the 'performative' relate to our common-sense understanding of the relationship between verbal texts and their theatrical performance?

Traditionally, the dramatic text has been seen as related to performance in a couple of ways, models that are evocative, too, of Austin's sense of the meanings of speech. Version one: the meanings of performances inhere in the text. Using Austin's terms, this might be said to be the 'Illocutionary' theory of dramatic performance, in which merely speaking the words performs an action because the action is inherent in the words: 'I promise' is a good example of illocutionary speech (it's actually quite difficult *not* to promise if you say 'I promise'); racial epithets are another (if we understand that the word itself is so injurious that uttering it causes injury to happen: this is, I think, the widespread consensus on the use of the 'N' word in the US today). Version two (in Austin's terms, a 'perlocutionary' theory of dramatic performance): the performance is a direct result of the text, in that the text, while not containing its performed meanings, produces a limited, predictable consequence in utterance: perhaps the phrase '*en garde*', or 'get lost' is a good example.[22]

The Finnish *A Midsummer Night's Dream*, however, appears to work against the perlocutionary force of the text:

> this is a production that created a unique kind of world that really did nothing that could have been predetermined from reading the play; it worked against the play in all kinds of ways yet resulted in a hugely memorable and challenging, conceptually rich production.
> (Worthen, 7)

DOING THINGS WITH WORDS

The Fifth Wall workshop took place, of course, at The Globe, where all kinds of unintentional twenty-first-century factors might be perceived as working against the plays produced within it. One despairing reviewer of the 2000 production of *Hamlet* asserts that 'the experiment fails … Shakespearean audiences probably had stronger legs, and certainly didn't have to contend with low-flying helicopters obscuring words 400 years removed from them'.[23] Yet I have been among the audience for a production of *The Comedy of Errors* in which the clown, Marcello Magni, playing both Dromios, eventually raised his eyes despairingly skywards at the rain that drowned his words almost as successfully as the *Hamlet* helicopters. He exhibited a degree of clownish pleasure at the state of the drenched groundlings in the pit, viewed from his dry position under the canopy – this, of course, a timeless rather than a late-modern irritation.

The theatre for which Shakespeare wrote, open to the air with its daylit audience, continually resists our ability to suppose 'a bush … a bear' (*MND* 5.1.22) and the meta-theatrical references in the plays continually underline this. I am reluctant to appear to be evoking once more the authority of performance so thoroughly dismantled by Bill Worthen, but it seems legitimate to wonder, standing in The Globe reconstruction being rained on, whether the rich resistances of the Finnish *A Midsummer Night's Dream* are not part of the 'grain' of plays written for such conditions. A swampy, wooded island offers, of course, a different kind of resistance to a purpose-built playhouse in which an audience may have done the work of supposing a bush a bear many times. It would be naive to suggest that my own sense of alienation when standing in an open-air theatre with parties of school children and tourists, watching men play women in Elizabethan dress, is the same as the experience of an early playgoer. However, I am ready to reiterate in this context the familiar reminder that that early theatrical experience would still have been a very different one to that of the indoor spectator in the darkened auditorium. A play written for a visible audience in a theatre that pronounces itself a theatre at every turn, leaves as its text not, perhaps, a perlocutionary blueprint for what must be done in production, but an openness to work against the grain that is part of the grain itself.

In Pimlott's *Richard II*, the extremes of meta-theatricality imposed on the play by the director's use of the space and what was outside it, seemed at once to alienate the world of the fiction and re-enforce the play's 'performative force',[24] as Worthen suggestively puts it. In the opening scene, Mowbray and Bolingbroke attempt to name one another traitor by throwing insults in ways that evoke literal physical attack.

'How to do things with words' is a central concern of *Richard II*. It is clearly foregrounded at the Other Place, as those who have lost their titles through banishment and deposition leave the playing space for the fictionally and theatrically meaningless car park.

Attempts at naming are further highlighted in this production by its use of the visible spectator. Various attempts at 'casting' the audience occur: Richard addresses us as his subjects at court; we are referred to as the commons, as an army, as supporters of Richard, as supporters of Bolingbroke. Varying degrees of power over us as subjects are assumed by Richard and Bolingbroke, most overtly when Bolingbroke demands that we rise to mourn for Mowbray when his death is announced. This is another awkward extra-diagetic moment in the play, as individual audience members get to their feet, some enthusiastic to participate, others visibly embarrassed and nervous as to what other forms of audience participation might be in store. Some do not wish to, or are physically unable to stand.

The impact of this moment lies, paradoxically, in the fact that it cannot entirely 'work' as part of the scene, that we are never entirely part of the fiction and always remain an audience that has paid to come and see a play. The visible audience can be addressed as if 'cast', but its members variously resist absorption into the play's world, resisting the meanings imposed upon them, rather as the car park outside the building resists labelling as the Tower of London or the place of Bolingbroke's exile. Moreover, this visible resistance of the audience to casting is particularly potent in a play about politics, just as the fictionally meaningless space of the car park is resonant at the points in the play where Bolingbroke's and Richard's titles – and their meaning in the society of the play – are stripped from them. That which cannot mean anything within the fiction draws our attention to who has power to make meaning or render others meaningless. The production resists the notion of a fictional world and a meta-theatrical world; it refuses the Brechtian shift from fiction to direct address. The play becomes a series of castings of, and addresses to, not only its fictional figures, but its paying audience, whose members are 'cast' in the knowledge of their potential resistance.

As we have seen, Bill Worthen critiques J.L. Austin's dismissal of theatrical performative language: 'a creature of print, he tended to see the meaning of plays to arise in the text, and so to be infelicitously falsified, betrayed or weakened – "etiolated" is his word – in stage performance'.[25] Austin's dismissal seems to arise from theatrical language's inability to 'do things' in the real world. On the one hand, performatives uttered by fictional figures can be said to imitate the performatives of real life and can be accepted as imitations by their audiences. A king can exile a magnate, and his words perform the act of exiling; a play in which this occurs exiles no one in reality, but simply tells the story of a performative that would be felicitous in the real world it reflects. According to this version of what plays do, their lack of actual performativity is so obvious as to not really be worth discussing. The effect of the RSC's *Richard II*, however, is to go beyond the reiteration of fictional performatives and attempt to do things *to the audience* with words. Here, the potential felicity of performatives is much less certain. We can refuse to behave like Bolingbroke's followers; his addressing us as such will not automatically perform an act of transformation.

I was not a member of the audience that tramped through trees and mud with Bill Worthen and the Viirus company cast of *A Midsummer Night's Dream*, but from his analysis, it seems that an uncomfortable but oddly productive focus upon the workings of language might have occurred here, as the theatrical power to evoke the imagination and say 'This, for the moment, is this' was undermined. If Shakespeare's plays are sophisticated struggles with the meaning of language and the ways in which language confers meaning, and thus power, productions that attempt to incorporate elements that resist meaning-making may be productively foregrounding that struggle.

DIVERGENCE?

So far, this analysis has suggested points of contact between academic and theatre practice concerned with difficulty and resistance in the theatre. Undoubtedly, a fitting conclusion would be to turn to The Fifth Wall discussion of Anne Bogart's future production of *A Midsummer Night's Dream* at San Jose Rep, and demonstrate how her thinking further underlines these connections. San Jose is a part of California that, Anne suggests, will not give its history up easily – or if it has, Anne's production promises to offer it back to modern Shakespeare audiences. Though artistic director Timothy Near has described San Jose as 'Silicon Valley's premier theater company',[26] Anne wants to find ways in which the California of the dust-bowl immigrants might inflect *A Midsummer*

Night's Dream. She poses the question, 'How do you make magic from nothing?' as central to her approach to the play; she refers to the material 'nothing' of the poverty that once inflicted immigrants to the state.[27] She does not suggest the play would work as an allegory for this period, or that 1930s California might serve as a setting in the conventional sense; rather that such an inflection might provide the productive resistance that will enable her to find something of the 'energy' of the play's 'original production'.[28]

Here the seamless connections made with Worthen appear to split a little. Here is the very discourse of authenticity that many academics have been eager to critique for the past 30 years. Recent movements in literary and performance criticism have resisted the notion that reading or production can reclaim original meaning or authorial intention. New historicism in the US and cultural materialism in the UK have held up every cultural artefact and form of discourse as an object for analysis and interrogation. The theatre academy, though not inclined to align itself with either, has begun to apply similar historicist and ideological critiques to the work of actors and directors. Bill Worthen himself interrogates the notion of reclaiming original identity in the essay on 'Shakespearean Performativity' cited earlier, and here was Anne suggesting that this was perfectly possible. As I suggested in the opening paragraphs of this chapter, however, it is awkward for the academic in dialogue with a theatre practitioner to read his or her work and descriptions of that work in ways that could be construed as negative. That tendency to admit that our livelihoods are not dependent on the fact that we are 'up there, doing it', leads us to give up questioning terms that might seem apolitical, ahistoricist or spuriously mystical because they are helpful to the people creating the work and therefore none of our critical business.

I wanted to resist this academic shyness and tackle Anne Bogart's 'energy of original production' head on. However, in attempting to do so, I am not inclined to make the kind of objection I thought The Fifth Wall encounter might provoke: the idea that the original energy of a piece of theatre is created in a historical moment of production and audience reception that is impossible to retrieve. A close reading of the way in which Anne Bogart uses the words 'energy' and 'original' takes us far from the essentialist rhetoric of the actor in my opening anecdote. The phrase emerged in response to a contribution from the floor, an account of an experience of directing *Macbeth* early in the speaker's career. Anne had spoken of her idea of magic emerging out of poverty and dust, a necessity in a society that seemed entirely un-magical. The contributor, Greg Doran, related this notion of necessity to a question he had found useful in staging the witches in Macbeth: 'What is the society we are creating in which there is this climate of fear which produces witches, or which needs witches … ?' (17). Bogart's response was 'who needs to perform this play? You don't need to recreate the original "look"', she argued, 'that's not the play – but it's not about simply putting it in a different place either' (18). Bogart's decision to set Steinbeck's California 'into a kind of constellation' (to return to an earlier phrase of Worthen's) with *A Midsummer Night's Dream* is not a means of recreating 'energy' in some mystical originary sense, but of offering her audience a framework in which the play becomes important, urgent, socially meaningful once again.

The ways Anne Bogart talks about working with text, space, body and audience are completely unlike anything a company of English Renaissance players might have done with a play by Shakespeare. Nevertheless, they offer a methodology for discovering how such a play might do the work of making meaning for which I am tempted to make large claims, in terms of their suitability for tackling a Shakespeare text. I imagine *A Midsummer Night's Dream* and Steinbeck's California in productive tension, the later world used as a means of flagging up the work that must be undertaken to make magic in the theatre, rather than as a way of smoothing its difficulties for a modern audience. I imagine a production that asks why a society might need a play about magic, an interrogation of the idea of transformation, as well as the celebration expected of *A Midsummer Night's Dream*. Acknowledging the histor-ical and cultural baggage of the region in which her production is to take place would seem on one level to offer resistance and contradiction to the play's own historical moment, rather than suggesting a means of discovering it. But Anne Bogart's intention is to find something of the original *energy* of a play, a term suggestive of live performance rather than fixed literary meaning. Permitting the actor's body, the architec-ture of the building in which she makes work, the baggage perform-ers and audience bring to a play, to produce meaning in rehearsal, might be reaching towards the ways in which plays made meaning in the out-door Elizabethan playhouse.

Interestingly, Anne talks of 'casting' the audience and recalls for me the addresses to the audience in Pimlott's *Richard II*: 'The audience are always cast' she says, 'whether they know it or not'.[29] She is still speculating as to how her audience for *A Midsummer Night's Dream* will be 'cast', how that play will seem to her and her company to address its spectators.[30] That the plays do consciously address their spectators would seem a commonplace. The connection I am making between Anne's work, Pimlott's *Richard II*, and the Finnish *A Midsummer Night's Dream* described by Bill Worthen, is that each appears to embrace the potential failure of that address to the world – the recalcitrant outside that may refuse to take the address as it is meant.

On the Finnish island of Worthen's account, Theseus comments upon the ease with which 'a bush [is] suppos'd a bear' (*MND* 5.1.22) while surrounded by trees that refuse to be anything but real trees, and fail to transform themselves into a magical forest just because actors are pretending to be fairies among them. I am suggesting that a theatre like The Globe, and the spectators who have paid to see plays in it, have something of this recalcitrant presence, and that the resistance to fictions they put up is part of the world of a Shakespeare play. How will this recalcitrant presence make itself felt in a production of *A Midsummer Night's Dream* – a play which, as Bill Worthen suggests, appears to offer as a theme the power of the imagination to transform? Perhaps it holds the potential for asking political questions about the imagination – whose imagination has the power to transform? Where might that imagination, or that power, fail? Anne Bogart intends to inflect her version with a notion of magic produced from conditions of material poverty. I can imagine her arrangement of this, the text, her mode of address to the audience and the gestural language of her performers, releasing an energy in the space between performer and audience that will permit us to watch the ways in which the play signifies, and to make meaning anew. I can also imagine productive failures of signification, both within the fiction and the auditorium. Anne's work and her future production of *A Midsummer Night's Dream*, the productively infelicitous performatives of Bill's Finnish experience and the meta-theatrical moments of the RSC's *Richard II*, all speak of the work these plays are conscious of doing in order to make meaning. At The Fifth Wall, these moments spoke to me anew of the ways in which the resistance of theatrical space to fictional transformation doubles back into Shakespeare's fictions, making the work of imagining difficult and examinable as well as magical and absorbing.

NOTES

1 'Practice as Research' is the phrase delineating the British Arts and Humanities Research Board initiative to evaluate practice in the arts for academic, scholarly and research potential.

2 There is one exception: Manchester Metropolitan University offers the only university-based conservatory course that trains actors for the stage.

3 Anne Bogart, *A Director Prepares: Seven Essays on Art and Theatre* (London: Routledge, 2001), back cover.

4 W.B. Worthen, essay written in preparation for The Fifth Wall research workshop, 6.

5 Charles Mee, 'Making up the Rules', in *Anne Bogart: Viewpoints*, ed. Michael Bigelow Dixon and Joel A. Smith (Lyme, New Hampshire: Smith and Kraus, 1995), 80.

6 For a fuller account of the Viewpoints, including the 'Viewpoints of Time', see Tina Landau, 'Source-Work, the Viewpoints and Composition: What are They?', in Dixon and Smith, *op. cit.*, 20–23.

7 *Ibid.*, 20.

8 *Ibid.*, 24.

9 *Ibid.*, 24.

10 W.B. Worthen, 'Shakespearean Performativity', in *Shakespeare and the Modern Theatre*, ed. Michael Bristol and Kathleen McLuskie (London and New York: Routledge, 2001), 117.

11 Robert Hurwitt, *San Francisco Examiner* (9 May 1997), in SITI Company Plays Archive, www.siti.org/going going gone press.html.

12 W.B. Worthen, essay written in preparation, 10.

13 Susannah Clapp, *Observer* (2 April 2000).

14 Michael Billington, *Guardian* (1 April 2000).

15 Jane Edwards, *Time Out* (5 April 2000).

16 Robert Butler, *Independent on Sunday* (2 April 2000).

17 Michael Billington, *op. cit.*; Alastair Macaulay, *Financial Times* (31 March 2000).

18 Philip Auslander, 'Task and Vision: Willem Dafoe and The Wooster Group', in Philip Auslander, *From Acting to Performance* (London and New York: Routledge, 1997), 42.

19 *Ibid.*, 42.

20 *Ibid.*, 42.

21 Worthen cites Michael Joyce, *Othermindedness: The Emergence of Network Culture* (Ann Arbor: University of Michigan Press, 2001), 3.

22 W.B. Worthen, essay written in preparation, 5.

23 Clive Johnson, 'Shakespeare's Big Mac', review of the new Globe's *Hamlet* held by The Globe Research Centre, source unknown.

24   W.B. Worthen, essay written in preparation, 12.

25 *Ibid.*, 5.

26 See http://www.sjrep.com/general/generalinfo.shtml accessed 16 February 2003.

27 Transcript, 17, and interview with Anne Bogart, New York (14 February 2003).

28 Interview with Anne Bogart, *ibid.*

29 *Ibid.*

30 Anne Bogart's *A Midsummer Night's Dream* opens at the San Jose Rep on 24 January 2004.

7

RETROSPECTIVE: JANELLE REINELT

FINAL SESSION (FINAL THOUGHTS) ON HEIGHTENED LANGUAGE: IMPASSE OR INTERCHANGE?

Nicholas Hytner (The National Theatre)
Janelle Reinelt (University of California, Irvine):
respondent
Ann Thompson (King's College, University of London)

The discussion uncovers impasses between the stage and page in areas of stage directions, punctuation and imagery, but also finds rapprochement as it opens up to wider debate, in ideas for working with language, and the changing expectations of theatrical and linguistic space and sound. The respondent for this essay takes on the task of looking retrospectively at the contributions to the entire collection, and considers institutional pressures, audience expectations, and disciplinary overlaps and differences.

I think unless we set out some real differences we might just *think* we're talking to each other, and actually we're just having mostly the good grace not to start our talk until someone else has finished, and to pick up some of their language as a sort of narrative device.

Emma Smith, The Fifth Wall research workshop, session six

Our workshop session on 'Shakespeare and Metaphor', coming at the end of an enormously stimulating colloquium, was faced with two difficulties. Nick Hytner was only able to join us for this one session, and so his remarks could not respond to the previous conversations, while being last meant we were nevertheless positioned to speak in relation to what had gone before. Ironically, this predicament yielded some useful insights as we both recapitulated several of the structural features that governed our discourses, and also went beyond those repetitions in some substantial ways. While the tensions between academics and practitioners had been an acknowledged aspect of our set-up, all of us seemed determined to make the interchange productive for both groups. This proved initially difficult during our session, thus renewing the tension between text and performance, those who study and those who perform. On the other hand, the clarity of some aspects of Shakespeare's language in performance seemed cumulative, and the topic of metaphorical or heightened language proved to be closely related to most other topics we had discussed over the previous two days.

A SERIES OF IMPASSES?

Stage directions

Ann Thompson, critic and editor, began by saying she did not want to dwell on editing, but she did want to observe that academic researchers are interested at least in part in 'how they might have done it at The Globe 400 years ago', while people 'who are using the stage now ask, how can we make it work today?' And so we began by being aware of several substantial incommensurabilities at the point of departure. We had agreed ahead of time to use *The Winter's Tale* as our common text, and specifically 2.3 as a scene that had a number of significant metaphorical constructions. Despite not wanting to dwell on editing, Thompson began by raising the kind of specific question that editors concerned with explicating the text might ask: 'What is the use of stage directions?' The opening of 2.3 exhibits a typical predicament: Leontes comes on with a number of other people (Paulina, Antigonus, Lords, servants), but speaks his first speech as a soliloquy; we know this because a servant interrupts him at line 9 and he says, 'Who's there!' – clearly he is not in the presence of this figure when he asks.[1] Thompson also points out that later in the scene when Leontes is threatening to kill his child, a lord says 'We all kneel' [152], but there is no stage direction or other indication of anyone getting up:

> Is that something that should be included in a Shakespeare edition or in the commentary to say they all kneel? It seems odd that if [someone says] 'We all kneel' they don't kneel, but that happens a lot on stage. The Oxford Complete Works edition is famous for having people kneel quite a lot, but the trouble with saying they

kneel is then you have to say they all get up again, and the Oxford famously doesn't! (3)

We chuckled about this but could not really propose a solution because, as Nick Hytner was to insist repeatedly, 'There are no rules' (4). Stage directions may or may not be rationalised by editors, and directors and actors may or may not consult them.

Punctuation

A second seeming impasse was reached later when the question of punctuation was raised in terms of its help or hindrance to actors. Thompson had pointed out that we picked *The Winter's Tale* for our discussion, in part, because it is one of the late plays where heightened and metaphorical language is taken to extremes and becomes the very language of the play as a whole. Leontes, in particular, is made to speak sentences with complicated or even impossible syntax, such that, for example, the Arden 2 editor 'resorts to the comment that Leontes is incoherent because he's so emotional. But if Leontes is incoherent, so is almost everyone else in the play; everybody talks this language, so perhaps it doesn't help to make that kind of point' (Thompson, 2). Hytner, who directed Alex Jennings as Leontes, responded that he thought the note was in fact correct – 'Leontes is incoherent and is having some kind of breakdown. I think those two huge soliloquies in the first scene were where he [Jennings] and I gave up and said, "We can't parse this, we just have to assume the words spew out"' (4–5).

Hytner tried to remember how Jennings had punctuated the opening speech, using as a guide the Oxford University Press edition:

> Nor night nor day no rest. It is but weakness
> To bear the matter thus; mere weakness, if
> The cause were not in being – part o'th' cause,
> She, th'adultress; for the harlot King
> Is quite beyond mine arm, out of the blank
> And level of my brain, plot-proof;

> [2.3.1–6]

and then consulting Arden 2:

> Nor night, nor day, no rest: it is but weakness
> To bear the matter thus: mere weakness. If

> The cause were not in being, – part o'th' cause,
> She th'adultress: for the harlot king
> Is quite beyond mine arm, out of the blank
> And level of my brain: plot-proof:
>
> (2.3.1–6)

He reconstructed their processing of the lines thus: 'Nor night nor day no rest, I'm tired, then bang, no link no link, this mind is leaping from "I'm tired" to "I'm weak, I'm pathetic, because I'm doing nothing about it"' (5). Responding to the question of punctuation, he said he thought they used a full stop after 'mere weakness', although at first he thought it might have been a semicolon. Since it was obvious that it was a matter of choice between actor and director how to punctuate this sentence, Thompson pressed on: 'Would your general preference be to have a script without any punctuation?', to which Hytner responded, 'Yeah, I think it's up to us' (6).

This discussion harks back to a similar impasse on the topic of punctuation in session four.[2] Lynne Magnusson had pointed out the unstable and historicised nature of punctuation in Shakespeare texts. She showed how moving from an Arden 3 edition back to a First Quarto version yields less punctuation and more possibilities for interpretation. She pointed out the possibility that early modern punctuation had more to do with breath, with physiology, than with syntax or grammar – a possible meeting ground with practitioners such as Peter Lichtenfels, who work with actors on breath placement and control in order to come 'on voice'. However, punctuation in the early modern text is insufficient as a guide for the actor because Shakespeare may have had nothing to do with it in either the quartos or folios, and also because the evolving history of print itself overlaps orality, meaning that both physiological and syntactical systems may have been in use simultaneously. Modern editors, in response to this ambiguity, often punctuate for reading, but do not make, as Magnusson put it, 'any effort at transparency' (Jenstad, Lichtenfels, Magnusson, 15), thus not providing any useful tools for actors, or indeed perhaps misleading them. In light of this discussion, Hytner's simple admission that he would rather not have punctuation in an edition does not seem so peremptory; there are sound reasons why this may not be one of the places where scholars and practitioners can easily meet.

At this point, I believed our session was staging the very difficulties between scholars and practitioners that The Fifth Wall workshop had been devised to dispel, and there was yet one more impasse ahead in terms of the heart of our topic, the role of metaphorical language for actors and audiences.

Imagery

Thompson raised with Hytner the key questions about handling heightened language: 'Whether the actor needs to visualise a metaphor in order to say it, and whether or not that visualisation needs to be conveyed to the audience?' (3). Embedded in this question was a variant of the concern, 'Of what use are we as scholars to you as practitioners?', that is, Thompson was trying to understand how much information and of what kind is useful to actors in their preparations. Does an actor need to understand and work with every aspect of heightened language? Should scholars expect to help them do that work? She brought forth two examples from the text. In the first, a single-line simile, Paulina chides Leontes' servants for not bringing him to his senses, saying ''Tis such as you / That creep like shadows by him and do sigh / At each his needless heavings, such as you / Nourish the cause of his awaking' (2.3.34–7). Thompson wanted to know if 'creep like shadows by him' is a cue as to how to present the lords, does it mean something to performance, or is it a simile that passes very quickly? 'The ultimate question is, can academic studies, academic editions, provide any help to performers grappling with a single line like this?' (Thompson, 4).

The second example, while more extended, was less immediately discernible as it compares the process of printing to the resemblance of father to baby: 'Although the print be little, the whole matter / And copy of the father – eye, nose, lip / The trick of 's frown, his forehead, nay, the valley, / The pretty dimples of his chin and cheek, his smiles, / The very mould and frame of hand, nail, finger' (2.3.98–102). Thus an actor or an audience member is being asked to visualise a baby – and often the stage baby is not, of course, a real baby – and to think of it as a copy of its father, as a book is copied by a press. 'Do we need to work through all those things if you are speaking or hearing those lines?' Thompson wanted to know. Hytner demurred: 'There are no rules in my experience … the two examples that you picked out … no, I would say it would be an unusual Paulina who visualised printing' (3–4). Impasse three.

WORKING WITH LANGUAGE: THE CHALLENGE
OF SHAKESPEARE

Were we to stop here, I would only have presented one version of our session, the one in which the academics seemed furthest from the practitioners. These very same topics and examples opened out into related discussions about the importance of language in relation to space (if not to stage directions), the demands of Shakespearean language for actors' training, unique abilities and shortcomings, and the roles of context, historical moment, and social class in relationship to the heightened languages of the stage.

Our discussions reaffirmed the undeniable fact that individual actors work with language variously, and directors use language creatively in individual ways as well. Greg Doran drew this to our attention when talking about how actors Antony Sher and Harriet Walter decided to assume that Lady Macbeth had previously given birth to a baby that died, and Annabel Arden remarked on Michael Gambon's 'perfect gesture' in Caryl Churchill's *A Number* when he glanced at his wedding ring in a climax concerning family breakdown and divorce.[4] In discussing *The Winter's Tale*, Nick Hytner had evoked Alex Jennings as someone who had an incredibly quick mind, and who was able to move through dense language and difficult syntax because he could make it sound like language actually coming from a character's train of thought. 'An actor like Alex makes the mental leaps so quickly and keeps an audience with him: he's mentally, and occasionally literally, bouncing off the walls' (Hytner, 6). Discussing scene 2.3, we realised that fire is one of the most frequently recurring images – six times according to Thompson – and Hytner stressed that although fire is a key to the character's (in this case Leontes') imagination and state, you would not stage a literal fire, but 'it depends on different individual's connections; different [people carry] different images within them' (6). In rehearsal, actors might reveal – or not – their personal connections to the image of fire, but actors would be using the image viscerally, none the less.

However, what if an actor, unlike Alex Jennings, does not have the lickety-split capacities of a lightening-quick mind? How does heightened language, densely packed, then challenge the actor? Hytner, speaking about casting the part of Williams in *Henry V*, said he would like to get someone who might have been cast in the television series *Soldier*

Soldier because he would want 'big strapping young guys'. But this might pose difficulties because of the kind of actor his chosen Williams might not:

> have been taken to see Shakespeare because the state schools don't have the money to afford [it]. So [the actor playing] Williams has probably been introduced to Shakespeare at drama school; it's not part of his world, it's not part of the fabric of the way he has experienced growing up, and the challenge is to persuade him that there is a world where people are fabulously articulate, even the squaddies.
>
> (10)

[Ed note: Many state schools in the UK teach Shakespeare as well or better than independent or fee-paying schools. Hytner seems to have been making a point about the fact that state school pupils are less likely to have seen a Shakespeare play being performed.] In an earlier session, Bridget Escolme had been speaking about how regional accents should not be ironed out of people at drama schools, and that these markings make speech interesting.[5] In the instance of *Henry V* and the part of Williams, clearly Hytner wanted to cast someone who had certain cultural markings, but then needed to help the actor meet the challenge of the strange, heightened language. Hytner referred specifically to a speech of Williams' that, while not in verse, has plenty of flourishes: 'That's a perilous shot out of an elder-gun, that a poor and a private displeasure can do against a monarch. You may as well go about to turn the sun to ice with fanning in his face with a peacock's feather' (*H5* 4.1.203–7). The elaborate figure of using a peacock's feather to perform such a monumental transformation as turning sun to ice needs to be delivered by this minor character as easily and elegantly as if it were a major soliloquy delivered by a protagonist (because, after all, as Thompson pointed out, the language is not only about characterisation, it also constructs the world of the play).

Hytner stressed two things: first, that 'what animates is physical reality', because the language is carried by the actor's specific associations of language with physical reality, and those will vary with the individual; and second, that in the end, the language does matter in its micro features, such that 'finding an internal and external reality to ground the language, even if you are not showing it to the audience, is terribly important: then you have to sit down and work out what it means' (5). For any actor, no matter what background or training, the issue will still be to find a way to provide a physical context for the lines. 'Where am I, what time is it, how tired am I, how long since the last scene, how long has the queen been in prison, how long has he been churning this over and over?' (5) – these are some of the questions Hytner suggested relative to Leontes' speech.

Tim Carroll chimed in at this point to support the notion of the importance of the physical characteristics of a scene, even if you are staging it on a stage like The Globe that is:

> absolutely hostile to the idea of very specific physical stagings. You will still need to have a sense of whether it is day or night, outside a bedroom or somewhere else; 'Am I tired?' – all of the things, in fact, that it is not a great idea to show on The Globe stage. These things still need conversation and decision, and it still makes a great difference to the play.
>
> (Carroll, 8)

This fundamental physical aspect to the acting process does not diminish in plays that feature elaborate, complex, extraordinary language; in fact, the physical anchor for the speeches is even more important, although the actors need to know what it is they are saying and how it can mean.

Even so, this preparation may not be enough to make the language work on stage and for the audience. One of the factors that proved critical in our discussion was speed – not just the mental agility of the actor, but the necessity for the words to proceed through utterances in rhythms, to keep momentum flowing. The actor from *Soldier Soldier* would need to be convinced and understand how he can pluck an image like a peacock feather out of the air. To some extent, this, too, is cultural and time-bound. As Hytner explained:

> There is a distinction to be made between an elaborately wrought image that needs to be invented on the spot and the image that slides in as part of a fast-working mind. There is a danger with creating on stage an elaborate image out of nothing; it lies in the split-second pause an actor takes to invent it, to mint it. There was a time

15 to 20 years ago when that kind of acting was very much in fashion, and the plays slowed down – and I think we know now that we need to restore momentum to the way we speak Shakespeare. When the actor believes in his ability to articulate Shakespeare's elaborate images and rhetorical structures, when he speaks Shakespeare fast, he is more comprehensible.

(4)

Speed had come up earlier in the workshop, specifically in the discussion of punctuation. Peter Lichtenfels, focusing on actor training, had remarked on his preference for the quarto editions because, 'The grammatical commas in modern editions, if taken as breath cues, produce many unearned pauses for the actor'. Unearned pauses interfere with the 'precision and consciousness of sound that arises when people are saying what they think, and thinking what they say'.[6]

What, then, are some of the ways that actors, particularly those whose experience of Shakespearean language is limited, can make this language so familiar that it comes easily and speedily from their tongues? Here, Joy Richardson, one of the actors who had been attending and occasionally performing for the workshop, made an important contribution. Pointing out that the directors in our group frequently spoke about working with actors, she charged that this obscured the work that actors do on their own to build relations with the text and develop character:

Away from the rehearsal room, actors work on finding the character, and often, very often, it's through observation. When I have a speech with a lot of heightened language, I ask, can I see any examples of it in the world we live in now? And there is so much! I go home and I live with my mother, and so much of what she says is what Shakespeare would have written. And it is amazing how loud, how expressive – the metaphors that people use! So often, when people I hear saying these things say them, they just race through them because they know what it is that they are trying to communicate; the person receiving it often gets the image clearly because it is given clearly.

(17)

Earlier, Greg Doran had talked about the text helping actors with 'oracy'. This word became a touchstone for using oral expression well. Here is how he defined it: 'Oracy is your skill in self-expression. It's your ability to put words together, to use your mouth. When I work on Shakespeare with actors, I tend to talk not about how to do Shakespeare's *verse*, but how to make the audience listen, because that is why he wrote the way he wrote: to reach an audience, *out there*, at the moment the words are uttered' (Bradby, Doran, Jackson, 12). This emphasis on 'using the mouth' in oracy skills to allow the words to reach people is essential for any actor.

Rapprochement

Here, then, a number of factors came together about heightened language in today's theatre: because of present-day conventions, the language must come speedily and easily; because the actor needs to link this language to physical actions, a full contextual sense of the material needs to be identified or created; because of the complexity of the syntax and images, the actual grammar and semantics need to be consciously pursued and mastered. Here is the first major *rapprochement* between scholars and practitioners: while actors and director can create physical associations and work on individual means of 'making the language their own', they can partner with scholars in search of precise meanings and the way grammar and syntax work. These scholarly tools are necessary but not sufficient for fully communicable performance. Indeed, The Fifth Wall discussion seems to validate what Ann Thompson (and John Thompson) had written in the introduction to *Shakespeare, Meaning and Metaphor*:

> Now it may very well be the case that Shakespeare's continuing communicability is largely a function of macro-level skills, of what would not be lost in translation … However, we have what is in our view strong experiential evidence of the contribution of the linguistic micro-level to the current life of the plays. This consists in the invariable awfulness of productions in which the actors try to get through the play without themselves quite understanding the lines. By contrast, intelligence of delivery at the verbal level seems capable of sustaining productions which in other respects may be very modest or even actively ill-conceived.[7]

PERFORMING SHAKESPEARE:
CHANGING EXPECTATIONS

In the process of discussing issues of speed and cultural familiarity with heightened language, our session moved into another fertile area. Observations about changing conventions of audience expectation with regard to speed led to a larger discussion about changing expectations concerning the size and scope of performances, both aural and spatial. To follow this trajectory, we can begin with Bridget Escolme's comment that contemporary audiences are seemingly much more aware of theatricality in performance, and actually enjoy a more open and direct relationship with the performers. She reinterpreted speed in delivery as 'urgent acts of communication', ones that don't take much time to execute because the audience is moving hand in hand with the performers: 'That means you don't have to ask people to have a little tiny psychological shift every time you say something, these acts of communication are becoming more urgent and flow more easily from a conscious theatricality between the audience and the performers' (12). Nick Hytner agreed with this idea, but linked it up to the effect of the physical scope of performance on audience expectation:

> The way audiences expect actors to be now is different from the way we acted 30 years ago, and very different no doubt from the way we acted 400 years ago. The biggest space at the National Theatre, the Olivier theatre, was designed to have Laurence Olivier standing centre stage doing what he did, but if you brought him back in his prime right now, we would find it uncomfortable, and cut-price imitations of Olivier are even more uncomfortable. The problem with heightened text now is that our notions of what's real, what's true, change all the time. In a studio space, there isn't a problem because of the intimacy of it and quite simply the way it tells an actor to be quiet: this removes the problems but it also removes the scale; emotional, physical, and intellectual scale. It's harder to do in a big space, but you can embrace the thousands and communicate with them directly.

(12)

This comment about the difference between playing Shakespeare in a studio space accommodating approximately 200 and a large auditorium seating upwards of 1,000, triggered a fascinating conversation about the relationship between the dynamics of sound and the style of Shakespeare performance. In a climate where audiences expect and want intimacy, one answer to producing in larger spaces has been to use microphones to amplify the actors' speech. Although stressing that he did not want to 'be negative' about Trevor Nunn's use of microphones when doing Shakespeare in the Olivier, Hytner used Nunn as an example of someone who has tried to solve the problem of preserving intimacy in a large space in this way. He insisted that using microphones diminishes the physical aspect of the language, the physicality born of projecting for a large space: 'I think the size of the spirits that animate these plays requires the size of physical engagement that goes with projecting your voice' (13). Actor Alan Cox, talking about what effective speaking requires in a large space without amplification, added, 'You have to engage your whole body and you are actually radiating a quality of energy as well as projecting a sound, that's metaphysical – you can't prove it' (14).

This topic of the modern desire for intimacy without sacrifice of the scope and power of big performances had clearly touched a cord with many of our session's participants. The Shakespeare Institute's Russell Jackson, for example, said that he wasn't expressing 'some kind of puritanical feeling', but rather fearing that a certain vocal homogenisation creeps into microphonic speech and that audiences will expect that they will always have privileged access to very softly spoken language, without realising that they give up something in order to have that effect. 'It's a bit like hearing all your music through CDs rather than being in the same acoustic space with people scraping and bowing.' He reminded us that one of the pleasurable paradoxes of big theatres is that they 'are places where people talk loud so that you can imagine they are speaking very softly'. Comparing the effect to opera where microphones are not used and where something extraordinary is going on physically, Jackson commented that in New York's Central Park, where microphones are necessary, the difficulty for actors is that when 'they've gone too loud for the mike and have to come back down, the level balancing clearly homogenises' (18–19).

Connecting with the session on gesture (Arden, Hendricks, Hunter), we were all reminded that language is linked in fundamental ways to embodiment, that gesture is as much a part of communicating the nuance of metaphor as punctuation, and that the size of the auditorium in which these gestures are spoken and the quality of sound, natural or amplified, will undoubtedly affect the meaning of the words, the perception of character, the world of the play. Amplified sound, as a technology, is one of the variables in this historical moment. In that session, David Bradby had said of the social nature of gesture, 'We're inhabiting the play in styles of physicality that were unimaginable 50 years ago, never mind 400' (Arden, Hendricks, Hunter, 19). We are also listening to the plays in ways that may have been unimaginable 50 years ago as well and, furthermore, we may be in the middle of a technology-driven transformation in our aural habits.

LANGUAGE, TIME AND SPACE

While the majority of our discussion had been closely linked to rehearsal and performance situations, the literary critics among us also frequently refocused our conversation by showing how the text itself carries some of the physical dimensions of time and space we were treating as issues of staging. Margo Hendricks, a critic but also a dramaturge, pointed out that beyond the way that physical stage space constructs the world of the play, language also produces a spatial concept of it, as when the baby in *The Winter's Tale* is taken away to be abandoned in Bohemia, throwing into relief the differences between Sicilia and Bohemia long before the actual Bohemian scenes take place.

> We also get the sense of two coexisting worlds in *Othello* with Cyprus and Venice, or in *As You Like It* with the Duke's court and the Forest of Arden. All these spaces are actually real in the text in terms of the language that is used to describe them.

(14–15)

Hendricks went on to question how the reality of a particular physical space could be – would have to be – used by directors to allow the spaces of the text to appear. This is not a question of design, of visually representing the spaces of the text, but rather of imagination, of how in a large space, for instance the Olivier theatre, an actor can create through text alone the specificity of the text's spatial architecture. Nick Hytner delineated three aspects to space in the Olivier: the present actual reality of actions taking place inside a theatre building; the imaginary space that an actor conjures to animate what he or she is saying (invisible, of course, to the audience); and the designed space built by the scene designer. For Hytner, the designed space is the least important, in part because he agrees with Hendricks:

In *Henry V*, there's a difference in the texture of the way they speak in 1.1 when in some kind of cave [antechamber]. We certainly don't need the walls and ceiling. The way the language – it's a technical matter – the way the language reaches another actor and then travels out to embrace an audience in a cavern [or small room] is plainly going to be very different to the way the language is used standing outside the walls of Harfleur. Those two scenes [1.1 and 4.1] side by side are entirely different, with entirely different prompts for the way an actor should physically embody the words as they come out.

(16)

This was not the only occasion when a director supported a claim for the determining power of the text.

Janelle Day Jenstad, speaking as a critic, raised a similar issue about metaphor and physical space that frequently comes up in her teaching. In *A Midsummer Night's Dream*, the overt reference to turning a green plot into a stage is, according to Jenstad, an example of meta-theatricality and metaphor collapsing in on themselves.[8] She wonders whether 'if you have the actor pointing at the tiring-house and saying "this hawthorn-brake" and you have two levels of metaphor going on, you don't have almost nothing in the end, the same way that the boy actor playing the girl playing the boy collapses into the boy' (*sic*, 17). While Jenstad seemed to imply that staging the play would get in the way of the appreciation of its metaphors, Hytner defended Shakespeare's ability to induce sophistication in his audiences:

There are instances where two parallel texts are going on, the play which is firmly rooted in the stage space and this other play that bounces out of the world we're performing it in. There is a kind of multi-layered effect going on when Quince refers to the 'hawthorn-brake', and my experience is that audiences can carry all of it in their heads at the same time.

(18)

CONCLUDING THOUGHTS

I found it striking how throughout the workshop, we participants were brought round to confront the differences of purpose for which we all do our work. At one point Lynne Magnusson cited Robert Weimann's suggestion that when exploring the intersection of the early modern writer's pen and the actor's voice, we need to recognise a fundamental disjunction (Jensted, Magnusson, Lichtenfels, 17). The writer's literary endeavours, derived from an education in written rhetoric and composition, are very different from the actor's largely oral rhetoric, physical, spectacular body-centred practices of performance and display. This *dis*continuity, writing and playing, pen and voice, allows for both reciprocity and difference at the heart of their relations in theatrical production.[9] A similar difference separates literary scholars from theatrical practitioners as well, although the director function sometimes summons a conceptual apparatus that approximates some forms of scholarly practice. The Fifth Wall workshop was devised as a search for reciprocity and difference between those of us whose function is education or intellectual reflection, and those whose function is theatrical production and performance.

Emma Smith was perhaps the most productively stubborn of us in her insistence that we not simply engage in polite accommodation. For her, our tasks are different:

> Criticism … requires us … to read asequentially, to read anachronistically, and to read for an academic, rather than theatrical, context, in which questions of history, language, reception and interpretation are interleaved with questions of the literary discipline, and its academic hierarchies … What works in the essay, or classroom, or monograph is not the same as what works in the theatre, and nor, perhaps, should it be.[10]

In the same session, director Tim Carroll made the needs of the rehearsal room clear when he talked about identifying the turning points in 'purposeful playing', and wished that critics would address those matters that would help clarify such points. Referring to a scene in *Twelfth Night*, Martin White observed that, 'an edition shouldn't be expected necessarily to offer a solution … but here the editors … failed to notice the question'.[11]

Most of the practitioners raised questions concerning the visual, aural and physical aspects of the texts – their materials, after all, are flesh-and-blood bodies and other empirical properties, while the material of scholars is print-based words. Here the pen and voice distinctions Weimann writes about prove most suggestive. The efficacy of performance will depend on the embodied utterances of actors; however, to the extent that 'Shakespeare' exists on the page as well as the stage, the different practices informing each will be intertwined. Just as we saw that orality and literacy did not succeed each other in two clean and disconnected moments, neither do performance and textual apprehension exist in isolation. This seems like a very important insight because it means we cannot really succeed without each other, following our separate *métiers*. In the session on 'Gesture and Language', Margo Hendricks and Annabel Arden came close to demonstrating this. Gesture seems to be of the body, but as Hendricks insists, it is also of the text. The text animates the actor's body, just as the actor's body animates the text. Arden agreed, and stressed that the body itself is a text. Thus, performance texts and literary texts are deeply entwined in performance.

But what about reading? Does reading require aspects of performance and display? Insofar as genre has retained any credit within our postmodern habits of thought, it can be argued that reading 'plays' invokes absent performances by their form, whether these are imaginary or conjured from the memories of readers. If we agree with Hytner that the meta-theatrical references of Quince can be held, multi-layered, by an audience watching a physical performance, perhaps in turn we can agree that hypothetical performances ghost any reading of a printed text. If so, then we scholars and practitioners really can't get quit of each other.

In a way, our Fifth Wall workshop conditions favoured the primacy of performance. Meeting at The Globe, including a number of actors, and involving many scholars who write about performance as often as text, the literary side of things could not help but seem secondary to the staging of the plays. Since the staging of plays is fundamentally concerned with the physical and bodily nature of the task, it seems that most of our conversations occurred within this implicit primacy of performance, or at least gave a certain privilege to it – one reason why I so admired Emma Smith's insistence on making sure the tensions of assuming a common purpose were clear. To the space of the theatre, she opposed the space of the library and charged us with denigrating it. She also staked out the materiality of her own subject matter: there are ways 'of thinking about words on the page which could never make it through into performance, because they're about words, they're about words visually, they're about the … patterns and … aesthetics of print'.[12]

Smith also discussed the particular work that recent gender and queer criticism have performed. It is not:

some kind of historicised representation of the early modern theatre. This is criticism – doing cultural work in university departments and beyond – which is about different voices being heard, which is about having, say, a queer or feminist stake in Shakespeare as a cultural icon.[13]

The validity of her points resides in the structural and institutional politics of literary studies in the academy. In order to achieve their goals there, scholars follow certain rules, conventions and practices just as directors follow certain theatrical ones. However, in the academy, the theatre and its practices are often dismissed as unintellectual if not downright illegitimate. The history of theatre studies in the British and American academy is a history of struggle for legitimation. Similarly, the kiss of death in journalistic reception of theatre productions is the perception of some performance as *too* intellectual, too academic.

While supporting Smith's claim that the institutions (university and theatre) require strict and sometimes mutually exclusive practices from their members, I would want to point out that the goal of doing cultural work, 'which is about different voices being heard, which is about having, say, a queer or feminist stake in Shakespeare as a cultural icon', has also been a priority among some performance practitioners as well. The project of these new theories and readings is not exclusively the domain of the university, and although performance cannot always 'make use' of all the insights of criticism, several of the directors present (Arden, Bogart, Carroll, Doran, Lichtenfels) were clearly up to date on much of the general contours of such scholarship. Tim Carroll affirmed this relationship through a negative pronouncement: 'There's no kind of criticism that could not influence the way I do a production'.[14] Perhaps we need a doctrine of separate but overlapping spheres.

Peter Lichtenfels exemplifies a blend, within one person, of these realms. In the first part of his comments for the workshop, he talked about methods for training the voice to speak Shakespeare, and here he was most embedded in the physical and bodily processes of the actor. He described exercises of breaking speeches into all vowels, or all consonants and talked about helping actors to release habitual tensions of the adult body, as well as generalising that 'consonants are allied to the actions, and the vowels to the emotions of the character'.[15] (Lynne Magnusson, performing her literary function, countered, 'Is it true?')[16]

However, Lichtenfels has also paid careful attention to the differences between the quartos, and links punctuation to its effects on the voice power of the character. In this research for *Romeo and Juliet* his concern is in concert with feminist scholarship – he is interested in giving Juliet the strongest voice possible within the text or within productions. Finding that the Q2 punctuation allows Juliet to express frustration through uttering an oath, he concluded that it emerged as the strongest choice. Trying out Q1 and Q4 in rehearsal and performance conditions, he searched for how different punctuation affected the actors.[17]

Here is a working practitioner able to harmonise through his labour two of the most seemingly opposed subjects (the voice/body of the actor and the punctuation of the various source texts). Of course, much of the work with the actor's voice and body may seem irrelevant to a scholar, just as much of the detailed archival or philological work of the scholar may seem irrelevant to the director, but the common political project and the uses made of punctuation analysis in aiding this goal illustrates the reciprocity that is always possible, if not always realisable, among scholars and practitioners.

Annabel Arden and Margo Hendricks came close to realising a similar chemistry in their dialogue about gestures. While Arden tended to emphasise the physical 'mystery' of the gesturing body, Hendricks gently held out for the gestures of the text, equally mysterious and powerful. Both agreed that they (body and text) animated each other. The body, as I suggested above, may be seen to ghost the text, even if it is not present palpably, materially, in print. Here, again, we can catch a glimpse of a productive and perhaps necessary relationship between director and critic.

I say 'perhaps' because I am less convinced the practitioner can do without the scholar than that the scholar can do without the practitioner. In arguing for the role of the 'linguistic micro-level' to the current life of the plays, Ann Thompson evidences bad productions in which the actors do not understand the lines, and in our session, Nick Hytner admitted the need to 'sit down and work out what it means' (5). I wonder if there is an equivalent validity when the focus is on reading. Hendricks and White clearly use performance to stimulate their criticism, but what about someone like Smith? Martin White uses Tim Carroll's experience of directing *Twelfth Night* to suggest that an editor may need the insights of performance to help recognise the turning points in scenes, and thus 'practice informs scholarshship'. White went on to argue that seeing an all-male cast perform at The Globe might encourage scholars to rethink their positions about how men play female roles. However, Smith remained relatively unmoved by these suggestions, and in particular seemed reluctant to give credence to 'the empirics of performance'. I think the more suggestive challenge is one offered elliptically by Lynette Hunter when she pointed out the materiality of the reading process: 'we've been talking about reading as though it is not a bodily experience, and I think reading *is* a bodily experience, it *is* embodied'.[18] The body of the reader joins up with the implied body of the spectator through the act of imagination. As the plays were written to be performed, they entail specific prompts to the audience's imagination of space, time, character – in short, world – not so different in kind as in degree from the theatre (more is left to the imagination in reading).

Although I don't know this to be true, I would venture to guess that most scholars who identify themselves as 'Shakespeare scholars' make use of actual performances and/or performance-based thinking in the course of their research and writing. This process, however, may exist almost below the surface, at an ideologically unconscious level, especially if they are predisposed to rule out such influences. As this level of speculation is inadequate evidence for any claim to parity, I believe we are left in our discourses with felicitous but inconclusive findings. Some, but not all, of our exchanges had seemed useful to participants. Some, but not all, of our concerns overlapped. Some, but not all, of our initial questions were answered. What did emerge was the possibility of a fruitful ongoing dialogue between performance practitioners who are interested in social, historical and literary matters as a stimulus or source for some aspects of their work, and literary theorists and critics who write about performance or for whom performance experiences can be seen as extending or enriching their reading of texts. I, for one, find great excitement and pleasure in the possibilities for that overlapping scholarly artistic practice.

NOTES

1 References are to the Oxford University Press edition, ed. Stephen Orgel (1996), and sometimes to the Arden 2 edition, ed. J.H.P. Pafford (1963), but only when identified as such.

2 See Chapter 1: 'Text and Voice', (19ff).

3 In session one (Chapter 3) Annabel Arden made the following comments about this passage: 'and the whole point is that you look at the baby, Paulina looks at the baby and says, "Look at it. Every detail is his. It's his baby. And he won't have it." And that's why we love Shakespeare: it's one of the most unbelievable, powerful theatrical things to do. It's not a real baby; I think probably in 99.9 per cent of productions there is no baby. But the gesture to that little object – whatever it is on stage, we've all seen babies. The language is so strong at that point, it's so simple as well, that the combination – you gesture to a tiny object like that and the words do the rest!' (5).

4 In sessions two and one (Chapters 4 and 5), respectively.

5 See Chapter 1, 33.

6 Quotations taken from a draft version of Chapter 1. See pp. 13–19, 23–5 in this volume for a fuller account of Lichtenfels' comments.

7 Compare Margo Hendricks' comments in the first session: 'the body animates the text and … the text animates gesture. And trying to think about what happens … In some of the worst productions I've ever seen … actors don't know what to do with their bodies, and their hands go over here, and [to Annabel Arden] you're right, it is that moment at which the line comes forth and then the hand or the body does something and you wonder at what point was there a cranial disconnect between those two' (Arden, Hendricks, Hunter, 7).

8   'This green plot shall be our stage, this hawthorn-brake our tiring-house; and we will do it in action, as we will do it before the Duke' (*MND* 3.1.3–5).

9 See Robert Weimann, *Author's Pen and Actor's Voice: Playing and Writing in Shakespeare's Theatre* (Cambridge: Cambridge University Press, 2000).

10 See Smith's extended comments in Chapter 2: 'Purposeful Playing? Purposeful Criticism?' The opening paragraphs lay out the issues clearly and starkly.

11 See Chapter 2, 51–2.

12 See *ibid.*, 53.

13 See *ibid.*, 56–7.

14 See *ibid.*, 57.

15 See Chapter 1, 16.

16 See *ibid.*, 26.

17 See *ibid.*, 31–2.

18 See Chapter 2, 54.

BACKGROUND TEXTS

Adamson, Sylvia, Lynette Hunter, Lynne Magnusson, Ann Thompson and Katie Wales (eds), *Reading Shakespeare's Dramatic Language: A Guide* (London: Arden Shakespeare, 2001)

Auslander, Philip, *From Acting to Performance* (London and New York: Routledge, 1997)

Austin, J.L. *How to Do Things with Words*, J.O. Urmson and Marina Sbisà (eds), (Cambridge, MA: Harvard University Press, 1962)

Barton, John, *Playing Shakespeare: An Actor's Guide* (1984; rpt. New York: Anchor Books, 2001)

Berger, Harry Jr; 'Text against Performance in Shakespeare: The Example of *Macbeth*', in Stephen Greenblatt (ed.), *The Power of Forms in the English Renaissance* (Norman, Oklahoma: Pilgrim Books, 1982), 49–79

Berry, Cicely, *Voice and the Actor* (London: Harrap, 1973)

——, *The Actor and His Text* (London: Harrap, 1987; later retitled *The Actor and the Text*)

——, *Text in Action* (London: Virgin, 2001)

Berry, Ralph, *On Directing Shakespeare: Interviews with Contemporary Directors* (London: Hamish Hamilton, 1989)

Bogart, Anne, *A Director Prepares: Seven Essays on Art and Theatre* (London: Routledge, 2001)

Bradley, David, *From Text to Performance in the Elizabethan Theatre* (Cambridge: Cambridge University Press, 1992)

Briggs, Julia, *This Stage Play World* (Oxford: Oxford University Press, 1997)

Bristol, Michael and Kathleen McLuskie (eds), *Shakespeare and the Modern Theatre: the Performance of Modernity* (London and New York: Routledge, 2001)

Brook, Peter, *The Shifting Point. Forty Years of Theatrical Exploration: 1946–87* (London: Methuen, 1988)

——, *Evoking (and Forgetting!) Shakespeare* (London: Nick Hern Books, 2002)

Buzacott, Martin, *The Death of the Actor: Shakespeare on Page and Stage* (London: Routledge, 1991)

Chambers, E.K., *The Elizabethan Stage*, vol. IV (Oxford: Clarendon Press, 1923)

Crewe, Jonathan, 'Punctuating Shakespeare', *Shakespeare Studies* 28 (2000), 23–41

Crystal, David, *The Cambridge Encyclopedia of the English Language* (Cambridge: Cambridge University Press, 1995)

Dawson, Antony B., 'The Impasse over the Stage', *English Literary Renaissance* 21 (1991), 309–27

Delgado, Maria M., *'Other' Spanish Theatres: Erasure and Inscription on the Twentieth-Century Spanish Stage* (Manchester and New York: Manchester University Press, 2003)

Delgado, Maria M. and Paul Heritage (eds), *In Contact with the Gods?: Directors Talk Theatre* (Manchester: Manchester University Press, 1996)

Dillon, Janette, 'Is There a Performance in this Text?', *Shakespeare Quarterly* 45, (1994), 74–86

Dixon, Michael Bigelow and Joel A. Smith, *Anne Bogart: Viewpoints* (Lyme, New Hampshire: Smith and Kraus, 1995)

Doran, Gregory, *Woza Shakespeare!* (New York: St Martin's Press, 2000)

Fischer-Lichte, Erica, 'Staging the Foreign as Cultural Transformation', in Erica Fischer-Lichte, Josephine Riley and Michael Gissenwehrer (eds), *The Dramatic Touch of Difference: Theatre, Own and Foreign* (Tübingen, Germany: Gunter Narr, 1990), 277–87

Gallén, Enric (ed.), *Romea, 125 anys* (Barcelona: Generalitat de Catalunya, 1989)

Greenblatt, Stephen, *Shakespearean Negotiations* (Oxford: Clarendon Press, 1988)

Habib, Imtiaz, *Shakespeare and Race* (Lanham: University Press of America, 1999)

Hawkes, Terence, *Meaning by Shakespeare* (London: Routledge, 1992)

Hendricks, Margo and Patricia Parker (eds), *Women, 'Race', and Writing in the Early Modern Period* (London: Routledge, 1994)

Holland, Peter, *English Shakespeares: Shakespeare on the English Stage in the 1990s* (Cambridge: Cambridge University Press, 1997)

Hooper, John, *The New Spaniards* (London: Penguin, 1995)

Howard, Jean, 'Crossdressing, the Theatre, and Gender Struggle in Early Modern England', *Shakespeare Quarterly* 3, 4 (Winter 1998), 418–40

Hunter, Lynette and Peter Lichtenfels, 'From Stage to Page: Turning to Theatre Practice for Ways to Talk About Character', in Shirley Chew and Alistair Stead (eds), *Translating Lives* (Liverpool: Liverpool University Press 1999) 53–73

——, 'Theatre Practice as a Guide to Textual Editing', in A. Thompson and G. McMullen (eds), *In Arden: Essays in Honour of Richard Proudfoot* (London: Thomson, 2002) 138–56

Jackson, Russell with Jonathan Bate (eds), *The Oxford Illustrated History of Shakespeare on Stage* (Oxford: Oxford University Press, 1996)

Jardine, Lisa, *Worldly Goods: A New History of the Renaissance* (London: Macmillan, 1996)

——, *Reading Shakespeare Historically* (London: Routledge, 1996)

Kastan, David Scott, *Shakespeare and the Book* (Cambridge: Cambridge University Press, 2001)

Kennedy, Dennis, 'Introduction: Shakespeare Without his Language', in Dennis Kennedy (ed.), *Foreign Shakespeare: Contemporary Performance* (Cambridge: Cambridge University Press, 1993)

——, *Looking at Shakespeare: A Visual History of Twentieth-Century Performance* (Cambridge: Cambridge University Press, 2001, 2nd edn)

Kiernan, Pauline, *Staging Shakespeare at the New Globe* (Basingstoke: Macmillan, 1999)

Kliman, Bernice W. (ed.), *Approaches to Teaching Shakespeare's Hamlet* (New York: Modern Language Association, 2002)

Knowles, Richard Paul, 'Shakespeare, Voice, and Ideology: Interrogating the Natural Voice', in James Bulman (ed.), *Shakespeare, Theory, and Performance* (New York: Routledge, 1996), 92–112

Lecoq, Jacques, *The Moving Body* (London: Methuen, 2002, 2nd edn)

Lichtenfels, Peter, 'Shakespeare's Language in the Theatre', in S. Adamson *et al.* (eds), *Reading Shakespeare's Dramatic Language* (London: Thomson Educational, 2000) 158–72

Linklater, Kristin, *Freeing the Natural Voice* (New York: Drama Book Specialists, 1976)

——, *Freeing Shakespeare's Voice: The Actor's Guide to Talking the Text* (New York: Theatre Communications Group, 1992)

McDonald, Russ (ed.), *Shakespeare Reread: The Texts in New Contexts* (Ithaca and London: Cornell University Press, 1994)

McGee, C.E., 'Performance Criticism', in Irena R. Makaryk (ed. and comp.), *Encyclopedia of Contemporary Literary Theory: Approaches, Scholars, Terms* (Toronto: University of Toronto Press, 1993), 133–8

Magnusson, Lynne, *Shakespeare and Social Dialogue: Dramatic Language and Elizabethan Letters* (Cambridge: Cambridge University Press, 1999)

Marcus, Leah S., *Unediting the Renaissance: Shakespeare, Marlowe, Milton* (London and New York: Routledge, 1996)

Orgel, Stephen, *Impersonations: the Performance of Gender in Shakespeare's England* (Cambridge: Cambridge University Press, 1996)

Parker, Patricia, *Shakespeare from the Margins: Language, Culture, Context* (Chicago and London: University of Chicago Press, 1996)

Pearson, Roberta E., *Eloquent Gestures: the Transformation of Performance Style in the Griffith Biograph Films* (Berkeley, CA: University of California Press, 1992)

Players of Shakespeare: Essays in Shakespearean Performance (Cambridge: Cambridge University Press): vol 1 (1965): ed. Philip Brockbank 1985, vol 2 (1988) and vol 3 (1993): eds Russell Jackson and Robert Smallwood, vol 4 (1998): ed. Robert Smallwood

Radloff, Bernhard, 'Text', in Irena R. Makaryk (ed. and comp.), *Encyclopedia of Contemporary Literary Theory: Approaches, Scholars, Terms* (Toronto: University of Toronto Press, 1993), 639–41

Rodenburg, Patsy, *The Right to Speak: Working with the Voice* (London: Methuen, 1992)

——, *Voice and the Text* (London: Methuen, 1993)

——, *Speaking Shakespeare* (New York: Palgrave Macmillan, 2002)

Rovine, Harvey, *Silence in Shakespeare: Drama, Power, and Gender* (Ann Arbor: UMI Research Press, 1987)

Slater, Ann Pasternak, *Shakespeare the Director* (Sussex: Harvester, 1982)

Smith, Bruce R., *The Acoustic World of Early Modern England: Attending to the O-Factor* (Chicago and London: University of Chicago Press, 1999)

Smith, Ian, 'Barbarian Errors: Performing Race in Early Modern England', *Shakespeare Quarterly* 49 (1998), 168–86

Stern, Tiffany, *Rehearsal from Shakespeare to Sheridan* (Oxford: Oxford University Press, 2000)

Thompson, Ann and John O. Thompson, *Shakespeare, Meaning and Metaphor* (Brighton: Harvester Press, 1987)

Thomson, Peter, *On Actors and Acting* (Exeter: Exeter University Press, 2000)

Weimann, Robert, *Author's Pen and Actor's Voice: Playing and Writing in Shakespeare's Theatre* (Cambridge: Cambridge University Press, 2000)

White, Martin, *Renaissance Drama in Action,* (London: Routledge, 1998)

Williams, David (ed.), *Collaborative Theatre: The Théâtre du Soleil Sourcebook* (London: Routledge, 1999)

Worthen, W.B., *Shakespeare and the Authority of Performance* (Cambridge: Cambridge University Press, 1997)

——, *Shakespeare and the Force of Modern Performance* (Cambridge: Cambridge University Press, 2003)

Wright, George T., *Shakespeare's Metrical Art* (Berkeley: University of California Press, 1988)

——, 'Troubles of a Professional Meter Reader', in Russ McDonald (ed.), *Shakespeare Reread: The Texts in New Contexts* (Ithaca and London: Cornell University Press, 1994), 56–76

INDEX